Routledge Revivals

Political Stylistics

First published in 1992, *Political Stylistics* draws together ideas about society and language from a range of theorists including Pratt, Bourdieu, Goody and Watt, and Bakhtin, to establish a political stylistics: a way of studying the formal properties of texts based on the principle that all linguistic production operates within the intricate network of power relations that structure the social realm. On a practical level, this methodology is used to analyse the representation of popular French and argot in three literary works where it extends beyond the speech of the characters and enters the narrative. The book is articulated along three axes: the trajectory of the French working class from mid-nineteenth century to the mid-twentieth century; the trajectory of popular language from social margin to literary centre; and the evolution of the novel from naturalism to modernism, to post-modernism. This book will be of interest to students of literature, linguistics, literary theory, and cultural studies.

Political Stylistics
Popular Language as Literary Artifact

Pascale Gaitet

First published in 1992
By Routledge

This edition first published in 2024 by Routledge
4 Park Square, Milton Park, Abingdon, Oxon, OX14 4RN
and by Routledge
605 Third Avenue, New York, NY 10017

Routledge is an imprint of the Taylor & Francis Group, an informa business

© 1992 Pascale Gaitet

All rights reserved. No part of this book may be reprinted or reproduced or utilised in any form or by any electronic, mechanical, or other means, now known or hereafter invented, including photocopying and recording, or in any information storage or retrieval system, without permission in writing from the publishers.

Publisher's Note
The publisher has gone to great lengths to ensure the quality of this reprint but points out that some imperfections in the original copies may be apparent.

Disclaimer
The publisher has made every effort to trace copyright holders and welcomes correspondence from those they have been unable to contact.

A Library of Congress record exists under ISBN: 0415059917

ISBN: 978-1-032-74886-3 (hbk)
ISBN: 978-1-003-47138-7 (ebk)
ISBN: 978-1-032-74887-0 (pbk)

Book DOI 10.4324/9781003471387

Political Stylistics
Popular Language as Literary Artifact

Pascale Gaitet

London and New York

First published 1992
by Routledge
11 New Fetter Lane, London EC4P 4EE

Simultaneously published in the USA and Canada
by Routledge
a division of Routledge, Chapman and Hall, Inc.
29 West 35th Street, New York, NY 10001

© 1992 Pascale Gaitet

Typeset in 10/12pt Times by
Selectmove Ltd, London
Printed in Great Britain by
TJ Press (Padstow) Ltd, Padstow, Cornwall

All rights reserved. No part of this book may be reprinted or reproduced or utilized in any form or by any electronic, mechanical, or other means, now known or hereafter invented, including photocopying and recording, or in any information storage or retrieval system, without permission in writing from the publishers.

British Library Cataloguing in Publication Data
Gaitet, Pascale
Political stylistics: popular language as literary artifact.
1. Literature
I. Title
808.02

Library of Congress Cataloging in Publication Data

Also available

ISBN 0-415-05991-7

To Nico Mann and Jim Ferguson

Contents

Acknowledgments	viii
Introduction	1
1 **A political stylistics**	6
2 **Zola's *L'Assommoir***	45
3 **Céline's *Voyage au bout de la nuit***	101
4 **Queneau's *Zazie dans le métro***	152
5 **Popular language as literary artifact**	198
Notes	217
Index	230

Acknowledgments

I wish to thank above all Suzanne Nash, who, from the very early stages of this book onwards, provided the constant encouragement, advice and constructive criticism that made its writing possible. Her contributions to my work, and to my life as a scholar, are invaluable. Many thanks also to my research assistant Martha Groves for her excellent editorial help, and for her patience and enthusiasm.

I am grateful to the many other friends and colleagues who read and commented on the manuscript, and to the Committee on Research of the University of California, Santa Cruz, for its financial support.

Introduction

> Then on th' Academy – staid dowager,
> Hiding "tropes" 'neath her petticoats away –
> And on the Alexandrine's close array
> I turned the revolutionary wind,
> The "Red Cap" on th' old dictionary bind.
> Henceforth no words of high or low degree!
> A tempest in the inkstand I decree![1]

With eruptive imagery and allegories that often plunge into the burlesque, Victor Hugo, in "Reply to an Act of Impeachment," celebrates the bond that links linguistic and political freedom. In this polemical piece which he proclaimed to be a defense of his literary innovations, the poet portrays himself as a heroic liberator of language as he sweeps into obsolescence the literary norms and values that the seventeenth century had established and the eighteenth century preserved: clarity, good taste, stilted versification and rhetorical forms. Rejecting the pre-revolutionary stylistic conventions that relegated local dialects and slang to low genres, overthrowing an aristocracy of words and conferring new dignity on the "vile, scorned, tabooed," Hugo demands that, rather than a stratified social order, as was the case in those monarchist days when "Some words were lords, some to the gutter sank," the French lexicon now reflect the republican virtues of liberty and equality. The writers' duty is to ensure the propagation of these values not only in the content but also in the form of their work. They must translate on a stylistic level, with a "democracy" of words unbridled by hierarchies, the spirit of 1789.

The ideals of lexical equality that Hugo advocates here with such fervor are, however, far from realized in his own literary production. Argot does find a place in two of his novels, *The Last Day of a*

Condemned and *Les Misérables*, but it never achieves the new dignity and status with which Hugo, in the poem, claims it ought now to be invested. *The Last Day of a Condemned* is a text that, according to the preface to the 1832 edition, Hugo wrote with the intention of popularizing an idea of a social, moral and political nature: the abolition of the death penalty. This work should be considered a plea "for all accused persons, present and future."[2] However, several straightforward allusions in the text indicate that the narrator, a prisoner condemned to death who recounts his last days before his execution in the form of a journal, is far from "universal." References to his past indicate a privileged social and cultural background that bears no resemblance to that of the other prisoners. He is also separated from them linguistically, as he reveals an aversion to their habitual mode of expression, argot, "that language at once sanguinary and grotesque."[3] The narrator views slang as a parasite, a wart, a hideous growth on the "normal" language. The negative power of these words is emphasized when they are spoken. It is the sound of argot that the "condemned" finds particularly offensive: "On hearing it spoken, the effect is like the shaking of dusty rags before one."[4] With a certain curiosity that rapidly degenerates into horror, he is later submitted to the gruesome celebration of the galley-slaves whose songs he describes as more raucous than the clanging of the chains which bind the men. The narrator's emphasis on the auditory effects of slang implies that he does not recognize this language as a vehicle for signification: he cannot perceive more than the materiality of the signifiers. So hellish does the narrator find the sight and sound of the shackled convicts that he is overcome by a malaise. As he recovers in the infirmary, his spirits rise when, through a window, he hears a song, not of the galley-slaves this time but of a young girl: "the pure, fresh, velvet voice of a young girl."[5] Contrary to his expectations, what she is singing is yet another lament in argot. This "idiom of crime . . . united to the voice of a young girl," these "monstrous words [that] proceeded from a fresh rosy mouth" cause him bitter disappointment and pain. Again, the words are described as deformed, repulsive.[6] The interaction of two elements which the narrator perceives as belonging to diametrically opposed and mutually exclusive categories – untrammeled beauty and innocence on the one hand, absolute subversion, ugliness and perversity on the other – appall him and catalyze his vision of the contaminating and deteriorating effect the prison has on all worthy things. Argot can be considered both the chief agent and symbol of deterioration as he reflects: "Ah! what infamous thing is a prison! It contains a venom which assails all within its pestilential reach. Everything withers there, even the song of a girl of fifteen."[7]

It appears, from these brief examples, that the narrator – the convict who, Hugo claims, represents all those in similar plights – abhors the language of the other prisoners. Above all, that language is foreign to him. The notion of a foreign, parasitical language is reflected in the manner in which the actual slang words are displayed in the text. In the French text, following the *condamné*'s first encounter with the language of the other prisoners, is a long list of argot terms printed in italics, with their translation given in parentheses. They are dissociated from the rest of the page, their singularity is underlined. Similarly, when a fellow convict recounts his life of crime, Hugo provides explanations of argot expressions in footnotes at the bottom of the page. It is quite obvious that the author considers slang to be unknown to the readers as well as to the persona behind the narrative voice. Their joint exclusion from this language creates a common ground between them, a bond that is the consequence of a linguistic strategy by which Hugo strives to induce the readers' sympathy and that is based on the recognition that they and the narrator share the same social and cultural background. This kind of recognition and complicity typically takes place to the detriment of another, in this case the mass of prisoners and their language, which clearly belongs to the world of crime.

Argot is also the subject of several chapters of *Les Misérables*. In a digression from the central plot, simply called "Slang," the concern is a theoretical one and the discussion of argot embraces linguistic, aesthetic and political points of view.[8] The description of this language is invested with imagery that suggests threatening and monstrous life: "that abject idiom which drips with filth," or "a frightful, living, and bristling polypus, which shivers, moves, trembles, demands the shadow again, menaces and glares." The words resemble "a lustreless and dull eye" or "the pincers of a crab."[9] When not reminiscent of creatures such as vipers, bats and centipedes, slang is compared, as in *The Last Day of a Condemned*, to abnormal growths, to warts, to parasites. As in the earlier novel, slang's otherness is reflected in the manner in which it is represented in the text. Hugo includes "translations" at the foot of the page.

In these chapters, Hugo explains at length his interest in argot, often invoking a moral justification. He sees his investigation as analogous to the scientific inquiry, experimentation and practice undertaken by doctors, biologists and surgeons: in all these areas, the end justifies the however unpleasant means of research: "Now, when did horror begin to exclude study? When did disease drive away the physician? . . . The thinker who would turn away from slang would resemble a surgeon who turned away from an ulcer or a wart."[10] Along with these practical motivations, the moral elements attached to duty, study and courage are also invoked:

> If a wound, a gulf, or a society are to be probed, is it considered a mistake to drive the probe too deep? We have always thought that it was sometimes an act of courage, and, at the very least, a simple and useful action, worthy of the sympathetic attention which duty accepted and performed deserves.[11]

Balzac, in a theoretical section of *Vautrin's Last Avatar*, also discusses his use of slang in his novel, first emphasizing the necessity of providing the reader with explanations concerning the world of criminals – its prisons, its way of life, and, particularly, its language.[12] In what clearly is an attempt to justify the presence of argot and to present it as a language entirely foreign to the reader and himself, he stresses its literary potential on the one hand, its frightening and repulsive aspect on the other. Argot is colorful, energetic, each word is "a bold metaphor, ingenious or horrible." Later Balzac concludes: "In this idiom, everything is savage." Not only are these descriptions strikingly close to Hugo's, but, as is the case in *The Last Day of a Condemned* and *Les Misérables*, slang is restricted to the directly reported speech of certain characters where the unexpected argot words or expressions are printed in italics, and translations are given in parentheses after each one.

Later in the nineteenth century, and during the twentieth, the demands that Hugo put forth in "Reply to an Act of Impeachment' but that he did not himself satisfy – that all words should be granted equal literary status, whatever their social origin – appeared closer to fulfillment in novels where popular language is not restricted to reported speech but extends to the narrative. It is this stylistic feature that I shall address in the following study, and whose evolution in a changing social and literary context I shall trace. Central to the investigation will be three key novels: Emile Zola's *L'Assommoir* (1876), Louis-Ferdinand Céline's *Journey to the End of the Night* (1932) and Raymond Queneau's *Zazie in the Metro* (1959). Apart from the shared representation of popular language outside of the directly reported voice of characters, these works bear a number of features that justify the prominent role that they will play here and that are worth mentioning briefly at this early stage. First, this representation does not occur only occasionally in these works, but is the main particularity of their style. The second feature has to do with historical context. The class to which popular language owes its origin and from which its study cannot be dissociated undergoes distinct change throughout this period, yet the French political field remains constant in its polarities. The period these novels span, running from the beginning of the Third Republic to the Fifth, is uninterruptedly ruled by the bourgeoisie and retains a stable political infrastructure. None the less, it is a time of significant economic and social evolution: beginning with modern capitalism and the emergence of an urban, industrial working class and ending in the late 1950s, with the first signs of a post-industrial society accompanied by, I shall argue, a loss of the working class's cultural specificity.

As well as punctuating different moments of a political trajectory contained within a set frame, the works mark three stages of a genre in the evolution of the literary field: the naturalist novel, the modernist novel, the postmodern novel. Another relevant feature is that *L'Assommoir*, *Journey to the End of the Night* and *Zazie in the Metro* belong to mainstream literature: consecrated by the academy as well as by a large and varied readership. They also met with immediate success. *L'Assommoir*, part of a corpus of works already accepted for publication, *Les Rougon-Macquart*, was the most financially rewarding of Zola's novels. *Zazie*, which soon after its publication was made into a film, is probably the best known of Queneau's novels, and Céline's *Journey* was a close contender for the Goncourt prize. All three books, now published in Gallimard's prestigious Pléiade edition as well as in Folio paperback, have achieved mass-distribution and success while belonging to what Mary Louise Pratt refers to as "honorific literature," that is, "a set of literary works that have passed a filtering process carried out by a specific group of people, namely scholars or intellectuals, according to standards associated primarily with the academy.'[13] This study will therefore be articulated on a crossroad of axes: the synchronic one on which the translation of a language from popular margin to literary center takes place will intersect with the diachronic trajectories of social class and novelistic genre.

1 A political stylistics

The introduction to this work suggests that, to the translation of popular language from social margin to literary center, I shall not seek to link psychological value and shed light on the author's personality; nor shall I catalogue formal features and uncover patterns, however complex, dissociated from anything other than the fact of their existence and internal structure. Rather, this study aims to establish and put to good use a *political stylistics*: an approach to the study of formal features of texts which is founded on the assumption that all linguistic production is conditioned by and operates within the intricate network of power relations that structure the social realm. Literary discourse is no exception and will be considered therefore not only to derive from, but also to participate in the dynamics of these power relations which, in all their superstructural ramifications, may be more or less removed from the economic base, more or less mediated by institutional forms of government. A word of caution, however. Today, we witness an unprecedented proliferation of academic discourses that (with the blessing of academic institutions) delight in detecting political signifiers in absolutely every area and aspect of social practice; this zeal, often accompanied by a marked disdain for classical marxism, is suspect, and, I would argue, serves as a strategy of diversion from the examination of more crucial political issues. If my understanding of the political does indeed include the ramifications of power relations, it is to the extent that these may be related to the economic base in a manner that does not call for an undue stretch of the imagination. When I assign a political foundation and potential to the representation of popular language in *L'Assommoir*, *Journey to the End of the Night* and *Zazie in the Metro*, I mean, by political potential, a possible and complexly mediated but none the less discernible role in the preservation or subversion of relations of production. It is with this basis and potential in view that the texts' formal features will be uncovered, described, analyzed and contextualized. Pierre Bourdieu, in *Ce que parler veut dire* ("What Speaking Means (To Say)"), suggests the trajectory that such an approach should observe:

> There is no science of discourse considered in itself and for itself: the formal properties of works reveal their meaning only if one relates them to the social conditions of their production on the one hand – that is, to the positions held by their authors in the field of production – and to the market for which they were produced on the other hand.[1]

Far more complex, however, than the movement that a political stylistics proposes to follow (from the social to the textual and back) is the method that will support its trajectory. Central to its elaboration is the development of socio-linguistic concepts and tools into ones which, in conjunction with more formal methodologies, will be fit for literary critical use. The term socio-linguistics immediately implies that a number of the premises and notions inherent to Saussurian linguistics and many derived critical approaches will have to be rejected or modified since they view language as a closed system and uphold the precise dichotomy that a political stylistics should overcome: the separation between internal and external linguistics, between the formal properties of language and its social uses. Saussure's notion of *langue*, because it denotes an abstract and normative system, will be of little use. Much more relevant will be that of a legitimate language.

LEGITIMATE LANGUAGE AND ITS POLITICAL FUNCTIONS

Legitimate language is the linguistic code that, within national boundaries, is officially designated and widely accepted as "correct." In this normative aspect it resembles Saussure's *langue*, from which it differs, however, in its unambiguously political functions: the very concrete manners in which legitimate language serves the interests of the state and/or ruling class. These functions can be grouped into two categories: processes of inclusion that encourage linguistic unification and ideological cohesion, and processes of exclusion that guarantee the preservation of an economic and cultural elite.

Linguistic unification ensures a certain level of communication necessary to the smooth functioning of relations of production, which is also facilitated by a minimum of ideological cohesion – the sharing of similar basic values. It is not unusual for governments to intervene directly and attempt to control linguistic use. Jan Knappert, in "Language in a Political Situation," recounts efforts towards language planning in southern Siberia, where three different Turkic dialects were originally spoken.[2] Soon after the October Revolution, different orthographies, based on the Roman script, were devised. In the mid 1930s, they were replaced by new ones, based on the Cyrillic script:

> This and many loan words gave the impression that the purpose of these languages is only to be a stepping stone for students whose higher degrees will all be in Russian. In this way, the speakers of the Turkic dialects will be tied to Russian as the central language of the country, and will be less conscious of their relations with their neighbors.[3]

Closer to home, between 1813 and 1823, the federal government of the United States urged states to pass statutes requiring English to be the language of instruction in public and private schools. In "Language and the Law: The Exercise of Political Power," Arnold Leibnitz ascribes this trend to "the religious and economic fears engendered by the increased immigration and the wartime xenophobia during those years."[4] In an attempt to assuage the social unrest caused by the Civil Rights Movements and the radicalism of the 1960s, the Bilingual Education Act was passed in 1968; however, two conservative decades later, we witness the legal designation of English as the official language of California and other states.

Perhaps nowhere more than in France has the institutionalized nature of legitimate language and its connection to political power been clearly displayed as, in conjunction with processes of political and cultural centralization, it worked towards verbal and ideological integration. As early as in the eighth century, Charlemagne attempted to unify his empire by encouraging linguistic cohesion with an educational system that promoted a normative and widespread use of Latin. If, in the tenth century, among the many dialects competing for legitimacy, *Francien* achieved supremacy over others, it is because the king Hugues Capet established his court in Paris, the place where it was spoken. Later, as Du Bellay suggests in his *Defense and Illustration of the French Language* (*Défense et illustration de la langue française*), the linguistic concerns that dominated the Renaissance – the efforts to create a rich and powerful French language – were very much linked to patriotic ideals:

> It seems to me, Reader, Friend of the French muses, that following those whom I have just named, you must not be ashamed to write

in your own language but that rather you must, if you are a friend of France – indeed, of yourself – give yourself entirely to this task, with the generous opinion that it is better to be an Achilles among one's own people than a Diomede, or even a Thersite, among others.[5]

These attempts to enrich, embellish and render the language more powerful were followed by an opposing trend in the seventeenth century. Correctness, good usage, and linguistic sobriety came to be highly regarded. They are promoted, for example, in Vaugelas' "Remarks on the French Language" (*Remarques sur la langue française*), a prescriptive text aimed not at reforming language but at establishing a socially based distinction between "good" and "bad" usage. As Vaugelas repeatedly states, good usage is set by a minority, the "elite of voices," the court: "It is the way of speaking of the best of the court, in conformity with the style of writing of the best authors of our time."[6] Vaugelas regards speech as a social act that engages one's responsibility, and he considers mimetism of the court as a means of protecting one's reputation and social prestige: "It takes only one word for a person to be subjected to public scorn."[7] It is also in the seventeenth century that the Académie Française, the primary guardian of the legitimate language and the highest authority in linguistic matters, was founded. From its origins onwards, the Académie was closely dependent on political power: Richelieu, hoping that a strong, refined and orderly language would help France achieve cultural hegemony throughout Europe as well as safeguard an internal coherence at home, ordered its formation. Indeed, its first dictionary was presented to the king. The Académie's role, unchanged to this day, is to preserve the purity and integrity of the French language, to establish norms and exercise censorship, and, as Nicolas Faret, one of its early members, stated at the first meeting: "to rid the language of the filth it had acquired."[8]

The effects of the Revolution on the French language were quite different from the ones that Hugo suggested. Rather than encouraging linguistic diversity, the post-revolutionary government called for the propagation of a unified "republican language," a national good that should be made available and common to all.[9] An immediate concern was to wipe out the alienating dialects that hindered the proper diffusion of a communal spirit. This project commanded a great deal of energy, and its implementation was approached in a systematic, bureaucratic manner. Committees were set up, reports ordered, and investigations carried out. The most powerful reform came with the decrees that, in October 1794, ordered the creation of state-run elementary schools throughout the country, with, as their two principal goals, the inculcation of republican ideals and the instruction of French. Increased literacy and ideological coherence were also to be gained by the proliferation and widespread distribution throughout the country of published material, such as simple instructional books or periodicals for adults and children, which were quite overt in their attempts at civic indoctrination. Linguistic reforms were often suggested at the time, but never materialized, even though, in 1792, a committee on public education set up an investigation to determine the most efficient manner of enforcing a new grammar and producing a new dictionary. The irony is that the notes used to compile this work turned out to be those which the (then suppressed) Académie Française had intended for a new edition of its own *Dictionnaire*.

It is clear that, rather than an elimination of authority, the Revolution brought a displacement of political and linguistic power. Good usage was no longer decreed by the court, as it was in Vaugelas' time, but by the state. As this passage taken from a text attempting to plan the appropriate holdings of a public library (*bibliothèque du peuple*) clearly implies, the primary issue was the propagation of normative French, not the popularization of the language:

> A work written in simple language will be understood even better by the people than a work written in a trivial style, and it will form its taste, so that one day the French language will be admired as that of Athens was in the past, and as today we admire the language of Florence.[10]

These ideas are far from original. As early as 1549, Du Bellay wished to make the French language superior not only to Italian but to Greek and Latin as well; and the values advanced here – simplicity, clarity, didacticism – would not have been out of place in the seventeenth century.

The republic did not last; its ideals, as well as its plans and projects, faltered. During the days of the Empire, little attention was paid to elementary schools; locally governed, they were left to their own devices and academic standards dropped drastically. Secondary and higher education was of far greater importance to Napoléon, who created the lycées that served the needs of the upper classes. These schools followed earlier traditions, emphasizing above all the study of Latin. The Imperial University, which the Emperor conceived as a highly hierarchical corporation, was centralized in Paris and assumed an obviously conservative function:

H. M. wants an institution whose doctrine will be protected from those little upheavals of fashion, an institution that will function even when the government slumbers, whose administration and statutes would be so deeply rooted that one would never dare to tamper light-heartedly with them. Should these hopes be realized, H. M. wishes to find in this institution a guarantee against any sort of pernicious and subversive theories – of one kind or another. There has always been, in all well-organized states, a body designed to regulate moral and political principles.[11]

Luckily, the linguistic and educational policies that sprang from the first years of republican idealism were not lost forever: they reappeared after the fall of the French Empire, when the Third Republic, in 1871, intent on suppressing all church influences and on overcoming the still widespread use of regional dialects, installed a system of free, compulsory and secular elementary schools. This system remains in operation today. As the 1932 Official Instructions for primary education clearly state, the teaching of French reflects a concern for linguistic, cultural and political homogeneity. The teachers, delegated by and accountable to the state, represent its authority in these matters: "Our teachers are well aware that to teach the French language is not only to work for the maintenance and expansion of a beautiful language and literature, it is also to fortify national unity."[12]

From Charlemagne's schools to Napoléon's Imperial University, from the republican schools of the 1790s to those of Jules Ferry and the present, the educational system, mediating between the government and the people, played a vital role in propagating and maintaining the forms and functions of the legitimate language. It is there that norms are implanted and upheld. With its abstract and regimented inculcation of syntactical and orthographic rules, schools set up criteria of linguistic correctness. In France, uniformity is guaranteed by the standardization of textbooks, curriculum, and examinations; in addition, decisions on the appropriate or acceptable forms of usage are issued by the Ministry of National Education.

As well as contributing to the first political function of legitimate language – the inclusive process which promotes linguistic and ideological unification – the educational system advances the second, the process of exclusion that guarantees the self-perpetuation of the ruling class. One of the functions of elementary education is to achieve the conditions for minimal linguistic communication, and to allow for the recognition, but not the knowledge, Bourdieu notes, of legitimate language.[13] The inequality of knowledge is due to the fact that the language that children first acquire, through imitation and within the context of their immediate surroundings, is that which is spoken in the family. The distance between this language and that which children will be taught in school is a direct function of their distance from the ruling class; therefore, the higher the social class, the easier the transition to "correct" language, the greater the scholarly success:

> The social value of the different linguistic codes available in a given society at a given time (that is, their economic and symbolic profitability) always depends on the distance that separates them from the linguistic norm that the School manages to impose in the definition of the socially recognized criteria of linguistic correction. More precisely, the value on the scholarly market of the linguistic capital available to each individual is a function of the distance between the type of symbolic mastery required by the school and the practical mastery initially provided by the individual's class education.[14]

Basil Bernstein, in his essay "Social Class, Language and Socialization," shows that significant class-induced differences reside in *how* language is used. He describes a study wherein children were asked to tell a story suggested by a series of pictures.[15] Those from the middle class related the sequence of events in a manner that enabled it to stand independently of the context – the picture – from which it derived ("Three boys are playing football and a boy kicks the ball . . . and it goes through the window . . . the ball breaks the window"); in the version of the lower-class children, the meanings were implicit, tied to the context ("They're playing football . . . and he kicks it . . . and it goes through there . . . it breaks the window"). Basing his conclusions on a wide range of studies and analyses, Bernstein suggests that only a very small percentage of the population has acquired the use of what he calls "the elaborated codes" that enable a speaker to produce meanings in which principles and operations are made linguistically explicit. One of the effects of the class system is to socialize the mass of the population to produce a discourse that is context-dependent and context-bound, rather than permitting a widespread access to "the meta-languages of control and innovation."[16]

Along with the ability to recognize legitimate French, what schools do manage to distribute equally among young children is a respect for that language and for those who use it, which automatically endows those who speak it properly with a status of power. Elementary education then, prepares for the preservation of an elite in two ways: by promoting this recognition and respect, and also by channeling unsuccessful students towards short studies in vocational schools, and the successful ones towards longer studies in secondary schools and universities. Secondary and higher education, of course, was also made inaccessible for economic reasons (the lycées remained costly until the end of the Second World War) to those working-class children who overcame the initial barriers. It is in secondary schools that the competence necessary to speak and write legitimate French is acquired, along with a solid grounding in the reading, understanding, and "appreciation" of French literature. Processes of selection continue to operate through stringent examinations and further divisions into more and less distinguished tracks, culminating, finally, in the separation of students who will attend the not-so-reputable universities from those who make it into the prestigious Grandes Ecoles.[17] Rather than erasing linguistic and social inequities, the schools clearly tend to reproduce them, by both drawing on and reinforcing the inclusive and exclusive functions of legitimate French. The use of language as a tool for exclusion and discrimination, reinforced by the inequities of the educational system, operates in the United States as well, perhaps never more obviously than when Southern states disenfranchised black voters with English literacy tests, a practice that was not seriously questioned until the Voting Rights Act of 1965.[18] In France, the scarcity of governmental efforts to improve immigrant workers' use of French reveals a similar attitude. Programs are designed to teach them what they need to know in order to function efficiently in the workplace, and no more; they are not welcome participants in the country's political procedures and ideological configurations.

LINGUISTIC HORIZON, DISCURSIVE SITUATION AND DISCURSIVE STRATEGIES

The discussion of the unequal and class-related distribution of competence necessary to the acquisition and usage of legitimate language brings us to another point on which I shall dissent from Saussure, who accounts for linguistic variation in terms of individual usage only. Here, linguistic variation will be considered as shaped by systems of constraints and privileges appertaining to the socio-economic position of the speaker, and to the situation in which it is produced. Three notions are vital to the discussion of such variations: linguistic horizon, discursive situation and discursive strategies.

What I call the *linguistic horizon* is determined by socio-economic position and social trajectory. It traces the limits of competence and circumscribes discursive possibilities. The linguistic horizon, then, contains all of the theoretically possible options that have been made available to the speaker through informal familiarization (which would hence contain the linguistic particularities of the social class into which the speaker was born) and formal inculcation, the length and thoroughness of which is also linked to socio-economic position. At any given moment, the linguistic horizon is fixed. It functions as a constraint on which the speaker cannot exercise choice. Among the possibilities contained within this framework, that to which one will resort depends in part on the *discursive situation*: the "market" situation in which linguistic production takes place. The socio-economic position of the speaker plays a role in determining, among other things, the discourse's "viability": whether a particular exchange will be allowed to take place, or whether a particular discourse will be allowed to be voiced. A number of other variables affect the discursive situation: to whom the discourse is addressed, the immediate conditions in which it is formulated and received, whether it remains internal to a social class, the symbolic or material gains at which it aims, the "method" best suited to the gain (threat, persuasion, seduction), and so forth. Overall, the discursive situation narrows down the number of linguistic options contained within the linguistic horizon. It eliminates some, encourages others. Among these possible *discursive strategies*, the speaker will decide which is the most efficient and appropriate.[19]

For example, when members of the lower classes interact with members of the dominant class in a non-confrontational situation, they are likely to adopt one of two strategies, both of which attempt to erase too-obvious signs of power imbalance: a tendency towards silence, or tense efforts at what Bourdieu calls hyper-correctness. Such efforts, William Labov points out, are usually incumbent upon women, traditionally called upon to communicate with doctors, teachers, bureaucrats, and so forth.[20] This type of hyper-correctness is also widespread in exchanges internal to the petite bourgeoisie, whose members attempt to signal to each other their separation from the working class and endow themselves with a distinctive feature of the bourgeoisie: "Hypercorrectness inscribes itself into the logic of pretention that leads the petit-bourgeois to try to appropriate early, at the price of constant efforts, the characteristics of the dominant class."[21]

If, in the situation mentioned above, members of the dominant class also wish to lessen the perception of power inequities, it is possible for them to resort to what Bourdieu calls a "strategy of condescension." For instance, Michael Dukakis, in his 1988 presidential campaign, attempted to win an Hispanic electorate with his use of Spanish; the campaign rally remains the only occasion on which such a person would resort to the language of a minority – and, probably, the main motivation for learning it in the first place. Such a strategy, whose function is demagogic seduction, takes place when a speaker's status, power and legitimacy are so clearly marked that they will not risk being challenged when the language used is lowered to that of the audience. Outside of the political and literary arenas, bourgeois appropriation of non-legitimate language is rare. Intellectuals in conflict with their class do not resort to this practice; Sartre did not address Renault workers in a discourse freighted with popular overtones.

In a confrontational situation involving speakers from different classes, the inverse effect is sought: rather than establishing common linguistic ground, distance is created as each group keeps to its own linguistic terrain and exacerbates its particularities. Not uncommonly, the lower-class person attempts to compensate for a lack of real power by trying to create its illusion with strong verbal aggression and vulgarities that might shock the bourgeois; unaccustomed to such linguistic displays, the latter might retort with a few well-chosen words, heavily loaded with threats and covert implications. Distance from the bourgeois can also be signaled in exchanges internal to the working class, as, for example, when Georges Marchais, First Secretary of the French Communist Party, performs a number of grammatical errors in his public speeches as a token of solidarity with the working class: another politician using language as a campaign tool – unlike Dukakis, of course, Marchais, on those occasions, does not resort to a language different from the one acquired through his own class upbringing (even though his social trajectory does enable him to avoid those mistakes).

This willful departure from legitimate language is also typical of less formal public verbal exchanges, internal to the working class, where norms are disregarded in a conscious and provocative manner. This is particularly the case in all-male groups, where transgression is paraded, and argot, the lexicon most removed from the official norm, predominates. Its use establishes not only distance but also intentionally subverts dominant values – linguistic, of course, but also aesthetic, moral, and emotional. Slang flaunts a rejection of bourgeois culture, denies a state of linguistic submission that efforts to use a more legitimate language would imply. Serving as a means of recognition crucial to the internal coherence of the group, creating and maintaining bonds and an exclusive atmosphere, slang participates in a phatic function: its role is as much to sustain communication as to convey information. It partakes, also, in the group's self-representation and constitution of an outcast identity.

Finally, the use of non-legitimate language to signify distance from or antagonism towards authority is not restricted to the lower classes. The discourse and/or practices of oppressed social groups can be invested with value by a certain "dissenting" segment of the dominant one. Examples of this are British punk, originally a working-class style that has been emulated by the middle class, or, as Norman Mailer describes them in *The White Negro*, "hip" whites using black language.[22] As James Baldwin points out in "The Black Boy Looks at the White Boy," the politically oppositional consequences of such appropriations are, at best, questionable.[23]

THE LITERARY TEXT, LEGITIMATE LANGUAGE AND THE LITERARY DISCURSIVE SITUATION

So far, the discussion of the socio-linguistic premises and concepts useful to a political stylistics has dealt with broad categories and general schemes: the political functions of a normative legitimate language, the relation of discourse to the socio-economic position of speaker and listener and to the discursive context. Remaining within the framework set up by these discussions, I shall address the specific linguistic product that this study will examine, the literary text. In light of the emphasis that the preceding pages have placed on the contextual determination of discourse, it is not surprising that our purposes will be served by a speech act theory of literature, such as that put forward by Mary Louise Pratt. As the point of departure of her arguments, Pratt demonstrates the inadequacy of Russian Formalist definitions of the literary: for Jakobson, a message where the aesthetic function is dominant; for Shklovsky, one whose linguistic techniques impede perception by aiming at defamiliarization; for Lotman, language that displays exclusive, inherent systems of signs and rules. In each case, these are essentialist conceptions that equate literariness to intrinsic textual properties. Pratt, illustrating her views with examples taken from Labov's *Language in the Inner City*, demonstrates that many such poetic properties (wordplay, rhythm, figures of speech – forms that call attention to themselves) exist outside of literary texts.[24] To this already thoroughly documented and convincing argument, I would add another: literariness can be as normative as it is deviant, and a strong interdependency links many literary texts – particularly prose – and legitimate language.

The most obvious institutional and symbolic embodiment of this relationship between literary and legitimate French is, perhaps, the long-standing Académie Française. Its forty members, representing the highest authority in linguistic matters, are selected from (and self-perpetuated by) some of the most acclaimed, or at least respected, authors of the time. From its origins onwards, the Académie Française demonstrated that a certain type of literary production attests to a privileged knowledge of and concern for legitimate language. As one of its first members, Arnaud, affirmed in his inauguration speech of 1771: "Those who have purified, ordered, fixed the character of our language are our good writers, whom the Académie Française has had the honor to count among its members."[25] I mentioned earlier that, in the seventeenth century, Vaugelas advocated the usage of the court. He considered "good usage" to be confirmed and consolidated when reflected in the work of writers: "The consent of good authors functions as a seal, or a verification, that authorizes the language of the court and that distinguishes between good and doubtful usage."[26] Voltaire, in his entry on language in the *Philosophical Dictionary*, wrote: "One must absolutely respect the manner in which good authors speak; and when there is a sufficient number of approved authors, the language is fixed."[27] Admittedly, matters become more complex in the nineteenth century, as Richard Terdiman demonstrates in *Discourse/Counter-Discourse*, with the proliferation of counterdiscourses whose oppositional features develop an increasingly formal nature, culminating, as far as the novel is concerned, in the *nouveau roman* of the twentieth century, where estrangement and defamiliarization are the main features.[28] Estrangement and defamiliarization, however, need not mean incorrectness; on the contrary, Bourdieu suggests that the two features can go hand in hand:

> The properties which characterize linguistic excellence can be summarized with two words: *distinction* and *correctness*. The work accomplished in the literary field produces the appearances of an original language by operating a set of derivations, the principle of which is a shift away from the most frequent usages, that is to say, common, ordinary, vulgar.[29] (my emphasis)

A move away from the ordinary can be accomplished without contradicting the rules of legitimate language. Furthermore, despite such stylistic trends (or as Barthes put it, the "problematic of language" that literature, since Flaubert, has become), grammarians continue to make use of literary texts to illustrate a particular aspect of legitimate language or to legitimize a new form.[30] Maurice Grévisse resorts to this process in his *Le Bon Usage*, the most authoritative guide to the French language, in which the preface to the sixth edition explains that examples taken from literary texts bear witness to each and every rule given there:

> The principal merit of M. Grévisse – vigilant and diligently informed recorder – is that he listens carefully to the best contemporary authors, to those who, by their consensus on a particular lexicological point, or a particular syntactical difficulty, temporarily fix French in a miraculous state of unstable equilibrium, threatened, but that must be defended.[31]

The interaction of grammarians and literary texts, this preface suggests, is twofold: on the unquestioned aspects of the legitimate language the text provides examples, and on acceptable innovations the grammarian establishes rules, so that the new element may be easily transmitted, with the help, as Bourdieu describes, of the educational system:

> writers, authors more or less authorized, must reckon with the grammarians who hold the monopoly over the consecration and canonization of writers and legitimate writing, and who contribute to the construction of a legitimate language by selecting, from among the products presented, those that they judge worthy of consecration and of incorporation into the realm of legitimacy through scholarly inculcation, and by submitting these works to a process of normalization and codification that renders them consciously controllable and hence easily reproducible.[32]

Dictations of passages from highly canonical texts, grammatical analyses performed on literary sentences, poems memorized to increase vocabulary – all these scholarly exercises strengthen the child's understanding that writers are, primarily, people who express themselves in good French. It is particularly during secondary education that literary texts, as well as being studied in themselves, play an important role in the inculcation of legitimate language. A correlation, therefore, exists between the "knowledge" of literature, and a competency in legitimate French.[33]

In addition to demonstrating that the intrinsic qualities of a work are not reliable criteria for establishing its literariness, Pratt develops a pragmatic, socio-cultural definition that is of far greater use to this study than an aesthetico-structural one. What constitutes the literary status, Pratt argues, is "a particular disposition of speaker and audience with regard to the message."[34] That particular disposition consists of the intentions, expectations and assumptions of writer and reader, which are based on the conventional procedures that govern the literary production and the literary market of a given society at a given time – in other words, on the literary discursive situation, which displays a number of constants, at least for the time and place that concern us here. Regarding the author's disposition (assumptions and expectations), the first relevant factor is that, in general, the literary text was written with the intention and the hope that it will be published, and published as literature. The author knows that, for this to happen, the text will undergo a selection process based on criteria that vary from publisher to publisher, but that the constant concern is the following: the text will have to be judged as acceptable to a certain public. Acceptability, in the eyes of the closely related publisher and audience, is dependent on what Jauss calls the horizon of expectations: the prevalent norms familiar to a given public at a given time.[35] Even though these prevailing literary norms evolve – literary standards at the time of the naturalist novel will be quite different from those at the dawn of postmodernism – and are constantly modified by new works as well as by social change, they determine, at any point in time, the framework within which the work will be read. The author is aware that the aesthetic distance that separates the work from the public's expectations must not be so great that the work will not even enter the literary field at all. Unlike when a member of the working class uses argot in an attempt to have the last word in an encounter with a member of the ruling class, the literary text, however confrontational, cannot completely break the communicative function. It can impede, complicate and question communication, but it must avoid causing all readers to close the book in desperation. Knowing this, authors take risks to varying degrees in the face of anticipated profits or losses, and more or less align their idea of the text with their idea of the audience's approbation.

Second, both the author and reader realize that once the work has been accepted as literature, it will carry that status with more or less authority, according to the type of publisher – whether widely recognized or a small press; and that the majority of readers are likely to accept the implied designation. By means of its reputation and publicity efforts, the publisher will play a large part in determining the size and nature of the audience. Also influential in shaping public opinion and attitude towards the work is its immediate reception by various agents – literary critics, the media at large. As it circulates in the market, the work's status is reinforced or discredited by judgments passed. Authors are no doubt conscious of all these intervening factors as they write, and no doubt take them into account during what Pratt calls the preparation process, which, in its unusual length and thoroughness, is another distinctive feature of the literary discursive situation. Both the writer and reader know that the literary work allows for more planning, correcting and cautious decisions about what is to be achieved and how to achieve it than most linguistic productions.

Operating alongside the shared factors – the literary intention, the awareness of the procedures that will confer the status of literature, the preparation process – a number of variables affect the literary discursive situation. As is the case for all linguistic production, the available strategies are restricted by an author's linguistic horizon. Among the writers of a given period, the degree of competence in different linguistic usages will not be uniform. Furthermore, the power relations that determine social hierarchy in general also operate within the specificity of the literary field to establish authorial status, which becomes another intervening factor in the work's acceptability. An unknown writer faces a far less favorable situation than one whose previous books have encountered a commercial success, perhaps accompanied by some official honors; the degree of respect and authority that such approval confers greatly facilitates a recognition of the new work's legitimacy and its propagation on the market. If there exists, at a given time, a common horizon of expectations, there will be variations among sub-groups, one or several of which the text might address: the author might have a particular audience in mind, and will write accordingly. Finally, onto the principal and common goal (to have the text published as literature) various secondary and different motivations might be grafted – Balzac's debts, Brecht's politics, for example.

POPULAR LANGUAGE AND ITS BOURGEOIS OBJECTIFICATIONS

Popular French will here be taken to refer to the modes of expression that predominate, usually for interactions internal to the group, among members of what can be considered the traditional French working class, a social group that came into existence with the rise of industrial capitalism in the mid- to late nineteenth century.

When an increasing centralization of labor needs brought an influx of workers from the provinces to Paris, the various local dialects, not yet entirely eradicated by previous efforts, lost their purpose. An urgent need appeared: the need for a means of communication that transcended the geographic origin of the speaker, and that also functioned as a distinctive feature, participating in the identity that this newly constituted subordinate class strove to create for itself. As Terdiman points out in *Discourse/Counter-Discourse*, this was a time when "increasing social and geographical mobility made group boundary lines much more uncertain. Under such circumstances, the use of cultural signs to indicate status becomes a much more subtle, less enforceable, yet at the same time more necessary calculus than previously."[36] Popular French emerged as the language of the Parisian workers who were removed from official culture, yet in closer physical proximity to the dominant class than when confined to villages of Brittany or Limousin. As this occurred, there became a pressing need for the dominant class to organize the political and ideological accommodation of an urban proletariat. Animated, on the one hand, by the intention to know and control the working class and, on the other, to distance itself from it, the bourgeoisie sought to confine this new class within the boundaries of a representation in which linguistic particularities played an important role.

In accordance with Volosinov's description of the word as "the most sensitive index of social changes, and, what is more, of changes still in the process of growth, still without definite shape, and not as yet accommodated into already regularized and fully defined ideological systems," the emergence of this new class and its specific mode of expression was underscored by a significant linguistic shift when argot, originally the secret code of a well-circumscribed and peripheral group, thieves and criminals, became connected to the popular language of the capital.[37] This shift has already been implicitly suggested here. In the introduction I referred to argot as a register available to members of the working class but showed that earlier, in 1826, it was characteristic of the inmates in Hugo's *The Last Day of a Condemned*. Such was the case for, approximately, the first half of the nineteenth century. As Louis Chevalier points out in *Laboring Classes and Dangerous Classes*, crime was an important theme in the literature of the time.[38] Argot also found a place in many texts of a "documentary" nature, the production of which was centered around the work of Eugène Vidocq, a reformed criminal who later joined the police force. His *Mémoires*, published in 1828, already contained many slang expressions, and was followed by numerous texts of the same kind, either directly inspired by Vidocq's or others very similar in outlook and origin.[39] For example, in 1829, there was a "New Argot Dictionary, by an Ex-Brigade Chief under M. Vidocq" (*Nouveau Dictionnaire d'argot, par un ex-chef de brigade sous M. Vidocq*), and the "Story of Vidocq, Chief of the Security Police" (*Histoire de Vidocq, chef de la police de sûreté*).[40] Works such as these, and others, such as "The Prisons of Paris, by a Former Inmate" (*Les Prisons de Paris par un ancien détenu*) and "Memories of a Pirate Philosopher" (*Les Mémoires d'un forban philosophe*), all of which include slang dictionaries, obviously satisfied the public's fascination with inside views of a subculture to which it did not belong.[41] This interest was camouflaged by claims to practical utility, as one of the earliest argot dictionaries, written anonymously by a "A Very Proper Gentleman," clearly suggests: it is described as a "Guide for worldly people, to guard them against narks, crooks, ladies of the night, and other fashionable people and lowly courtisanes of that sort" (most likely it was principally with the ladies of the night that a Very Proper Gentleman would have any contact with the underworld).[42]

Vidocq's second book, "Thieves" (*Les Voleurs*), also asserts a practical purpose: it is called "a work that discloses the tricks of rascals and destined to become the *Vade Mecum* of all honest people."[43] With this remark, Vidocq strives to put himself in the privileged position of one who, having belonged to the underworld, now finds himself on the respectable side of society and who works for the common good, with, of course, first-hand knowledge of his subject: "I wanted to paint thieves as they are in reality."[44] Slang finds more than an occasional place in this work: "Thieves" takes the form of an argot dictionary and is entirely dependent on this language. The world of criminals is thus conveniently reduced and classified, submitted to an order imposed from the outside. The slang terms are defined both geographically and according to "types" of thieves: "I indicated as often as I could to which group the individual belonged who named an object in such a manner, and in what region he ordinarily lived."[45] Vidocq distinguishes between thieves from Brittany, Normandy, or Paris, for instance, and between those associated with various "professions": peddlers, prostitutes, travelling merchants, showmen. He justifies his primarily linguistic approach by claiming that a familiarity with these people's mode of communication is indispensable to a knowledge of their world. Argot, here, is restricted to criminals, and retains much of its original identity and function: the arcane language of outcast and subversive groups that came into being in the fifteenth century. At that time, the economic ruin and disorder that followed the Hundred Years War led a certain segment of the population to reorganize itself independently of established society. Out-of-work peasants, merchants and laborers, soldiers who had fled the army and escaped convicts were the main components of what was known as the Corporation of Beggars (Corporation des Gueux). They formed a highly structured group, with its own social hierarchy and language (then called *Jargon*), army, legal jurisdiction, and so forth. Although the Corporation of Beggars went through many changes, it remained in existence until the reign of Louis XIV; *Jargon* was called *Narquois* in the sixteenth and seventeenth centuries and *argot* thereafter.[46]

The translation of argot from the language of criminals to the language of the people is reflected in many works, particularly dictionaries, that appeared at the time. In a scholarly work published in 1856, Francisque-Michel describes the relationship that links slang and popular language. First he notes the existence of "another language, that exists alongside the language spoken by respectable and learned people."[47] He then goes on to describe how slang now finds a place in this other language: "French argot, as I have briefly described it, does not only belong to the idiom of criminals. *It also finds a place in popular language*" (my emphasis).[48] Another example is a dictionary by Lorédan Larchey, first called, in 1859, "The Eccentricities of the French Language" (*Les Excentricités de la langue française*). The sixth edition, published in 1872, was renamed "Historical, Etymological and Anecdotal Dictionary of Parisian Slang" (*Dictionnaire historique, étymologique et anecdotique de l'argot parisien*).[49] There is a shift in these titles, one suggesting an element of frivolity (eccentricities), the other a more scientific project (etymological dictionary), and a specifically Parisian language. In the introduction to the 1872 edition of his dictionary, Larchey refers to this trend and quotes an article from *Le Figaro*, written in 1862:

> "Reading the list of words previously typical of the conversations of thieves and crooks, one guesses, on the one hand, that a good number of them will not last long, and one realizes, on the other hand, that *a good many of them have found a place in public usage*."[50] (my emphasis)

Also in *Le Figaro* (26 March 1866), a favorable review was written in response to Delvau's "Dictionary of Crude Language" (*Dictionnaire de la langue verte*), which was seen as an interesting and necessary

24 Political Stylistics

reaction to a linguistic invasion: "Argot is invading us – our Parisian Thebes, rather than a hundred gates, has a hundred languages."[51] The first and second editions of "The Dictionary of Crude Language" were published in 1866; a third appeared in 1883, and a fourth in 1889. They were well received, with, as the supplement to the third edition tells us, "much ado and a great deal of curiosity."[52] In the preface, Delvau explains why his work is valuable; first, because the terms given in the dictionary are so widely used that a foreigner, or even someone from the provinces, would not be able to understand what he heard in the capital if he were not familiar with argot. Second, although Delvau admits that slang has a brutal aspect, he believes that, none the less, a high value should be placed on its ability to evoke strong images through vivid metaphors. His attitude towards those who routinely use this language is one of unabashed superiority. Although he describes himself as a "child of the streets of Paris," issued from generations of working people (attempting, like Vidocq, to prove an authentic familiarity with his subject), he too considers himself to have now risen above his origins. He gains distance through the process of writing, classifying and translating popular language – that is, by partaking in the bourgeoisie's strategy of representation, and this distance automatically translates into a position of moral righteousness:

> There where many delicate people do not dare to go for fear of dirtying their sense and spirits, I was not afraid to go, for we moralists have the double privilege of salamanders and ermines: we may cross through flames without being scorched, and through mud without being soiled.[53]

Much can be learned about the bourgeoisie's strategy of representation of the working class, by looking into the professed motivations and the justifications of those who, from the outside, were concerned with popular language. In particular, it is worth noting how they differ from those of the authors who wrote about the argot of criminals. A practical aim was assigned to texts of the latter sort as well; a knowledge of argot was judged potentially useful, but as a protective measure. Any contact the reader might have with criminals was assumed to be (and probably was) defensive ("a work that discloses the tricks of rascals"). Delvau, however, claims that his dictionary might help a person from the provinces visiting the capital (without suggesting that this might be in a dangerous situation), and one of his other works, "Underground Paris" (*Les Dessous de Paris*) is something of a guide for brief and entertaining excursions into the underworld. Condescending amusement replaces the fascinated horror that had been aroused by the unknown underworld of criminals and its obscure linguistic code.[54] Francisque-Michel describes popular language as "cheerful, witty, insolent" and the *Figaro* article comments: "And take note how [members of the working class] are well skilled in the art of talking cheerfully about sad things. Rather than say 'to die,' they say 'to go fishing for fried fish in the river Styx.' Isn't that ingenious!"[55] Such stances, like all those that delight in the picturesque, were not innocent. Part of a trend common at the time, they established distance from the object of which they attempt to construct a positive image – in this case that of the "good worker." Such a strategy barely concealed the bourgeoisie's anxiety in the face of the working class's potential power. This ambiguity is quite apparent in Delvau's attitude, for instance: his admiration for the vivid imagery and metaphors of popular language is accompanied by contemptuous references. These are linguistic translations of another tactic, motivated by the same fear: the representation of the "bad worker," the negativity of which is sharpened when the voice of criminals is still made to resonate in popular language. Such a perception is particularly useful to the bourgeoisie: it enables its fear of the proletariat's potential power to masquerade as fear of moral disorder.

A similar attitude also informs *Le Sublime* by Denis Poulot, a work of the 1870s that purports to be both descriptive and preventive.[56] The first part consists of eight portraits of different types of workers, of their attitudes and activities, and offers many examples of conversations where argot expressions appear in italics and are clarified by footnotes. In the introduction, Poulot apologizes for the harshness of the language, which, he explains, has to be given in all its crudity because academic French has no expressions to translate the popular terms. The workers are ranked according to the degree to which they exhibit qualities such as eagerness to work, ability to save money, sobriety, and respect for the boss: the "true worker" comes first, whereas what Poulot ironically calls the "sublime" (the bad worker) comes last. Poulot proposes measures that would solve a difficult and pressing problem: the demoralization of the working class. Improvement should be achieved by providing the greatest possible well-being for all, while respecting the law and justice, under the general guidelines of improved education and morality. The underlying aim of the work, and the moral pretext that covers a conservative political stance, emerge very clearly in the last sentence:

> To all the reformers who, to attain the much anticipated regeneration, cry out "down with capital, down with interest, down with God, down with family, down with ownership!" we answer, with the cry of our conscience and our deep conviction: "Down with lazy workers!"[57]

I showed, in the introduction, how argot and popular language in *The Last Day of a Condemned*, *Les Misérables* and *Vautrin's Last Avatar* were represented in a manner that drew immediate attention to their dissociation from the body of the text: their singularity was underlined with italics, footnotes, parentheses and translations. Unlike the novels to be considered here, the unexpected expressions were always restricted to the characters' directly reported utterances. Establishing a bond between writer and reader, and excluding the lower classes by an objectifying representation, these words function as boundary markers. Another work in which the distancing and objectifying functions appear with glaring clarity is Eugène Sue's serial novel "The Mysteries of Paris" (*Les Mystères de Paris*), first published in 1842 in the then right-wing *Le Journal des Débats*. Recounting the daily lives, with numerous anecdotes and picturesque incidents, of lower-class characters, the work met with enormous success and enjoyed a very large readership. As in Hugo's and Balzac's novels, slang words in this text are separated from others; they are printed in italics and explanations are provided in footnotes which very often include deprecatory comments, such as: "We shall not for too long have recourse to this awful argot language, we shall only provide a few typical examples" and "We are ashamed of these details, but they concur with these strange customs."[58] Also like Hugo and Balzac, Sue recognizes a certain poetic potential in argot. Reflecting on the name of one of the characters, Fleur-de-Marie, he writes:

> Bizarre contrast, strange accident! the inventors of this dreadful language have hence elevated themselves to saintly poetry! They have added an additional charm to the chaste thought that they wanted to express in their hideous language; for the frightening thing, worthy of the attention of thinkers, is that these men are numerous enough, united enough, to have their own language, as they have their own customs and their own part of town.[59]

Sue does not view argot as merely poetic, however. It is also threatening, for it symbolizes the people's unity: "the frightening thing . . . is that these men are numerous enough, united enough to have their own language." Again, a political menace underlies the entertaining picturesque. A similarly ambivalent attitude is displayed by Hugo who, in *Les Misérables*, repeatedly depicts argot in repellent terms: "It is a horrible, toad-like tongue, which goes, comes, hops, crawls, slavers and moves monstrously in that vast grey mist . . . ." To hear that language spoken gives one the impression of "a hideous murmur, sounding almost like human accents, but more like a yell than like a speech." Yet, Hugo is not without recognition of its poetic aspects, its strength and vitality, its powerful metaphors: "It is proper that a language which wishes to say everything and yet to conceal everything abounds in figures." He acknowledges, therefore, that "this strange dialect has by right its own place in the great impartial museum where there is room for the rusty copper coins as well as the gold medal, and which is called literature."[60]

Hugo's novel is also significant in that it reflects the displacement of the linguistic specificity of criminals and its absorption into that of the people. Unlike the hordes of prisoners in *The Last Day of a Condemned* (1829), the characters who resort to slang in *Les Misérables* (1862) are often sympathetic. The use of argot, here, extends to a group specific to Hugo's social vision, *la misère* (which can be translated as wretchedness), the status of which is not without ambiguity. The ambiguity, combining the two meanings that Victor Brombert in *Victor Hugo and the Visionary Novel*[61] discerns in Hugo's use of the term *misérables* (abject, despicable scoundrels on the one hand, and unhappy and potentially sublime victims of the social order on the other), is well illustrated in the following description:

> the people who labour, suffer and wait, oppressed woman, the dying child, the secret warfare between man and man, obscure ferocities, prejudices, conventional inequities, the subterranean consequences of the law, the secret evolution of souls, the indistinct tremors of multitudes, those who die of hunger, the bare-footed, the bare-armed, the dis-inherited, the orphans, the unhappy, the infamous and all the ghosts that wander in darkness.[62]

Similarly, Hugo considers argot to express both misfortune and transgression: "There is darkness in misfortune, and greater darkness still in crime; these two darknesses amalgamated compose slang."[63] The deplorable socio-economic conditions under which the people live are responsible for what Hugo here calls misfortune. In these passages, both the Revolution and the people are glorified. Hugo goes on to suggest, however, that his abstract ideal of the enlightened, morally righteous class may not be retained. The present deterioration of social conditions is such that the "grand forward march of the minds" may be hindered: "Apoplexy is no longer to be apprehended, but another illness, consumption, is present. Social consumption is called wretchedness."[64] Therefore, he argues, it is the duty of all enlightened thinkers to turn their attention to this dangerous situation and prevent further aggravation, according to what he calls a "social philosophy." Such concerns are surely motivated by fear as well as generosity: "Social philosophy is essentially the science of peace. Its object is, and its result must be, the dissolution of passions by the study of antagonisms. It examines, scrutinizes, and analyzes; then it recomposes."[65]

Unlike criminals (whose lot the bourgeoisie had no interest in improving), the people could not be categorically condemned, outwardly and unequivocally despised, but had to be contained within a strategy of representation that allowed both accommodation and control. The preceding discussion shows how the emerging linguistic specificity of the working class attracted much attention and was used in the construction of an image that represented the people as a foreign, threatening, distant entity, one that could and should, nevertheless, settle in a place of necessary subjugation. A *strategy of accommodation* showed the people and its language, viewed through supposedly indulgent eyes, as a good-natured and inoffensive provider of entertaining idiosyncrasies. A *strategy of control* constructed this class and its language as a subject of enquiry to be approached in a scientific manner and in need of nothing other than enlightened didacticism and humanitarian reform. In both cases the bourgeoisie launched its project of objectification and control, in which the representation of popular language in literary texts played an important role.

From the rise of industrial capitalism to the emergence of monopoly capitalism, the economic and cultural profile of the working class evolved. During this period, its language also changed, with particular ease because of many synchronic variations, and because it was not crystalized in a written form. To this day, however, a bourgeois representation of the working class remains in existence, which strategically refers to it, Bourdieu notes, as a typically and reassuringly French entity. The myth, he explains, draws on romanticized representations, such as Marcel Carné's movies rather than on actual observation. "It excludes without a second thought all immigrant workers, Spanish or Portuguese, Algerian or Moroccan, Malian or Senegalese, who occupy a more important place among the population of industrial workers than in the imaginary proletariat."[66]

POPULAR LANGUAGE AND ITS SUBVERSIVE POTENTIAL

In all the cases reviewed above, the bourgeois appropriation of popular language participates in an objectifying representation of the working class that aims at its political containment and control. In the literary texts, this strategy restricts popular language to the voice of characters. By visibly dissociating the unfamiliar expressions from the rest of the text, and by offering deprecatory comments about them, the author clearly distances himself from that idiom and those who speak it. Barthes notes, in *Writing Degree Zero*, that the nineteenth century was a period during which "the bourgeoisie found good-humoured entertainment in everything situated on the fringe of its own preserve." Entertainment, however, was not operating alone and innocently, but in conjunction with a serious political agenda.[67] The novels discussed above are literary works in which a particular stylistic feature contributed to reinforcing the political structure of the society from which they emerged. In *L'Assommoir*, *Journey to the End of the Night* and *Zazie in the Metro*, popular language is represented without the obvious marks of objectification that accompany its presence in earlier texts. It is, therefore, not illogical to assume that, because they depart from a stylistic strategy that reinforces the bourgeoisie's domination, they may perform an oppositional political function. To what extent this transformation is realized, and whether it indeed operates as a political subversion, are the central questions that this study addresses. There are a number of ways in which the rupture with previous literary practice could suggest a challenge to the established order; some might only be revealed by the texts themselves, and others merit theoretical exploration at this early point. It is also worth noting (another word of caution) that a number of resistances, both internal and external to the text, may well be at work to hinder this disruptive potential.

It is a well-known and much regretted fact that classical marxist criticism has never paid attention to style. For Lukács, to cite one critic among many others, form should be totally transparent; literary works should put forth a mimetic representation of reality invariably moving towards socialism, according to a pre-set historical process:

> The more "artless" a work of art, the more it gives the effect of life and nature, the more clearly it exemplifies an actual concentrated reflection of its times and the more clearly it demonstrates that the only function of its form is to express this objectivity, this

reflection of life in the concreteness and clarity with all its motivating contradictions.[68]

Here and now, social realism knows few advocates. Much of contemporary political criticism is derived from the views advocated, from an unorthodox marxist position, by the Frankfurt School. Condemning social realism and engaged works, Adorno, in his essay "Commitment," which concludes his debate with Benjamin by criticizing all politically direct art, celebrates texts where "language jolts signification" and whose stylistic resistance, tension and negation have a deeply unsettling effect that shocks the reader out of complacency: "It is not the office of art to spotlight alternatives but to resist by its form only the course of the world which permanently puts a pistol to men's heads."[69] Marcuse, in *The Aesthetic Dimension*, also articulates a strong critique of mimetic representation and argues in favor of an aesthetic transformation. It is by virtue of its form that literature can contribute to the struggle towards liberation: "The aesthetic transformation is achieved through a reshaping of language, perception and understanding so that they reveal the essence of reality in its appearance: the repressed potentialities of man and nature."[70] Works that do not rely on unchallenged communication to convey a mere reproduction of dominant ideology would, through disorientation, bring the reader to new attitudes. These positions are not without their problems, and many charges have been brought against them. Elitism is the first that comes to mind. As Leenhardt put it:

> Among its very limited public, this kind of text will ultimately organize a permanent exchange of ingeniousness in which a given cultural heritage will always play a dominant role. The reader toward whom this literature is directed is thus an academician bristling with erudition.[71]

Also addressing problems of readership, Terry Eagleton, in a critique of reception theories, brings to attention Wolfgang Iser's remark in *The Act of Reading* that readers with strong ideological commitments are likely to be inadequate, since they are not likely to be open to the transformative power of works that disconfirm routine habits of perception. The ideal reader, Eagleton concludes, would have to be someone whose beliefs are only provisional in the first place: "The only good reader would *already* have to be a liberal: the act of reading produces a kind of subject it also presupposes" (Eagleton's emphasis).[72] And, launching his critique from a different angle,

Adorno himself warns that a cultivation of the unintelligible easily falls into the facile:

> The loss of tension evident in works of painting and music which have moved away from objective representation and intelligible or coherent meaning has in many ways spread to the literature known in a repellent jargon as "texts." Such works drift to the brinks of indifference, degenerate insensibly into mere hobbies, into idle repetition of formulas now abandoned in other art forms, into trivial patterns.[73]

Finally, it is worth noting that there is no guarantee that a liberated sensibility induced by works whose multiple, unstable meanings suggest a questioning of the world as we know it will operate as a space for a revolutionary conscience to develop. Barthes, in *The Pleasure of the Text*, suggests that there is no better response to such a writing than, all critical faculties set aside, to submit to the engulfing, exalting and above all pleasurable power-play of language.[74]

The consequence of the disorienting effect that the presence of popular language in *L'Assommoir*, *Journey to the End of the Night* and *Zazie in the Metro* might have on the reader is certainly an area worthy of investigation. Because the public's horizon of expectations changes with time, there will be variations, of course, in how unexpected that stylistic feature actually is for each novel. But, in all cases, the presence of popular language contradicts what does remain a shared belief, inculcated by the educational system: writers express themselves in good French. These novels might also problematize the communicative function to a certain degree: not because of a syntax that produces ambiguity of meaning (except in the case of *Journey*, but, as we will see, this is not due to the presence of popular language alone) but because the reader might be unfamiliar with certain expressions. An important difference between the works to be reviewed here and those that Adorno advocates is that their style not only departs, deviates from legitimate language, but also contradicts its rules. Unlike the works by Kafka or Beckett, or even Philippe Sollers, these novels display grammatical mistakes. This opposition to legitimate language can be viewed as an opposition to its political functions and to the institutions that promote them.

If this study has focused on the discussion of legitimate and popular language, this is by no means to suggest that these are the only two idioms that operate within a society. A wide array of intermediaries between these two extremes forms a hierarchy that reflects that of society. The model used here corresponds to Bourdieu's, which views the linguistic field as a system of power relations founded on the unequal distribution of linguistic capital, a differential structure that reproduces that of the unequal distribution of economic wealth.[75] Admittedly, linguistic variations also occur with a number of other factors – geography, gender, and generation, to cite a few – but these will not be relevant here. They do enter, however, into Mikhail Bakhtin's conception of heteroglossia, as he discusses it in *The Dialogic Imagination*. Even though, in this work, linguistic diversity is not as closely bound to class notions as it is here (and includes, for example, different professional jargons, different generic written styles), Bakhtin's attempts to bridge the gap between "an abstract formal approach and an equally abstract ideological approach" will provide crucial critical tools for this study.[76] Particularly useful, at this point, is his argument that the word gains meaning not only from its relation to other words but also from its connection to the social realm; even when syntactically isolated, the word is pervaded by previous contexts, previous usages and social conflicts.

Popular language, when used by members of the class from which it originates, often plays a phatic role: to construct the cohesiveness of the group, and, often, to signal distance from and antagonism towards the ruling class. In the bourgeois appropriations discussed above, we have seen that this language is used for quite different ends, and, Bakhtin notes, sometimes becomes divorced from its original functions:

> for the speakers of the languages themselves, these generic languages and professional jargons are directly intentional – they denote and express directly and fully, and are capable of expressing themselves without mediation; but outside, that is, for those not participating in the given purview, these languages may be treated as objects, as typifications, as local color.[77]

The bourgeoisie, as it seizes the instrument that, in its original use, helps the working class construct its identity and constitute itself as an adversative position of potential power, reverses its function: popular language is transformed into a tool for reinforcing the working class's alienation. Volosinov suggests that, in cases such as these, when one and the same language is used by different classes, "differently oriented accents intersect in every ideological sign; sign becomes an arena of the class struggle."[78] If traces of the word's history, and of its uses in previous contexts were still present in the bourgeois appropriations prior to *L'Assommoir*, they were rendered inactive by the very clear objectification: the "accents" of bourgeois domination won over that of working-class expression. In the conflict these representations expressed, the ruling class clearly had the upper hand. Such, however, may not be the case for the works to be examined here. Traces of the previous contexts, history, and functions of popular language may remain dangerously active; its ties to the social class from which it originates may not be controlled.

The presence of popular language in *L'Assommoir*, *Journey to the End of the Night* and *Zazie in the Metro*, by disconfirming routine expectations and habits of perception, might have a transformative effect on the reader's view of the world. Further, the grammatical incorrections that the texts display, by opposing the rules and norms of legitimate language, might suggest an opposition to its conservative political functions. And, in popular language, antagonistic accents towards the ruling class might still resonate. All of these effects would be, of course, closely interlinked, and would operate in conjunction with each other. A last possibility (also closely related to those mentioned above) for subversive political efficiency derives from the linguistic re-stratification that, Bakhtin suggests, the literary text allows:

> Therefore, the stratification of language – generic, professional, social in the narrow sense, that of particular world views, particular tendencies, particular individuals, the social speech diversity and language diversity (dialects) of languages – upon entering the novel establishes its own special order within it and becomes a unique artistic system which orchestrates the intentional theme of the author.[79]

In the new order that an artistic reworking organizes, popular language may play a role that is no longer one of subordination. The novel's stylistic structure, then, would suggest a new social order under which the working class escapes the domination in which it has been previously held; in that case, the political effectiveness of literary utopia would have to be closely scrutinized.

FROM THE SOCIAL TO THE TEXTUAL AND BACK

The previous discussions have outlined a set of socio-linguistic models and critical tools that will be relevant to a political stylistics. Each of the following three chapters will be devoted to one novel, and will investigate the text's production, its formal particularities, and its effects in the socio-political realm, according to an approach that needs to be delineated at this point. The final chapter will synthesize the vital points uncovered in each work.

The social grounding of the study of each novel will investigate two areas: the place from which popular language is removed and the circumstances that participate in its displacement. The place from which popular language is removed is, of course, the working class; its evolution, from the rise of industrial capitalism to the dawn of post-industrial society will have to be taken into account. Even though the *peuple* will remain the most oppressed class and will continue to be ruled by the same social group throughout the period that concerns us, there will be changes in a number of areas: in, for example, the amount of economic hardship and the extent of revolutionary potential; in the degree of cultural specificity; in the manner in which the working class and ruling class see each other. World historical forces – wars, revolutions – from the late 1870s to the late 1950s will, of course, affect the internal politics of France, while more localized transformations, such as of the educational system, will directly influence the linguistic field. Clearly, popular language itself will evolve throughout this period in its place and functions within the literary and political arenas, as well as in its formal particularities. Its original profile, at each moment of its displacement, from 1876, to 1932, and 1959 (the publication dates of the three novels), will be traced.

As for the circumstances that contribute to the displacement of popular language, they are constants and variables that in part make up the literary discursive situation. The stylistic choices that this situation offers are dependent on a number of factors, the first of which is the author's linguistic horizon: what modes of expression are available to him, given his original class position and social trajectory. Should he be of working-class origin, one might ask whether popular language finds a place in his work because of a lack of competence in the usage of legitimate language (an unlikely, but theoretically plausible situation). If not, the necessarily unusual manner in which the author acquired legitimate French (such as Céline's autodidactic experience) will influence his attitude towards that language. If he does not belong to the working class, the manner in which he gained his knowledge of popular language will be relevant: Zola, for instance, relied on dictionaries and documentary works. In this case, the language of the working class was not directly displaced, but mediated. The author's intellectual as well as material position *vis-à-vis* the class from which popular language originates will also influence its transposition. We have seen that one of the important variables of the literary discursive situation is whether the exchange is confrontational or not; however, the degree of solidarity with, or enmity towards the people that the author might profess will not necessarily be unambiguously reflected in the text – in their literary representation, political attitudes might also undergo displacement and transformation, or, at least, refraction.

The public's horizon of expectations, shaped by previous literary experience, the educational system, and the particular configuration of the literary field varies with time and will have to be determined in each case; the author's status, and the particular section of the reading public that he might aim to address will also be taken into consideration. Queneau's literary reputation, for instance, was well established before he wrote *Zazie*; he did not rely on that text alone to establish his legitimacy. He was also a reader for Gallimard and knew that this novel, like his previous ones, would be published there. Such was not the case for *Journey*, Céline's first work, initially anonymously submitted to and rejected by the same publisher. Finally, the preparation process will be looked at, along with factors related to the stylistic choice in a more direct way: previous works, drafts, and the author's statements, public or private, about his project. The task, then, will be to circumscribe those elements that intervene in what Bakhtin calls the choice of a language: "With each literary-verbal performance, consciousness must actively orient itself amidst heteroglossia, it must move in and occupy a position for itself within it; it chooses, in other words, a language."[80]

Next, the place to which popular language is brought, the novel, will be examined. A crucial point that the textual analysis needs to take into account is that underlying the representation of popular language in these literary works is the mutation of a primarily spoken code into a written one. The representation, therefore, entails not only a change of context (from the social to the literary) but a change of form: from the oral to the graphic. We have seen that, whatever the response of individual readers might have been when slang found a place in several novels of the nineteenth century, such as *The Last Day of a Condemned* and *Vautrin's Last Avatar*, no official censorship was exercised against its occurrence in some reported conversations in these texts. However, at the beginning of the Second Empire, official authorities strongly reacted against the presence of slang on stage. In 1853, the Minister of the Interior advised theater directors not to allow artists to insert in their roles "sentences that have not been submitted to censorship, especially argot sentences." In 1858, the Minister of State informed them that "The Censorship Committee has received strict instructions against the use, in the theater, of terms borrowed from argot."[81] Even though both instances occur in a literary context, argot spoken in the theater appears more threatening to governmental authorities than its written counterpart. The 1853 memo suggests that part of the problem was that actors spontaneously added sentences that did not belong to the original script and thus evaded censorship; but the government's concern must also have had to do with the fact that slang on stage is dangerously closer to its original, primarily spoken form, whereas the written representation neutralizes its potency, not only by symbolically distancing the language from its social roots, but also by carrying out a transformation on its original structures. For writing is not simply a transcription of speech into a written state; rather, the two modes of expression are quite distinct in their form, function, and manner of acquisition.

Generically and in degree of usage, speech has primacy. Language, in individuals and societies alike, is first spoken, and not always written. As Jack Goody and Ian Watt point out in "The Consequences of Literacy," uncertain criteria – such as whether a system actually qualifies as writing, and the degree to which the knowledge has penetrated the society – make rigid distinctions between literate and non-literate societies difficult to establish.[82] The trajectory of the written word has been traced back to pictographs (series of pictures directly representing the object, in a more or less standardized manner). These were followed by logograms whereby a symbol represents an entire word, to form a complex system available only to a small and powerful elite. Such inscriptions were tied to primarily religious, administrative and commercial contexts. Goody and Watt also suggest that writing systems served a profoundly conservative function, allowing the literate elite to cling to the privilege that determined its existence and power. A relative democratization of writing occurred with the appearance of alphabetic systems. Phonetic principles seem to have been first introduced in Sumeria, in about 3000 BC, again to record economic transactions and laws; it was not until a thousand years later that Middle Eastern syllabaries, from which all alphabets derive, came into existence. Only in sixth-century Greece was widespread literacy achieved, and it played a vital role in the country's cultural and political unification. However, if alphabetic systems of writing are more accessible than those that preceded, Goody and Watt point out that degrees of participation in literate cultures vary greatly within a society at a given time: "the literate mode of communication does not impose itself as forcefully or uniformly as was the case with the oral transmission of a cultural tradition."[83] Furthermore, writing upholds the normative aspect of legitimate language and is central to the conveyance and diffusion of discourses of authority.

Because the written word is realized in fixed and verifiable form, it remains. It is more open to control than its spoken counterpart, it carries a degree of finality and juridical weight and projects its meaning to many readers over a long period of time. Because the written text may always be looked back upon, it affords a more complex, analytical structure and develops, as Barthes points out, into a seed-like growth that expands ramifications along subordinate sentence structures.[84] Speech, on the other hand, has a more aggregative nature; its flow is linear and additive. Since listening cannot be retroactive, repetition is necessary to keep both the speaker and listener on the right track, in a movement of expansion that is counteracted by one of reduction: syntagms tend to contract into shorter units, words are sometimes omitted. To compensate for omissions and ambiguities, spoken communication relies heavily on phonetic information (intonations, pauses, exclamations) and non-linguistic signs (gestures, situational context). It is far less precise, less ordered, and more fragmented than writing, containing gaps, liaison words and phatic elements that establish an atmosphere of social contact rather than provide information. On the other hand, since writing has to be self-contained, it carries a greater amount of clearly encoded linguistic information, and because it establishes a material line of continuity, it is able to take a more complex form: an ordered structure within which each word has a precise grammatical function indicated by its position, spelling, and the surrounding syntax. Many more forms, syntactical and lexical, are judged acceptable in speech, for its standards of correctness are less rigid and therefore allow for linguistic innovation. Only after neologisms, or syntactical drifts, have gained spoken currency does one discover their occasional use in texts. Then they must appear numerous times before they are authorized to enter the revised version of a dictionary or grammar book, the official seal of approval.

Unlike speech, which is acquired through familiarization, and whose practice is available to all, writing requires formal training: graphic technique, the learning of rules, the memorization of orthography. This knowledge is acquired in school where, in a highly normative way, writing is taught to represent and reinforce norms of correctness: it is the legitimate language that the child is taught to write. So unsuited is writing to reflect adequately any language but this one that linguists have devised a phonetic code in which most characteristics of speech, including accents, pauses, stresses, regional particularities and intonations are indicated with precision. Otherwise, when a written form is given to a spoken expression (whether it be in police reports, interviews in the press, or characters' utterances in literary texts) one cannot talk of transcriptions but representations. Since it is impossible to include every feature of the spoken code, the representation necessarily involves a transformation. Because popular language, with its syntactical particularities and words that are not officially recognized, is even more removed from legitimate language than the one that the upper classes use in everyday conversation, its representation in writing will necessarily involve further alterations; these are not only related to writing's inadequacy in representing a primarily oral code, especially one that is significantly distant from legitimate language, but also to the lack of familiarity of a writer who might be removed from the social situation and conditions in which popular language is spoken.

Bakhtin argues that when a "social language" is represented in the literary text, "typical aspects of the language are selected as characteristic of or symbolically crucial to the language."[85] The forms by virtue of which popular language is represented I shall refer to as popular markers. Not only, of course, will these forms be selected because the author perceives them as typical but also because they best suit his stylistic intentions. Is popular language primarily represented by lexical, syntactical or phonetic markers? Among the lexical ones, how removed are the words from legitimate vocabulary – are they only slightly colloquial, or clearly popular? Are they attached to a particular subject matter? There will also be variations in the degree of syntactical error. Are the grammatical forms in question typical of spoken language and hence deviate only slightly from the norm, or do they clearly oppose it? Among the popular markers, do different types occur more readily at different points in the text? In their adaptation to the written mode, what type of transformation do they seem to have undergone? These are some of the questions that will first be addressed, along with an initial analysis of popular markers in terms of their internal structure. Bearing in mind that popular language, as it appears on the printed page of the literary text, is, as Terdiman puts it, a very tangible outcome of "the struggle for the control of the sign's use,"[86] the first step will help indicate how forcefully the accents of antagonism towards the ruling class still resonate. Furthermore, it will offer information on the vitality with which these forms oppose the rules and norms of legitimate language. Often, Bourdieu remarks, the written representation is far removed from its original form:

> Because of their concern to treat it like a "language" – that is, with all the rigor that one ordinarily reserves for legitimate language – all those who have attempted to describe or write "the popular," linguists or writers – have condemned themselves to produce artifacts almost entirely unrelated to the ordinary language that speakers the most foreign to legitimate language use for internal exchanges.[87]

To these more or less attenuated traces, new accents are added by the word's new literary status, written form, and surrounding context. An analysis of the markers' relation to their surrounding context, and of their role in the overall stylistic structure of the novel, are the next two steps the analysis should take. Bakhtin suggests:

> The linguistic and stylistic profile of a given element (lexical, semantic, syntactic) is shaped by that subordinated unity to which it is most immediately proximate. At the same time this element, together with its immediate unity, figures into the style of the novel as a whole, itself supports the accent of the whole and participates in the process whereby the unified meaning of the whole is structured and revealed.[88]

The notion of stylistic effect, which Riffaterre puts forth in his "Essays in Structural Stylistics" (*Essais de stylistique structurale*), will be useful to analyze the interaction between popular markers and their immediate context.[89] Dismissing the importance of an external norm that is brought to bear on the reading from outside experience, Riffaterre introduces the notion of internal context: the habitual (because repeated) pattern of linguistic forms that the text establishes and to which the reader becomes accustomed. If several breaches of the same type take place successively, the context is modified as the previously unpredictable elements become part of the reader's new expectations. We will look, then, at where popular markers first occur, in particular where and how they are introduced outside of the directly reported speech of characters. Further on in the text, their density at different points may vary. In some sections, they may remain stylistically disruptive, but scarce. Elsewhere, they may become predictable enough to form the context and, even though quantitatively prevalent, will lose the impact they created when first present, for the reader will have grown accustomed to them. It will be important to note whether routine habits of perception are suddenly disconfirmed or gradually so – and whether, once this has occurred, the reader will be constantly jolted by a variety of stylistic surprises,

40   Political Stylistics

or become used to a stable structure that the text has created. Even though, on those occasions, popular language will command less attention, it will be the dominant feature of what Bakhtin calls compositional or stylistic unities:

> The stylistic uniqueness of the novel as a genre consists precisely in the combination of these subordinated, yet still relatively autonomous unities (even at times comprised of different languages) into the higher unity of the work as a whole: the style of the novel is to be found in the combination of its styles. The language of a novel is the system of its "languages."[90]

Also worth investigating, then, is the manner in which the stylistic unities interact with each other, and the place and role of popular language in the unity of the novel will have to be established. It is in relation to the other stylistic unities that a re-stratification might occur to suggest a social utopia whereby the popular might not be maintained in a place of subordination.

The stylistic structure of the novel will not, of course, be analyzed independently, but in conjunction with its narrative structure. Even though the distinguishing stylistic trait of *L'Assommoir*, *Journey to the End of the Night* and *Zazie in the Metro* is that popular markers occur outside of the directly reported speech of characters, they also occur within it; it will be important to note whether this is the case for the speech of all characters, and how it might differ according to their social definition, role, situation, and so forth. When popular markers do find a place outside of directly reported speech, this might be in the narrated speech. On which occasions this occurs, with what type of popular markers, and the manner in which the speech is narrated (with, for example, devices such as indirect and free indirect style) will have to be determined. Whether or not popular markers also occur in the narration of events, and, if so, to relate what kind of event, are other questions worth raising. Furthermore, they can play a significant role in the narrative structure when linked to certain types of focalization. I hasten to add that the stylistic structure and narrative structure will not be regarded and analyzed separately, as their consecutive discussion here might suggest, but, rather, in relation to each other; the interactions between how the story is put together, the language used to tell it, and how one affects the other are, of course, crucial. Just as this chapter, rather than formulating a methodology that is to be unremittingly applied, seeks to construct a set of critical tools and suggest how they can be used in conjunction with each other, the rigidity with which the textual analysis is outlined here will disappear in practice. The analytical procedure will be very much guided by the text itself. Certain parts of the investigation will appear particularly relevant and interesting, some may provoke further and unexpected developments, whereas others might prove less effective. This outline is not a model to be applied in the same manner to three very different works, but a set of guidelines to areas worthy of attention.

The analysis provides a description of the structures to which a reader might react, in a way related only to the work itself, not to the horizon of expectations brought in from the outside. The reader that it assumes is not dissimilar to the one that Wolfgang Iser puts forth in *The Act of Reading*, the implied reader, whose character and historical situation are not predetermined: "The concept of the implied reader is therefore a textual structure anticipating the presence of a recipient without necessarily defining him."[91] The implied reader, then, is merely an abstraction, an abstraction that served a temporary purpose. Iser moves away from that abstraction with his conception of the realization of the text: the procedures whereby the given structures undergo processing and manipulation (with acts of selection, organization, and so forth) until all converge into a pattern that is coherent for the individual. This operation depends on each reader's past feelings, views and values, and history. Factors such as these cannot be documented within the scope of this study. What will have been documented, however, in the discussion of the literary discursive situation, is the horizon of expectations that Jauss, who accounts for reading as an essentially collective phenomenon, proposes as the common set of attitudes towards the text. These expectations must be brought to bear on the information that the stylistic analysis yielded, and will certainly modulate whatever oppositional potential was suggested.

Even though one may safely assume the existence, for a given society at a given time, of a common set of expectations, not all are shared; Jauss's horizon can be viewed only as the lowest common denominator. Furthermore, what will significantly vary are the reactions to the fulfillment or non-fulfillment of these expectations. Jacques Leenhardt, in "Towards a Sociology of Reading," attempts to establish whether different sociological groups read differently.[92] He submitted a set of questions regarding two novels, one French, the other Hungarian, to five hundred readers of different backgrounds in France and Hungary. Since similar questions were put to all informants, the research did not seek to determine whether the readers responded to similar aspects of the novel, but how they reacted. Leenhardt found out that the answers could indeed be grouped into four systems for each national category. One can therefore talk not of a unified public, but of various publics, each with a particular reading system. It is obvious that, in reality, the reading public of a given work at a given time is not as diverse as the one Leenhardt observes – he purposefully questioned a wide sample of social groups, some of which might not otherwise have read the novels. It is also clear that a similar investigation cannot, for our purpose, be undertaken. However, it is possible to document reactions based on a distinction that often can, but not necessarily does, reflect socio-economic position: political allegiance. To the hypothetical reading deduced from the synthesis of the textual analysis and the general horizon of expectations, the last section of this study will add a discussion of the responses to the work's publication in the press of various political tendencies.

Not only will these responses be endowed with a certain degree of typicality, they will also partake in the determination of other readers' reactions. The literary text does not arrive before the eyes of the reader in virgin state. Already conditioned by the status of the author and publisher, the work is also shaped by the reception it encounters when it is launched on the market. The reactions of the public at large are undoubtedly shaped by the judgments passed by official readers in an institutional framework, and the press, with its increasingly important role, will be a crucial mediating agent. Pointing out that between 1830 and 1880 the circulation of newspapers in Paris had increased forty times, Terdiman describes the period that concerns us here as one during which "newspapers as institutionalized discourse would experience an extraordinary multiplication in its pervasiveness of the world of words and social representation".[93] Unlike those in more specialized publications, the assessments of the work in the press address a much wider audience than the novel could ever hope to reach; and by providing unabashed value judgments and clear-cut interpretations these reactions will help determine by whom the work is read, as well as how.

Since the readings that will concern us here are those grounded in and aiming to serve a specific political viewpoint, we will turn our attention to reactions (and there were many) in those publications that were officially affiliated to or informally supportive of a particular party or position. At the time of *L'Assommoir*, in 1876, organized political forces were still polarized between republican and anti-republican, with some variants, of course, in each camp. Both sides were geared, ultimately, towards controlling the working class –

particularly after the Commune uprisings – with different tactics, more or less overtly recognizing its existence as a social force to be reckoned with. Later, for *Journey to the End of the Night* and *Zazie in the Metro*, the left of the official political spectrum extended to the communist party, offering a radically different view of the situation, function and future of the proletariat. As for the right, it included, at the time of the publication of Céline's novel, not only traditional conservatism but fascist movements as well. In all cases, varying assumptions, divergent versions of history and interpretations of present-day situations, as well as different attitudes towards the working class and its language, provide the framework within which the work is read, and affect reactions to its style: political allegiance is founded on and produces different belief systems, and hence different reading systems. These reading systems will determine which aspects of the text will draw attention, how they are organized into a coherent whole, how the novel will be interpreted. Furthermore, not only will the novels be read from different viewpoints and with different sets of assumptions in mind, they will also be presented to the public with a political intention – to promote the cause a particular newspaper supports. The critics will all have investments in a particular representation of the popular, and it is likely that they will attempt to make the work serve that agenda. In a very conscious manner, certain aspects of the text will be emphasized, others will be ignored, connections made and parallels drawn to achieve this end. In short, the text will be manipulated and used as a very tangible propaganda tool. These critics will not be reading the novels as purely sensuous experiences, nor will they present themselves as being, or assume their audience to be, bristling with erudition. Our study will end at a place where the stylistic and political are brought to bear directly on each other.

2 Zola's *L'Assommoir*

In the preceding chapter I described how, during the second half of the nineteenth century, the need for a centralized, urban workforce brought a modern working class into being. Simultaneously, a popular language developed, drawing on an argot vocabulary that, previously, had been restricted to criminal groups. I outlined two strategies that the bourgeoisie adopted towards the people: a strategy of accommodation that allowed a representation of the oppressed class in terms of picturesque and inoffensive difference on the one hand, and, on the other, a strategy of control that established the workers as a subject of scientific inquiry, and that suggested occasional reforms from which they might benefit. Both attitudes, founded on an effort to objectify, reveal a double impulse: to know the working class, and to establish a distance from it. These initial steps, however, were not sufficient. In 1871, what the bourgeoisie had feared and attempted to avert through its earlier efforts occurred: a violent uprising of the working class: the Commune. Unlike what had happened in earlier revolutions, or revolutionary attempts, the enemy was not the aristocracy, against which both bourgeois and laborers were temporarily united, but the bourgeoisie itself. The Commune, in 1871, crystalized the opposition to capitalism. Strong repression, naturally, ensued. The *Communards* were not amnestied until 1879, and prohibitive laws were passed, such as that which made it a penal offense to belong to the Workers International. These events certainly heightened the workers' awareness of the possibility of revolution while, at the same time, reminding them of the strength of the oppressive forces against which they were pitted. To the bourgeoisie, the Commune brought the realization that its initial fears were justified, and that forceful domination was now warranted. Proletarian revolt ceased to be an abstraction. Five years later, in 1876, Zola's *L'Assommoir* was published.

Zola was born bourgeois. His father was a much respected civil engineer in Aix-en-Provence whose early death brought a sudden decline in the family's fortune, but the only child was nevertheless brought up according to the privileges of his class, attending a private school (Collège Bourbon in Aix) and a prestigious lycée (Saint Louis in Paris) where he did not do very well. Much has been made of the two years that Zola spent in relative poverty when, having failed his baccalauréat, he could not find suitable work. It would probably be more accurate to consider this period, which soon ended when Zola was employed by the Librairie Hachette in 1862, and later headed its publicity department in 1864, as an exercise in bohemianism. Even though he probably did come into close contact with the working class, he was, clearly, an outside and passing witness. There is no doubt that Zola did not learn popular language through what Pierre Bourdieu calls familiarization; his social status gave him the opportunity to acquire legitimate French which he put to use in his work for Hachette, and later, as a journalist when he wrote literary chronicles and political commentaries, often in a satirical vein. His professed position was republican, of the liberal sort, but not until the Dreyfus affair, in 1898, did Zola become active in the political field. During the Commune, he remained an observer, working as a parliamentary reporter for *La Cloche*, and then for *Le Sémaphore* in Marseilles. His newspaper reports on the meetings of the Assembly in Versailles show no signs of sympathy for the workers' struggle; one detects only the hope that a settlement between the opposing forces would soon be reached.

While he was still a journalist, Zola first entered the literary field with *Ninon's Tales* (*Les Contes à Ninon*), a collection of short stories that he published in 1864, followed by, a year later, *Claude's Confessions* (*Les Confessions de Claude*), an assemblage of mood descriptions in the first person. Like *The Mysteries of Marseilles* (*Les Mystères de Marseille*), which it directly preceded, *A Dead Woman's Wish* (*Le Voeu d'une morte*) was a serial published in the daily press and claimed no literary qualities. *Thérèse Raquin* and *Madeleine Ferrat* depart from these early works in that they suggest a literary experiment in observing, investigating and presenting facts according to the analytical methods of science. Drawing on Hippolyte Taine's theories which advocate the transposition of the exact analysis of biological, historical and social determination into literature, Zola declares in the preface to the second edition of *Thérèse Raquin*: "my aim was primarily scientific . . . I simply performed, on two living bodies, the analytical work that surgeons perform on corpses."[1] Zola later theorized the novelistic approach that the term *naturaliste* implied in *The Experimental Novel* (*Le Roman expérimental*), after having developed it in practice in the first volumes of *Les Rougon-Macquart*. In 1868, Zola first mentioned to the Goncourt brothers his intention to write the history of a family under the Second Empire. The resulting collection of several novels served a double purpose: in addition to the focus on the reign of Napoléon III, the series would also address questions of heredity and environment through a set of interlinked characters.

"AS THEY THEMSELVES SEE IT"

Factors such as the author's understanding of the main characteristics of a genre at a given time, and perception of the public's expectations, determine in part the literary discursive situation and hence the choice of a style. Zola's views of his predecessors and contemporaries is provided in the critical work, *The Naturalist Novelists* (*Les Romanciers naturalistes*), which he published in 1881. There is no reason to believe that the opinions expressed there are significantly different from those which Zola held a few years earlier when he wrote *L'Assommoir*. In the first chapter, I discussed some aspects of the novels of Hugo and Balzac, the two towering literary figures that preceded him. Zola appreciated the extensive, sweeping, all-encompassing nature of their work. In Balzac, he was attracted to the monumental aspect of *The Human Comedy* (*La Comédie humaine*), a representation of society that spanned the Restoration and the July Monarchy, and which established the possibility of literary works as testimony to a historical period. Admiring Balzac's vivid representation of social reality, Zola referred to him as the master of the modern novel who struck a death blow to outdated genres and inaugurated the literary future with a work that formed a vast epic, an immense fresco in which a whole society lives:

> He created the naturalist novel, the exact study of society, and, with one stroke, and with brilliant audacity, he dared to bring to life, in that vast fresco, an entire society, a copy of the one which existed right before his eyes. It was the most explosive affirmation of modern evolution. He killed the lies of obsolete genres, he inaugurated the future.[2]

Elsewhere, however, Zola expressed a slight criticism: contrary to Balzac's proclaimed aim (to be the secretary of his century), some aspects of *The Human Comedy* uncover strange inventions, extraordinary adventures; on occasion, its author lost himself in dream.³ In the preliminary notes pertaining to *Les Rougon-Macquart*, Zola very clearly stated what else separates him from Balzac:

> Unlike Balzac, I do not wish to pass judgment on the affairs of men, to be a politician, a philosopher, a moralist. I shall be content to be a scholar, to say what is, while seeking the intimate reasons.⁴

In the "Notes on the general progress of the work," he was even more forceful in his rejection of the political:

> I do not want to establish or defend a politics or a religion. My study is a simple corner of analysis of the world as it is. I simply establish facts. It is a study of man placed in a social milieu, without sermon. If my novel must have a result, it will be this: to say *the human truth*, to dissassemble our machinery, to show the secret mechanisms of heredity, the effects of our environment. After that, legislators and moralists will be free to take my work, to draw conclusions, and to contemplate dressing the wounds which I will have shown.⁵ (Zola's emphasis)

A "simple corner of analysis of the world as it is" points to what Zola admired in Flaubert, his contemporary, and whose work, he says, brought value to impartial observation. In Flaubert, an apparently neutral narrator presents a cold, objective analysis of facts, disappearing behind the action without offering a moral or a conclusion: "The author is not a moralist but an anatomist who is content with telling what he finds in the human cadaver."⁶ On the points that separate Flaubert from Balzac, Zola lavishes his praise: there is no trace of the *romanesque* whatsoever in Flaubert's writing. His novels are an exact reproduction of life. The author's effort towards composition concerns only the choice of scenes, and the characters are not inflated but represented as they are. As well as admiring his impartial observation and neutrality, Zola applauds Flaubert's aesthetic concern, his sober and striking style, and his superb and exact images: works that are "truth clothed by a poet."⁷

While he shuns the political, Zola stresses the importance of heredity and environment, obviously referring to Taine's theories on biological and social determinism, theories that will play a large part in *L'Assommoir*. The Goncourt brothers, with whom, as with Flaubert, Zola enjoyed personal relations, were also of influence. Zola was struck by the exactness of their descriptions, by the novelty of their subjects, and by their ability to render nervous energy through style.

His favorite of their work, about which he wrote an article in "My Hatreds" (*Mes Haines*), was *Germinie Lacerteux*.[8] In this assessment that pre-dates *L'Assommoir*, Zola draws a parallel between *Madame Bovary* and the Goncourts' novel about a servant whose subdued and humble days contrast with an uninhibited and somewhat unfortunate love life at night:

> To those who claim that the Goncourts have gone too far, I answer that there can be no limit in the study of truth. Different epochs or languages tolerate more or less boldness; thought is always audacious. The crime, therefore, is to have said out loud what many think silently. The timid will oppose Mme Bovary to Germinie Lacerteux. A married woman, the wife of a doctor, that may be acceptable; but a domestic, an old maid of forty, that is insufferable. Furthermore, the love affairs of M. Flaubert's characters are elegant, refined, whereas those of the Goncourts live in the gutter. In a word, there are two different worlds: a bourgeois world, obeying certain social rules, still placing a certain measure in its passion; and a world of the working people, less cultivated and more cynical, in action as in speech. These hypocritical times allow us to paint one, but not touch the other. Ask why, while pointing out that the vices are exactly the same. No one will know what to answer.[9]

The study of truth, of which, says Zola, there can be no excess, serves to justify the representation of a subject that, until then, had not been considered worthy of high literary attention: the working-class character. For the artist to close his eyes on this stratum of society, Zola adds, would be hypocrisy, for it is now well understood that he has acquired the right to "pry deep into the human nature, to hide nothing of the human corpse."[10] The idea of scientific inquiry and objectivity, which Zola later brought to bear on Flaubert, and which, sometime earlier, Hugo had applied to his own work, is also suggested here. Novels such as *Germinie Lacerteux*, Zola argues, are products of their time, for there exists a close relationship between "modern man, the product of an advanced civilization, and this novel of the gutter, with its pungent and acrid smell."[11]

In their preface to *Germinie Lacerteux*, the Goncourts begin by apologizing – as was so often the case – to those readers who might be shocked by this "true novel," this "book that comes from the street," for such is not their aim; rather, they wish to "contradict habits."[12] The novel as a genre, they claim, now participates in literary and social inquiry as well as psychological analysis and research; it cannot represent the upper classes only, but must take into account the lower classes also. There is no reason, they add, for the reader's interest and emotion not to be aroused by this subject. The Goncourts, however, make a point of contrasting *Germinie Lacerteux* with the "naughty little works," the "whores' memoirs," the "bedroom confessions" and "erotic filth" that had been around for some time. There were, indeed, many such accounts, the most famous of which, perhaps, had been Eugène Sue's "The Mysteries of Paris" (*Les Mystères de Paris*), a serial novel published in 1843. It is not irrelevant that in 1867 Zola had tried his hand at this kind of literature with *The Mysteries of Marseille*, serialized in *Le Messager de Provence*. *The Mysteries of Marseille* was based on famous court cases that Zola reconstructed from law reports and press cuttings. He needed the money, and justified his venture to a friend in these terms: "Unlike you, I cannot afford to fall asleep, to isolate myself in an ivory tower, under the pretext that the crowd is stupid. I need the crowd, I go to it in whatever way I can, I try every means to master it."[13]

In his work that preceded *Les Rougon-Macquart*, Zola had practiced low literary genres, and addressed a wide audience. He was aware of the existence of and the need for a mass readership, which he was not afraid to court. Clearly, he expected to aim higher in the literary sphere with *Les Rougon-Macquart*. But the experience of this early work remained vital, and was not entirely foreign to his future project. The contract with his publisher Lacroix, and later Charpentier, stipulated that the novels would appear as serials in the press before being published in book form. To Zola's experience and knowledge of the prerequisites for mass-readership, the Goncourts' *Germinie Lacerteux* added the precedent of a work that, with high literary standards and presumptions, represented a working-class character.

In the initial prospectus that he sent to his publisher Lacroix, Zola included a preliminary list of ten *Rougon-Macquart* novels; he described the forthcoming *L'Assommoir* as the painting of a modern working-class family. The novel would illustrate the drama of the Parisian worker's demoralization under the deplorable influence of slum and tavern life. Unlike the Goncourts' strange Germinie, the characters were to be typical, the story extraordinarily banal. The work emphasizes the responsibility of the environment for the workers' misfortunes, and the idea of an inevitable degradation is suggested on the first page of the "preparatory dossier," the preliminary notes to the novels which I shall discuss in greater depth later. Among some very general remarks concerning the number and length of chapters, Zola briefly outlines what he sees as the aim of the novel: "To explain the people's customs, the vices, the falls, the moral and physical ugliness in terms of the environment, of the living conditions to which this society submits the workers."[14]

Also on this page appears a laconic but vital remark: *le style à toute volée* (the style, full force). However vague, this phrase suggests, with the term *volée*, movement, speed and surprise. One may already say, at this point, that the originality of *L'Assommoir* lies in the primacy given to two factors: the representation of the people, and the style, the importance of which Zola underlines at this point; the novel is initially conceptualized around these two poles. Although Zola had begun to collect information for *L'Assommoir* long before the summer of 1875, only then did he concentrate on producing what was to be called, initially, "Gervaise's Novel" ("Le Roman de Gervaise"). A letter he wrote while on vacation to Paul Alexis on 7 September 1875, suggests that Zola was aware that its style would be crucial to the novel; he did not yet know, however, what form it would take:

> I have the outline, but I need Paris to fill out the details. I have opted for a very large and very simple tableau, with an extraordinary banality of facts, daily life. There remains the style, which will be hard to find.[15]

Many traces of Zola's search for a style are apparent in the preparatory dossier, which, far removed from the final text, is a collection of notes, outlines and documents, consisting of 217 folios divided into several sections. In the "Complete outline," the projected chapters are first summarized, then developed at some length. Within this section Zola interspersed eclectic notes, such as a diagram of the streets where the action is to take place, an inventory of street names, an argot list and so on. Next is "On alcoholism," an account of the physical effects of alcoholism directly taken from a then famous scientific work on the subject by a Docteur Magnan. Zola added a tentative transposition of these effects in the case of a central character, Coupeau. Following this, "The district, the streets, the cabarets and the dance halls," is also of a documentary nature but not based on a technical work this time: Zola took down first-hand observations, sketches and descriptions of several streets, of the people who walked them and of the restaurants found there. The characters of *L'Assommoir* are listed in a section called "Characters," where each is profiled with details on age, physical particularities, personalities and genealogy. Their relative importance is indicated, each is assigned a precise function, whether it is to play a key role or to remain a silhouette in the background. "Notes taken from *Le Sublime*-Argot dictionary" refers to the work by Poulot which I discussed earlier (p. 25). From this text Zola took notes, copied passages and argot expressions which he either included in the transcriptions themselves or in a list at the end of the section. In all likelihood, the next section of the reconstructed manuscript, the "Sketches" (a somewhat muddled collection of notes sketching the rough profile of the work), constituted the first part of the dossier which ends with "Various information": more observations, newspaper cuttings and various descriptions of the technical aspects of professions to be described in the novel. Even though *Les Rougon-Macquart* purported to be the portrayal of a family under the Second Empire, it is quite clear, from these notes, that it was from contemporary society that Zola was drawing his information.

The dossier shows what an enormous amount of preparation, thought and planning went into Zola's literary production, and it uncovers the important role of detailed documentation and learned references. Zola applied such methods to the creation of his other novels. This meticulous process of conception is not peculiar to *L'Assommoir* and has already been thoroughly analyzed elsewhere.[16] Here, the distinctive features are, of course, the specific linguistic material gathered and the sources chosen for this documentation. And an important piece of information is that Zola had originally planned to restrict popular language to the reported speech of characters, and he marked, in his notes, the places in the text where it seemed imperative to do so. For example: "Gervaise dragging herself to the *Assommoir* to see Coupeau . . . an argot conversation . . . use the rest of the drunks' argot" (fol. 61). Two other documents suggest that the innovation of extending popular language to the narrative was not a choice made prior to the final writing. It had not been included in the theoretical conception of the work, but suggested by the actual realization of the text. The first is a simple remark by Paul Alexis, who, in "Emile Zola, Notes of a Friend" (*Emile Zola, Notes d'un ami*), mentions that only after Zola had completed two chapters of his novel did he think of including slang in the narrative.[17] The other source, also of a rather anecdotal nature, is a newspaper article published in *Le Figaro* on 7 December 1930. While he was writing *L'Assommoir*, the story goes, Zola explained to Paul Bourget the motivations behind its style:

The atmosphere that surrounds [the characters] must not be as I see it, but, rather, as they themselves see it. It is hence not in my writer's language that I must describe it, but in theirs, in the language that they speak. A while ago, as I waited for the omnibus, I thought about one of them, Lantier, and thought: Lantier, if he were in my place? well, he would say "Je fais le poireau sur le trottoir." Lantier would not have said it any other way, and that is exactly how I must say it.[18]

[The literal translation of "Faire le poireau sur le trottoir" is "to stand as a leek on the sidewalk." It is a slang expression that means to waste one's time waiting in line.]

The popular expressions that Zola initially planned to include in *L'Assommoir* are contained in three lists that appear in the dossier. The longest, consisting of 606 terms, is found in the section called "Various information." Although no source is cited, Zola, defending himself against an accusation of having plagiarized Poulot's *Le Sublime*, mentions in a letter to *Le Télégraphe* (18 March 1877) that he used several works of reference, one of which was Alfred Delvau's 'Dictionary of Crude Language.'[19] Since all the terms in this list, and the occasional explanations that accompany them, correlate with those given in Delvau's work, one may conclude that this was, indeed, one of the sources used. Zola's reliance on Delvau and Poulot substantiates the fact that, as his class background indicates, he did not acquire popular language through familiarization as a child. It is important to note, however, that out of all the terms jotted down, Zola noted the meaning of only 76, approximately one-sixth. He obviously understood the others. This relative acquaintance with popular language is explained by his bohemian years and by the fact that, even when he had achieved some degree of financial security, he lived close to working-class districts of Paris. Just as a member of the working class hears, recognizes and understands legitimate French without speaking it, Zola must have been accustomed to hearing, and to some extent understanding, popular language, though not using it himself. It is likely, then, that he compiled the list while reading through the dictionary and took down expressions that he had been accustomed to hearing (without explanations) or those that were of particular interest to him (with explanations). The available linguistic material, as it appears in the preparatory notes, is the product, then, of both an external source and personal experience. Paul Alexis claims that Zola was familiar enough with argot to have established the list only as a reminder: "He had gone through argot dictionaries, not seeking to learn that language from scratch, but wanting to refresh his memory, so as to choose without forgetting any of those words that he had most often heard the workers use."[20]

Zola, however, did not consider the reader's memory to be in need of refreshment: unlike Hugo, Balzac and Sue, he did not provide explanatory footnotes, or include a glossary at the end of *L'Assommoir*. This can be explained in part by the fact that, at the end of the nineteenth century, argot was gaining far more widespread use beyond the realm of criminal groups. Still, the discrepancy between Zola's expectation that the reader of the time would understand the popular language represented in the novel with the help of the context only (since no explanations were provided), and the fact that he himself relied on a specialized source, indicates that the reference works he used might have played a role more symbolic than practical. Their function was not purely informational; acting as mediation, they must have served as a means by which Zola, more or less consciously, posited his distance from popular language in its social context, and hence from those who routinely used it. Furthermore, the reliance on an external source, the rigid, linear aspect of a list, and the arbitrariness of an alphabetical classification might have been means by which Zola assumed a "scientific," analytical attitude.

The other source from which Zola gathered information is Poulot's *Le Sublime*, which I discussed in the first chapter.[21] The section of the work that describes and ranks workers according to moral and behavioral criteria contains numerous examples of workers' conversations in which argot expressions appear in italics and are explained in footnotes. Zola made a list of these expressions, classified not alphabetically, but taken down in the order in which they appear in *Le Sublime*. He compiled forty-five terms altogether, half of which he gives with an explanation. Perhaps Zola was less familiar with the slang that appeared in Poulot's work. It is more specialized, usually related to the workers' activities in the workplace. Prior to this list are ten pages of notes which Zola gathered as he read through Poulot's book. On occasion, Zola does not immediately take down specific information but just notations: for instance "argot, p. 16" and "conversation in argot, p. 139," to remind himself to include, in the list that follows, the slang expressions found on those pages. Unlike Delvau's dictionary, *Le Sublime* provides details of not only the lexical but also the syntactical particularities of popular discourse, for Poulot transcribes entire conversations as well as isolated expressions.

Both Poulot and Delvau were intent on distancing themselves from their popular origins. Poulot guarantees that his observations are first hand – he himself had been a worker for several years. He stresses, however, that he later became a foreman and then a business owner. This certainly seems to be the side on which he rallies: for, as the preface to *Le Sublime* indicates, his work is motivated by an anti-revolutionary concern, and is directed towards a bourgeois reader to whom he gives advice on how to keep the masses in place. The second part puts forth guidelines for improvement in a gesture that, as Poulot suggests in his *Explication* to the second edition, is hardly philanthropic: "One must, at whatever cost, get rid of bad workers. . . . It is not a question of fraternity, it is a question of security."[22] A year before the Commune, it is clear what Poulot has in mind. Delvau also forsakes his working-class origins: he now calls himself a moralist, claiming that this enables him to write about the people without being contaminated by what is degrading about them. Implied by the author's attitudes, by the mere format of a dictionary in Delvau and the footnotes in Poulot, is the bourgeoisie's strategy of accommodation and control through objectification. Zola's sources represent typical, conservative stances. Neither showed any hint of an intention to invest popular language with a new dignity, to allow a silenced voice to be heard, or to provide a place for it in the literary field.

Finally, the dossier indicates that, contrary to his claims, Zola did not, on all occasions, account for the people's hardship in terms of the social environment. The influence of Taine's theory of environment is apparent in the "first outline" where, as a solution to the working-class's problems, he advocates "fresh air, light and education for the lower classes" and, in the "Sketches" section of the dossier the same attitude is suggested:

> The novel must do this: show the working-class environment, and explain working-class lives in terms of that environment; how in Paris, drunkenness, the degradation of family life, domestic violence, the acceptance of all shames and all miseries derive from the very conditions of workers' lives, the rough work and the slovenliness. (fol. 157)

However, in other parts of the dossier a radically different conception of the workers' situation emerges. The principal document that highlights this discrepancy is an article by Francisque Sarcey on the Parisian working class which Zola took from the newspaper *Le Gaulois* of 8 September 1870. Here, the workers are classified into three types: the ideal worker, sober, thrifty, industrious, eager for education and self-improvement at one extreme; at the other, the "big mouth" ("mauvais braillard"), a lazy and dissatisfied political agitator. The more typical is the "joker" ("rigoleur"), dissipated and lacking in foresight. Caution and self-discipline, Sarcey concludes, is all the Parisian worker needs to improve his condition, and by changing his habits he will achieve more for his own good than any social reform ever will. A view of the workers as free individuals, able to make choices regardless of external conditions is, of course, at odds with the theory of environment. Furthermore, even though the second part of *Le Sublime* proposes measures to improve the situation of the people, the first part classifies workers into eight categories and suggests that the "ouvrier vrai" (ideal worker) exists under present conditions; and Poulot himself tells us that, thanks to his hard work, he progressed from worker to owner. A belief in moral determinism is also apparent in Zola's notes on Goujet, a character whose role is to "mark a contrast." He characterizes him as follows: "Goujet, a blacksmith, muscular effort, good-looking fellow. Somewhat somber. Loves Gervaise. Use him in the dénouement. *Good worker*"[23] (fol. 163, my emphasis).

Later, Zola makes clear what he means by a good worker: "The good worker, with a full acceptance of that terminology (see notes)." The reference, clearly, is to Poulot's typology, and shows that Zola accepts, and will include in his work, the possibility of moral as well as social determinism. As David Place points out in "Zola and the Working Class: The Meaning of *L'Assommoir*," the dossier displays two positions at odds with each other.[24] Another set of contradictory positions that emerges from the "Dossier" is equally significant. In some early notes concerning *Les Rougon-Macquart*, Zola emphasizes his apolitical position. As I mentioned above, he claims that he does not wish to defend a type of government, that his work is designed as a simple analysis of the world as it is, and that moralists and legislators, rather than the author, should draw conclusions from his novel. Elsewhere, however, he writes that *L'Assommoir* will explain the behavior of the people by showing the conditions in which workers are made to live, and he advocates fresh air, light and education as a means to improve the lot of the worker. *Vis à vis* the working class, Zola seems to oscillate between a position of neutrality and distance, and a very specific negative stance: humanistic reformism, which was certainly not uncommon, either earlier on in the century, or after the Commune. The working-class rebellion was followed by two typical impulses on the part of the bourgeoisie: stronger repression was the option chosen by the conservatives, and slight improvements in the workers' lives, just enough to avoid further uprisings, by the liberals.

At the time of *L'Assommoir*, the working class was no longer merely in formation, but was a social entity that had made its weight felt and for whom the Commune uprisings had provided a strong sense of identity, forcing the bourgeoisie, who had been overtly assailed as the oppressor, to devise new strategies of control. Even though Zola's reactions to the Commune were among the most liberal, he was neither opposed to the ruling class, nor free from its preconceptions and attitudes. It is true that his social trajectory, conditioned in great part by the death of his father and his desire to be a writer, allowed him to be more flexible than his solidly bourgeois origins might have suggested. He was, however, provided with many of the opportunities that the ruling class offers. His itinerary, if it led him away from the typical channels of his class, was chosen, initially, for reasons of personal ambitions rather than political sympathies. The preparatory dossier, as well as providing a great deal of information on the forthcoming novel, also illustrates Zola's relationship to the working class and its language. On many occasions, this document shows that he acknowledges the important effect of living conditions on behavior, but, concerning this issue, two remarks are necessary. First, theories of environment do not, by any means, examine class interaction and the mechanisms of oppression – they do not bring the political to bear on the analysis. And, second, Zola displays occasional slips towards an acceptance of very conservative theories of moral determinism. His generally liberal position is not, however, without, a certain degree of ambivalence. That he belies his uncertainty is also suggested when, during the preparatory process, he gathers information from works in which argot appears in written and ordered form, even though he had probably been accustomed to hearing those words spoken in their original social context. Zola was not in conflict with the bourgeoisie, nor was he in conflict with legitimate language and dominant discourse. His traditional education (Collège Bourbon, Lycée Saint Louis) certainly encouraged the acquisition of legitimate language; and the style of his press articles and literary works that preceded *L'Assommoir* is not unconventional.

Concerning the public's horizon of expectations, it is safe to assume that it did not include the representation of popular language outside of characters' utterances, nor did it encompass novels primarily concerned with the working class. As Auerbach notes:

> With the first great realists of the century, with Stendhal, Balzac, and even with Flaubert, the lower strata of the people, and indeed the people as such in general, hardly appear. And when it appears,

it is not seen on its own premises, within its own life, but from above. Even with Flaubert (whose *Coeur Simple*, by the way, did not appear until a decade after *Germinie Lacerteux* . . .) the working class is on the whole represented by servants and background figures only.[25]

The centrality of a working-class character in *Germinie Lacerteux* was a departure from this tradition, but, as Auerbach also points out, the representation was not of the class as a whole, but of one intriguing character, and that which draws the Goncourts to the subject matter of the novel was "the sensory fascination of the ugly, the repulsive and the morbid."[26]

Before the publication of *L'Assommoir* (the work that brought him fortune and fame), Zola was not unknown in the literary field, in which the eclecticism of his work had created a wide and varied readership. The first six novels of the *Rougon-Macquart* series had gained a respectable – if not overwhelming – success. Among these, only *The Belly of Paris* (*Le Ventre de Paris*) contained occasional and peripheral representations of the working class. Nothing led the public to expect a work as drastically innovative as *L'Assommoir*. Zola's position in the literary field was established and secure enough to the extent that *Les Rougon-Macquart* had been accepted for publication, but it was not without need of consolidation. Material gain was a strong motivation, for the royalties that he would receive from these novels were to be his sole source of income. As he said earlier: "I need the crowd." The fact that he agreed to have the novels serialized in the press prior to their publication in book form indicates a willingness to address as broad a readership as possible. Unlike *The Mysteries of Marseille* and *A Dead Woman's Wish*, however, this work was not solely a commercial project, but born out of serious literary concerns and ideals that would, for example, incorporate the monumental scale of Balzac's *The Human Comedy*, the impartiality of Flaubert's representations, and the Goncourts' conviction that the lower classes may now enter the literary text. *Les Rougon-Macquart* was not meant to break entirely with tradition. What does set Zola apart from his predecessors are his claims to scientific methods, his concern with questions of heredity, and his systematic documentation. Yet, prior to *L'Assommoir*, nothing indicates that questions of stylistic innovation were central to his concerns. It appears to be the subject matter of the novel that brought on the change; to represent "realistically" the utterances of working-class characters is a choice that correlates with Zola's overall project. To extend their discourse to "the atmosphere

58 *Political Stylistics*

that surrounds them" does not, and apparently grew out of the novel's realization.

POTENTIAL AND RESISTANCE

It appears from the preparatory dossier and reported anecdotes that Zola had at first planned to represent popular language only in the reported speech of characters. This is, indeed, how it is primarily introduced in the novel. The first conversations, however, involving Gervaise, Madame Boche (her neighbor), Lantier (the father of her two children), and Coupeau (whom she will later marry), are not significantly different from those in Zola's previous works: they contain only a small number of colloquial or familiar expressions. It is during a heated verbal and physical exchange at the washhouse, "au milieu des bruits d'écluse des seaux d'eau jetés à toute volée" ("amidst the noise of pails of water thrown with full force") where Gervaise confronts Virginie "qui venait de l'atteindre à toute volée sur son bras nu" ("who had just hit her bare arm with full force") that the "style à toute volée" ("the style, full force") initially appears.[27] The analysis of a short extract of this lengthy interchange (8 pages) will be sufficient to review the manner in which Zola first realized his stylistic project:

> "Ah! le chameau! répétait la grande Virginie. Qu'est-ce qui lui prend, à cette enragée là!"
>
> Gervaise en arrêt, le menton tendu, la face convulsée, ne répondait pas, n'ayant point encore le coup de gosier de Paris. L'autre continua:
>
> "Va donc! C'est las de rouler la province, ça n'avait pas douze ans que ça servait de paillasse à soldats, ça a laissé une jambe dans son pays . . . Elle est tombée de pourriture, sa jambe . . ."
>
> Un rire courut. Virginie, voyant son succès, s'approcha de deux pas, redressant sa haute taille, criant plus fort:
>
> "Hein! avance un peu, pour voir, que je te fasse ton affaire! Tu sais, il ne faut pas venir nous embêter, ici . . . Est-ce que je la connais, moi, cette peau! Si elle m'avait attrapée, je lui aurait joliment retroussé ses jupons; vous auriez vu ça. Qu'elle dise seulement ce que je lui ai fait . . . Dis, rouchie, qu'est-ce qu'on t'a fait?
>
> – Ne causez pas tant, bégaya Gervaise. Vous savez bien . . . On a vu mon mari, hier soir . . . Et taisez-vous, parce que je vous étranglerais, bien sûr!

Zola's L'Assommoir 59

– Son mari! Ah! elle est bonne, celle là! . . . Le mari à madame! Comme si on avait des maris, avec cette dégaine! . . . Ce n'est pas ma faute s'il t'a lâchée. Je ne te l'ai pas volé, peut-être. On peut me fouiller . . . Veux-tu que je te dise, tu l'empoisonnais, cet homme! Il était trop gentil pour toi . . . Avait-il son collier, au moins? Qui est-ce qui a trouvé le mari à madame? . . . Il y aura récompense. (pp. 617–18)

("Oh, the cow," repeated Virginie. "What's the matter with her, that crazed woman!"

Gervaise stood still, chin thrust out, face contorted, but she made no retort, having not yet learned the Parisian back talk. The other went on:

"Look at that! It's tired of whoring around in the provinces, it wasn't even twelve when it served as a mattress for soldiers, it left a leg back home – it rotted and fell off, her leg . . ."

A laugh went around. Virginie, seeing her success, made two steps forwards, drawing herself up to her full height, screaming even louder.

"Hey! Just come and see, I'll take care of you! You know, we don't want you pestering us here . . . Me, I don't know her, that bitch! If she'd caught me, I wouldn't half have pulled up her skirts! Would have been a sight! Why doesn't she only say what I did to her . . . Say, slut, what did we do to you?"

"Don't talk so much,' Gervaise stammered out. "You know all right . . . my husband was seen last night . . . and shut up, because I'll strangle you, you can be sure!"

"Her husband! that's good one, that! . . . the lady's husband! As if one could get a husband, looking like that! . . . It's not my fault, if he dumped you. Search me . . . If you want to know, you nagged him to death, that man! He was too good for you . . . Was he wearing his collar, at least? Who found the lady's husband? . . . There'll be a reward.")

Popular markers appear very prominently on a lexical level, with vulgar expressions such as *rouler la province, paillasse à soldats, faire ton affaire, elle est bonne, dégaine,* and the insults *chameau* and *roussie*. A heavily abusive tone is also conveyed by the demonstrative *ça*, a contraction of *cela* (it), which is in itself representative of spoken language, and which is here used to designate Gervaise rather than, as is usually the case, objects: *ça servait, ça n'avait pas, ça a laissé* (it served, it was, it left). Equally pejorative and also referring to Gervaise are the expressions *cette enragée là, cette peau* (that crazy woman, that bitch), where the demonstrative *cette*, serving to establish complicity between speaker and audience (in this case the crowd gathered at the washhouse that is intently observing the fight) is followed by the designation of a person in terms of physical or personality traits. The pronoun *on* can be used as the indeterminate "one" as, for example, in many proverbs (*Comme on fait son lit on se couche*). As a substitute for the first person plural *nous* (we), it is typical of spoken language. When it refers to a clearly determined person or group, such as is the case here in *comme si on avait des maris* (as if one could get a husband), where Virginie refers to Gervaise, or *on peut me fouiller* (search me), where Virginie addresses Gervaise (*tu*) or the crowd (*vous*), it takes on a decidedly popular tone and expresses scorn and disdain. A number of expressions in this passage convey no semantic information, but they are important components of spoken discourse, indicating the emotional state of the characters and creating a particular atmosphere – here, one of excitement and hostility: *Ah!, Va donc!, Hein!* Similarly, the expressions *dis, tu sais, bien sûr*, and *pour voir* do not add informational value to the sentences in which they occur, but they secure verbal contact, provide emphasis and participate in the phatic function.

There are also some syntactical features of spoken and popular language in this passage. One is the *rappel*, in which a group of words performs the grammatical function of subject or object, but follows the use of a pronoun that takes its place in the body of a sentence. Examples of this are (my emphasis):

- Qu'est-ce qui *lui* prend, à cette *enragée-là*? (What's the matter with her, that crazed woman?)

- *Elle* est tombée de pourriture, *sa jambe*. (It rotted and fell off, her leg.)

- Est-ce que *je la* connais, *moi*, cette *peau*! (Me, I don't know her, that bitch!)

Such constructions, where the abstract elements come first and the concrete ones last, are used, Leo Spitzer notes, by those who, uncertain of their enunciation, want to make sure that their train of thought is understood, and, with the repetition, seek to add emphasis and insistence to their discourse.[28] The profuse punctuation of this passage – exclamation marks, interrogations, ellipses – translate the intonation of an animated exchange, fragmenting the flow of utterances which appear as a paratactic succession of short phrases, some of which are verbless. Furthermore, since Virginie addresses Gervaise and the audience alternately, no continuous semantic line is discernible.

Zola's L'Assommoir 61

The initial situation in which popular markers appear with some density is rather typical, both in literary and social terms. The discourse is internal to the working class, confrontational, and occurs before an audience: a crowd avidly watches the two women engage in an increasingly violent fight where all sense of decorum is dropped as Gervaise and Virginie rip each other's clothes off and hurl buckets of water at each other. We are also told that Gervaise does hesitate to respond verbally to Virginie for she has not yet mastered "Parisian back talk" implying that popular language, particularly in its aggressive use, is specific to the capital. Comedy is not absent from this encounter; there is even something of the farce in this famous "washhouse scene" – the genre in which, prior to the nineteenth century, popular language was traditionally considered acceptable. Throughout the novel, a high density of popular markers in the characters' directly reported speech is associated with a loss of control, anger, alcohol. For example, a drunk Coupeau mocks his daughter Nana's first communion dress in these terms:

"Je t'en ficherai, des robes blanches! Hein? c'est encore pour te faire des nichons dans ton corsage avec des boules de papier, comme l'autre dimanche? . . . Oui, oui, attends un peu! Je te vois bien tortiller ton derrière. Ça te chatouille, les belles frusques, ça te monte le coco . . . Veux-tu décaniller de là, bougre de chenillon! Retire tes patoches, colle moi ça dans un tiroir, ou je te débarbouille avec!" (p. 847)

("I'll give you white dresses! What? so that you can make yourself some tits with crumpled up paper, like last Sunday? yes, yes, just you wait. I see you wriggling your backside. They tickle you, those fancy rags, they go straight to your head . . . Get the hell out of here, damn little brat! Take off those clothes, stick them in a drawer, or I'll wash your face with them!")

Popular and vulgar words and expressions abound: *ficherai, nichon, décaniller, frusques, chenillon, tortiller ton derrière, monter le coco*. There is the usual contraction of *cela* into *ça*, a *rappel* (*Ça te chatouille, les belles frusques*), several fragmented, incomplete sentences, and phatic expressions (*Hein? Oui, oui, attends un peu*). A final conversation is worth consideration; it occurs at *L'Assommoir*, the bar that lends its name to the novel. Here, Coupeau urges Gervaise to drink with him and other workers:

"Dis-donc, Marie-bon-bec, ne fais pas ta gueule! cria Coupeau. Tu sais, à Chaillot les rabat-joie! . . . Qu'est-ce que tu veux boire?

– Rien, bien sûr, répondit la blanchisseuse. Je n'ai pas dîné, moi.

– Eh bien! raison de plus; ça soutient, une goutte de quelque chose.

Mais, comme elle ne se déridait pas, Mes-Bottes se montra galant de nouveau.

"Madame doit aimer les douceurs," murmura-t-il.

– J'aime les hommes qui ne se soûlent pas, reprit-elle en se fâchant. Oui, j'aime qu'on rapporte sa paie et qu'on soit de parole, quand on a fait une promesse.

– Ah! c'est ça qui te chiffonne! dit le zingueur, sans cesser de ricaner. Tu veux ta part. Alors, grande cruche, pourquoi refuses-tu une consommation? . . . Prends donc, c'est tout bénéfice." (p. 867)

("Say, Marie-bon-bec, don't make a face!' shouted Coupeau. "To hell with wet blankets, you know! . . . What will it be?"

"Nothing, of course," replied the laundress. "Me, I haven't eaten."

"So? all the more reason; it'll keep you going, a drop of something."

But, because she still hesitated, Mes-Bottes became gallant once again.

"Madam surely likes things sweet," he murmured.

"I like men who don't get drunk," she said, becoming annoyed. "Yes, I like them to bring home their wages, and keep their word when they have made a promise."

"Ah! that's what bothering you," said the zinc worker. "So, stupid, why won't you have a drink? Take it, there's nothing to lose.")

The detailed analysis of many such passages would confirm the fact that Zola represented popular language in directly reported conversations by means of numerous lexical terms and three main syntactical forms: the contraction of *cela* into *ça*, the fragmentation of the sentence with phatic elements, filler terms and interjections, and *rappels* (*je n'ai pas dîné, moi; ça soutient, une goutte de quelque chose*). As I mentioned earlier, Zola's knowledge of popular language was gained both from experience and from documents such as Delvau's "Dictionary of Crude Language" and Poulot's *Le Sublime*, which includes examples of conversations between workers in a variety of situations: at home, at work, and, particularly, when drinking. This latter source provided Zola not only with lexical material, but also with syntactical models that could be reproduced as such, or altered. Zola could have performed no transformation whatsoever on Poulot's model; he could have multiplied the number of popular markers, or could have ironed out the edges of what seemed too harsh and incorrect a discourse. He chose the latter course. The comparison of characters' utterances as they are represented by Poulot and Zola shows that many of the popular markers in *Le Sublime* do not appear in *L'Assommoir*. Those withheld are, primarily, the more potent ones. On Poulot's material, removed already from actual instances of popular discourse, Zola operated a secondary transformation which brought the utterances closer to correctness. His caution in the use of popular linguistic material is also revealed by the manner in which it first appears in an unrefined scene where two working-class women publicly provoke and fight each other – such is the low subject matter that initially authorizes the low language of *L'Assommoir*. The characters who primarily resort to popular language throughout the novel are Gervaise and Coupeau, increasingly so as their life deteriorates, as well as the workers, like Mes-Bottes and Bibi-la-Grillade. Significantly, Goujet, the worker whom, in opposition to the others, Zola conceived of as exemplary, does not. He is renowned for his sobriety and silence, and when he does speak, he shows few signs of incorrectness.

In the passages analyzed above the characters' utterances are clearly shown to be words-of-others, unambiguously marked by a set of recognized signs, as is always the case for directly reported speech: punctuation, a change of tenses (from past to present), a first-person pronoun. But, as we know, popular language in *L'Assommoir* is also represented outside of directly reported utterances. The way in which this occurs, imperceptibly at first, is with a specific stylistic device, the indirect and free indirect style of which Flaubert, before Zola, made important use. Both forms, allowing the characteristics of words-of-others, permit the retention of a specific individual expression, while, at the same time, effacing the signs that indicate a breach in narrative. In indirect style, the characters' thoughts or utterances are reported in a subordinated clause, introduced by a declarative verb: they said, they remarked, they hoped, etc. With free indirect style, there is no such verb, the act of reporting is not suggested in the text. Thus, there is no indication as to whether what is being represented is an utterance or a thought. An isolated instance of this form appears in the first chapter of *L'Assommoir*:[29]

> C'était un grand gaillard, à cou énorme. Il riait, il jouissait des morceaux de peau que les deux femmes montraient. *La petite blonde était grasse comme une caille. Ça serait farce, si sa chemise se fendait.* (p. 620, my emphasis)

(He was a big thick-necked fellow. He was laughing, enjoying the glimpses of flesh that the two women were showing. *The little blond one was as plump as a quail. It would be fun, if her shirt split open.*)

The sentences in italics relate the fellow's hopes for further excitement at the "washhouse scene." These could be silent thoughts, a loud exclamation, or a hushed remark to a worker standing nearby. In indirect style, they would translate as *il pensa que la petite blonde était grasse comme une caille* (he thought that the little blond one was as plump as a quail); in direct style *il pensa: la petite blonde est grasse comme une caille* (he thought: the little blond one is as plump as a quail). However, this is only an assumption, for, as Ann Banfield argues in "Narrative Style and the Grammar of Direct and Indirect Speech," it is impossible to deduce with certainty, from either an indirect or free indirect statement, the direct utterance that would serve as its deep structure.[30] In both indirect and free indirect style there is a change of tenses: present becomes past, future becomes conditional and past becomes pluperfect. Indirect and free indirect style also warrant a change of pronoun. For instance, a directly reported statement such as *la petite blonde en face de moi est grasse* (the little blond one opposite me is plump) would become *la petite blonde en face de lui* (the little blond one opposite him). However, free indirect style often appears to remain closer to the actual utterance than indirect style. For example, the fellow here refers to Gervaise as *la petite blonde* (the little blond one) for he does not know her name, she is new to the neighborhood. Indirect style, however, would allow *il pensa que Gervaise était grasse* (he thought that Gervaise was plump). Free indirect style, then, is in the paradoxical position of allowing a greater fidelity to the spoken or thought words, but displaying less formal signs than indirect style that these are words of others.

As I mentioned, the instance discussed above is an isolated one in the first chapter. Free indirect style becomes increasingly current in the third chapter and beyond; indirect style already appears with some insistence in the second chapter, which is mainly composed of subdued conversations between Gervaise and Coupeau: *Et elle se mit à rire plus fort, parce que Coupeau lui racontait que Virginie, désolée d'avoir tout montré, venait de quitter le quartier* (And she laughed louder, because Coupeau was telling her that Virginie, ashamed to have shown all, had just left the district – p. 628). Coupeau's utterance is contained in a subordinate clause, introduced by the verb *raconter* and the conjunction *que*. It ends with the end of the sentence. The fact that these words are clearly attributed to Coupeau allows the inclusion of a colloquial expression, *tout montrer*. It is important to remember, however, that it is impossible to reconstruct Virginie's actual utterance or thought, or Coupeau's representation of it; indirect and free indirect style can report anything ranging from the substance alone, to the substance and form of an utterance. Zola could just as well have written that *Virginie, désolée de son humiliation, venait de quitter le quartier* (Virginie, ashamed of her humiliation, had just left the district). In the following example, Gervaise's utterance is first introduced in the indirect style by *répétant que*:

> Son visage, pourtant, gardait une douceur enfantine; elle avançait ses mains potelées, en répétant qu'elle n'écraserait pas une mouche; *elle ne connaissait les coups que pour en avoir joliment reçu dans sa vie.* (p. 628, my emphasis)
>
> (Her face, however, retained a child-like gentleness; she put her plump hands forward, repeating that she wouldn't hurt a fly; *she knew beatings only because she had been subject to them many times in her life.*)

Grammatically, it is a little less clear whether the italicized sentences represent Gervaise's utterances or a statement put forth by the narrator to explain her attitude. However, the function of *répétant* could extend beyond the semi-colon. It could also be an instance of free indirect style, as in the following example:

> "Oh! c'est vilain de boire!" dit-elle à demi-voix.
> Et elle raconta qu'autrefois, avec sa mère, elle buvait de l'anisette, à Plassans. Mais elle avait failli en mourir un jour, et ça l'avait dégoûtée; elle ne pouvait plus voir les liqueurs. (p. 630)
>
> ("Oh! it's bad to drink!" she said in a hushed voice.
> And she explained that she used to drink anisette with her mother, in Plassans. But she almost died of it once, and that put her off it; she could no longer stand liquor.)

Here, again, after a clear instance of indirect style, it is grammatically uncertain whether the last two sentences represent Gervaise's utterance or not. The verb tenses could be those of a narration of past events. Semantically, however, the reader probably understands that she is explaining to Coupeau why she does not drink, in an instance of free indirect style that allows for the popular markers *ça* and *pouvait plus voir*. In the next example, Mes-Bottes' voice is introduced in the indirect style, by the two verbs *traiter* and *accuser*:

66 Political Stylistics

On entendait Mes-Bottes traiter le père Colombe de fripouille, en l'accusant de n'avoir rempli son verre qu'à moitié. *Lui, était un bon, un chouette, un d'attaque. Ah! zut! le singe pouvait se fouiller, il ne retournerait pas à la boîte, il avait la flemme.* Et il proposait aux deux camarades d'aller au Petit Bonhomme qui tousse, une mine à poivre de la barrière Saint Denis, où l'on buvait du chien tout pur. (p. 632, my emphasis)

(Mes-Bottes could be heard calling old Colombe a stingy good-for-nothing, accusing him of only half-filling his glass. *As for him, he was a good fellow, he was all right, on top of things. What the hell! the boss could hunt for him high and low, he was not going back to work in that dump, he couldn't be bothered.* And he suggested to his two pals that they go to the Petit Bonhomme qui tousse, a watering hole up near Saint Denis, where they served it up straight.)

The italicized sentences do not have a logical semantic connection to what Mes-Bottes says about old Colombe. It is possible, but not necessary, that Mes-Bottes suddenly becomes the subject matter of his own discourse. It is also possible that these sentences are part of a narrative that sarcastically describes the attitude of the worker. The fact, however, that they are followed by one where there is a clear case of indirect style introduced by *et il proposait* (and he suggested) indicates that in all likelihood, they too are meant to represent the character's voice.

In this overview of examples taken from the second chapter of *L'Assommoir*, cases of indirect style precede and serve to introduce free indirect style, and sometimes, as in the instances quoted above, frame it. These forms, then, where popular markers are not dissociated from the narrative, do not strike the reader as unexpected or unusual. No stylistic effect is created by a clear contrast, as would be the case, for example, if a sharply demarcated, directly reported utterance preceded one in indirect style. A point worth repeating is that indirect or free indirect style provides little information with regard to the actual utterance. It is quite possible for the substance of the message alone, rather than the substance and the form, to be reported. Although indirect or free indirect style allows popular markers, the syntax does not require their presence. It simply allows it. These grammatical forms have also raised questions as to whether they provide stylistically conveyed information concerning the person who is doing the reporting. For Chomskian linguists, the phrase

"Nixon said that the portraits of comrade Lenin should be banned" could only have been spoken by a Communist. However, Claude Perruchot asks, could one deduce, from the sentence in *Madame Bovary* telling us that Emma "aimait la brebis malade ou le pauvre Jésus qui tombe en marchant sur sa croix" ("loved the sick ewe, or poor Jesus who fell as he carried his cross") that Flaubert must have been a very pious man?[31] "Comrade Lenin," or "poor Jesus," may belong to the voice reporting the utterance, or to the utterance itself. Indirect and free indirect style function precisely as a means for eroding boundaries and establishing an ambiguous demarcation of the speaking subject.

The uncertainty regarding to whom certain components of the discourse belong increases in the third chapter of *L'Assommoir*, as a detailed analysis of a section of the opening paragraph will show:

Mais Coupeau se récriait: on ne pouvait pas se marier comme ça, sans manger un morceau ensemble. Lui, se battait joliment de l'oeil du quartier! Oh! quelque chose de tout simple, un petit tour de balade l'après-midi, en attendant d'aller tordre le cou à un lapin, au premier gargot venu. Et pas de musique au dessert, bien sûr, pas de clarinette pour secouer le panier aux crottes des dames. Histoire de trinquer seulement, avant de revenir faire dodo chacun chez soi.

Le zingueur, plaisantant, rigolant, décida la jeune femme, lorsqu'il lui eut juré qu'on ne s'amuserait pas. Il aurait l'oeil sur les verres, pour empêcher les coups de soleil. Alors, il organisa un pique-nique à cent sous par tête, chez Auguste, au Moulin d'Argent, boulevard de La Chapelle. C'était un petit marchand de vin dans les prix doux, qui avait un bastringue au fond de son arrière-boutique, sous les trois acacias de sa cour. Au premier, on serait parfaitement bien. Pendant dix jours, il racola des convives, dans la maison de sa soeur, rue de la Goutte-d'Or: M. Madinier, Mlle Remanjou, Mme Gaudron et son mari. (p. 649)

(But Coupeau protested: you couldn't get married just like that, without eating a little something together. Him, he didn't give a damn about the neighborhood. Oh, something very simple, of course, a little outing of some kind in the afternoon, to pass the time before biting into a rabbit, at the first restaurant on the way. And no music after the meal, of course, no clarinet to make the ladies' asses wobble. Just to have a drink together, and then, everybody sleeps, each in his own home.

The zinc worker, joking, laughing, convinced the young woman when he swore that there would be no fooling around. He'd keep an eye on the glasses, to make sure that no one got pissed. So he organized a meal, at a hundred sous per person, at Auguste's Moulin d'Argent, boulevard de La Chapelle. It was a small, cheap wine shop that had a dance floor in the backyard under the three acacia trees. In a room on the first floor, it would be just fine. For ten days he got hold of guests, from his sister's building, rue de la Goutte d'Or: M. Madinier, Mlle Remanjou, Mme Gaudron and her husband.)

Here, Coupeau's utterance is introduced by *se récriait* (protested) and followed by three sentences in free indirect style, until *chacun chez soi* (each in his own home), that include numerous popular markers of a lexical type: three that appear on the lists that Zola had drawn up in the preparatory dossier (*se battre l'oeil, le panier aux crottes, le gargot*) and several other expressions, more colloquial or familiar than decidedly popular (*comme ça, manger un morceau, tordre le cou à un lapin, faire dodo, tour de ballade*). Three verbless sentences semantically but not syntactically depend on *se récriait*. Because they can be understood as part of Coupeau's conception of an appropriate wedding celebration and logically follow the one in which his utterance is represented, the reader assumes that these words are still his. Furthermore, they are not interrupted by a clearly narrative statement. Similarly, in the second paragraph, the verb *jurer* (to swear) introduces a second case of indirect style, then sentences in free indirect style extend to *coups de soleil* (getting wasted). After that comes a narrative statement, introduced by *alors*, that marks a breach, recounting events rather than discourse: *Alors il organisa un pique-nique, à cent sous par tête, au Moulin d'Argent, boulevard de la Chapelle* ("So he organized a meal . . ."). *Par tête*, rather than *par personne*, is clearly popular and so are, in the description of the restaurant, *bastringue* and *dans les prix doux*; however, these sentences are not clearly attributed to a character. The use of the pronoun *on*, in *au premier on serait parfaitement bien*, marks a return to a character's voice. Then, the pronoun *il* in *pendant dix jours il racola des convives* (for ten days he got hold of guests) marks a return to the narrative. Another such ambiguity is present in the following passage:

Seule maman Coupeau s'était mise à pleurer, en disant qu'elle partirait plutôt en avant pour se cacher dans un coin; et on avait promis de l'emmener. Quant au rendez-vous de toute la société, il était fixé à une heure, au Moulin d'Argent. De là, on irait gagner la faim dans la plaine Saint-Denis; on prendrait le chemin de fer et on retournerait à pattes, le long de la grande route. La partie s'annonçait très bien, pas une bosse à tout avaler, mais un brin de rigolade, quelque chose de gentil et d'honnête. (p. 650)

(Only mother Coupeau began to cry, saying that she would rather get there ahead of time, and hide in a corner, so they promised to take her. The gathering was planned at one o'clock, at the Moulin d'Argent. From there, going to the plaine Saint-Denis would give everyone an appetite, getting there by train and then walking back along the main road. The outing looked good, not a fancy time, but a bit of fun, something nice and honest.)

As in the previous examples, there is first a clear case of indirect style in *en disant qu'elle partirait* (saying that she would rather get there) but the following sentences, starting with *quant au rendez-vous*, are not clearly assigned to a character at all, and include popular expressions: *gagner la faim, à pattes, pas une bosse à tout avaler, un brin de rigolade*. The progressive introduction of popular language, in the second and third chapters of *L'Assommoir*, is accompanied by a blurring of the boundaries between characters' speech; ambiguity as to whom is speaking often sets in. In these instances, the popular markers differ from those in directly reported conversations: they take on a primarily lexical form. Incomplete sentences are common, but there are fewer contractions and *rappels* than in other places.

In the examples discussed here, which are typical of the second and third chapters of *L'Assommoir*, the popular markers present in instances of indirect and free indirect style take on a lexical, rather than syntactical form. Incomplete sentences are common, but contractions and *rappels* are not as frequent as they are in directly reported conversations. Although there are a few instances of popular markers in the narration of events, they typically occur in the narration of speech, or to express characters' reactions, views, and opinions. The perspective in this novel is, most of the time, internally focused: the reader is told only what the characters know. For example, at the beginning of the novel, when Lantier fails to return one night, our knowledge of where he might have been is conveyed to us through Gervaise's perceptions. And in all the passages discussed, it is the characters' views that are represented. If the answer to the question "who speaks" is uncertain, it is clear who sees. However, as will become clear, breaches do occur, and these are accompanied by a clear stylistic change.

The third chapter, describing in a quick-moving and often comic manner Gervaise and Coupeau's wedding, the promenade through

Paris, the visit to the Louvre and to several restaurants, is in large part composed of the characters' utterances, directly or indirectly reported. There is a passage, however, that differs from the rest. The tone is elevated and the theme is of some importance to the arguments that follow. It is a description of the Paris sky, which is not seen through the eyes of the characters, even though it is preceded by their perception of the city landscape. The scene takes place at the top of the Colonne Vendôme:

> Mais M. Madinier, sur la plate-forme, montrait déjà les monuments. Jamais Mme Fauconnier ni Mlle Remanjou ne voulurent sortir de l'escalier; la pensée seule du pavé, en bas, leur tournait les sangs; et elles se contentaient de risquer des coups d'oeil par la petite porte. Mme Lerat, plus crâne, faisait le tour de l'étroite terrasse, en se collant contre le bronze du dôme. Mais c'était tout de même rudement émotionnant, quand on songeait qu'il aurait suffi de passer une jambe. Quelle culbute, sacré Dieu! Les hommes, un peu pâles, regardaient la place. On se serait cru en l'air, séparé de tout. Non, décidément, ça vous faisait froid aux boyaux. M. Madinier, pourtant, recommandait de lever les yeux, de les diriger devant soi, très loin; ça empêchait le vertige. Et il continuait à indiquer du doigt les Invalides, le Panthéon, Notre-Dame, la tour Saint-Jacques, les buttes Montmartre. Puis, Mme Lorilleux eut l'idée de demander si l'on apercevait, sur le boulevard de La Chapelle, le marchand de vin où l'on allait manger, Au Moulin d'Argent. Alors, pendant dix minutes, on chercha, on se disputa même; chacun plaçait le marchand de vin à un endroit. Paris, autour d'eux, étendait son immensité grise, aux lointains bleuâtres, ses vallées profondes, où roulait une houle de toitures; toute la rive droite était dans l'ombre, sous un grand haillon de nuage cuivré; et, du bord de ce nuage, frangé d'or, un large rayon coulait, qui allumait les milliers de vitres de la rive gauche d'un pétillement d'étincelles, détachant en lumière ce coin de la ville sur un ciel très pur, lavé par l'orage.
>
> "Ce n'était pas la peine de monter pour nous manger le nez," dit Boche, furieux, en reprenant l'escalier. (p. 662)

(But M. Madinier, on the platform, was already pointing out landmarks. Mme Fauconnier and Mlle Remanjou never left the staircase; the mere thought of the pavement, down there, gave them the creeps; and they were content with a few glances through the little door. Mme Lerat had more nerve, and walked around the narrow platform, hugging herself against the bronze dome. But it was really scary, when you thought that all it would take would be to slip a leg over. Good God, what a fall! The men, a little pale, looked down at the square. You felt you were up in the air, cut off from everything. No, really, it froze your guts. M. Madinier, however, advised everyone to raise their eyes and to look straight ahead, far into the distance; it stopped you from feeling giddy. And he went on pointing to the Invalides, the Panthéon, Notre-Dame, the Saint-Jacques tower, the hills of Montmartre. Then it occurred to Mme Lorilleux to ask if one could see, on the boulevard de La Chapelle, the wine merchant who would be providing lunch, the Moulin d'Argent. So, for ten minutes, a search went on, an argument even broke out; everyone picked a different place. Paris, around them, spread its grey immensity, its bluish horizon, its deep valleys where waves of rooftops rolled; the entire right bank lay in the shade, beneath a great ragged sheet of coppery cloud; and, from the edge of this cloud, fringed with gold, a large sunbeam fell, that lit up the thousands of windows on the left bank with outbursts of sparks, bringing to light this part of the city under a very pure sky, swept clean by the storm.

"There was no point in coming here to squabble," said Boche, furious, walking down the stairs.)

At first, this passage relates the characters' impressions, their attitudes and their actions, in indirect and free indirect style, and with many popular markers, as they contemplate the city that surrounds them (*on, ça, quelle culbute, sacré Dieu, tourner les sangs, plus crâne, rudement émotionnant, froid aux boyaux*). After the wedding party has glanced at several well-known monuments, the center of interest changes and becomes the location of the wine merchant where they are to dine later. Suddenly, with *Paris, autour d'eux* (Paris, around them), there is a break both in the style and perspective, which is no longer focused through the characters. The vision that was fragmented, narrow and downward-looking becomes sweeping and progresses beyond the buildings of the city to include more cosmic elements: sun, clouds, sky. The grand scale of this landscape is reflected in the style of this passage. The prose is now sophisticated, lyrical in places, and contains many forms that Jean-Louis Vissière, in "L'Art de la phrase dans *L'Assommoir*" ("The Art of the Sentence in *L'Assommoir*") considers to be the hallmark of *écriture artiste* (artistic writing).[32] The chief characteristic of this style is the fragmentation of one long sentence by semi-colons, to form what Vissière, and Marcel Cressot, in *La Phrase et le vocabulaire de J. K. Huysmans*, call the *phrase tableau*, or the *phrase impressioniste*.[33] Also typical is the subject–verb disjunction in *Paris, autour d'eux, étendait* (Paris, all around them, spread) caused by the presence of an adverbial group, and the subject–verb inversion in *où roulaient des houles de toitures* (literally: where rolled waves of rooftops). The structure *et, du bord de ce nuage, frangé d'or* (and, from the edge of this cloud, fringed with gold) is also common to *écriture artiste*: there is first a conjunction (*et*), a complement indicating place (*au bord de ce nuage*), then an adjectival group (*frangé d'or*). There are great numbers of adjectives and *recherché* imagery throughout this passage: *houles de toitures, haillon de nuage cuivré, pétillement d'étincelles* (waves of rooftops, ragged sheets of coppery clouds, outbursts of sparks). Vissière, who comments on the passage, adds the rhythmic balance: a recurrent syllabic count of ten and the repetition of the vowel *i*.

Before reaching this passage, the reader has grown accustomed to the presence of popular markers, first introduced in the directly reported speech of characters, then almost imperceptibly, through a gradual stylistic shift, the markers extend beyond their conventional boundaries. What is unusual here and draws attention to itself by standing out in opposition to the context is the passage in *écriture artiste*. Furthermore, the vision it conveys, a lofty, elevated description of the sky brightened by sunrays, is opposed to the other passage which is focused through the characters, banal (the famous monuments), parochial and internal to the group (the search for the wine merchant), and downward-directed. As important to the novel as is the actual presence of various stylistic unities is the dialogical angle at which they meet, and their relation to each other. This particular shift is abrupt; the characters' perceptions of Paris and the description of the sky interact through opposition. The reader, then, engrossed in a style heavily imbued with popular markers, and having witnessed Gervaise and Coupeau's wedding in all its comic trivia, is suddenly reminded of a superior world-view and style. Furthermore, the fact that the Colonne Vendôme is central to a textual moment that establishes a hierarchy of discourse and world-view is not without importance. On 16 May 1871, one of the more theatrical moments of the Commune was the demolition of this monument in tribute to the victory of Napoléon's Grande Armée. In *The Emergence of Social Space: Rimbaud and the Paris Commune*, Kristin Ross interprets this destruction as an antihierarchical gesture, an attempt to level the vertical, an action symbolizing the Communards' revolt against social regimentation.[34] In this passage, not only do the working-class characters react to the height of the monument with ridiculed awe and bewilderment (as opposed to the superb aplomb that served its demolition), but Zola, through linguistic means, also restores the Colonne as a locus of hierarchy, both social and linguistic.

The third chapter of *L'Assommoir* has revealed an important amount of information crucial to this study: the extensive use of indirect and free indirect style, resulting in a certain ambiguity as to the dividing line between the characters' utterances and the narrative, and hence as to the status of popular markers. And there is a sudden breach in style that draws attention to opposing world-views. Another key chapter to be looked at now is the twelfth chapter, two-thirds of which are composed of Gervaise's soliloquy, as, in the depths of misery, she searches for food, wanders the streets, and attempts to prostitute herself. In the preparatory dossier, Zola had written that in these pages "the style must be somber and depressed, poignant. A scene with a continuous and persistent effect." The twelfth chapter contains the highest concentration and most constant stream of popular markers:

> Ce devait être le samedi après le terme, quelque chose comme le 12 ou le 13 janvier, Gervaise ne savait plus au juste. Elle perdait la boule, parce qu'il y avait des siècles qu'elle ne s'était rien mis de chaud dans le ventre. Ah! quelle semaine infernale! un ratissage complet, deux pains de quatres livres le mardi qui avaient duré jusqu'au jeudi, puis une croûte sèche retrouvée la veille, et pas une miette depuis trente-six heures, une vraie danse devant le buffet! Ce qu'elle savait par exemple, ce qu'elle sentait sur son dos, c'était le temps de chien, un froid noir, un ciel barbouillé comme le cul d'une poêle, crevant d'une neige qui s'entêtait à ne pas tomber. Quand on a l'hiver et la faim dans les tripes, on peut serrer sa ceinture, ça ne vous nourrit guère. (pp. 903–4)

> (It must have been the Saturday after rent day, something like the 12th or 13th of January, Gervaise wasn't exactly sure anymore. She was losing her mind, because it had been ages since she'd put anything warm in her stomach. Ah! what a hellish week! a total clean-out, two four-pound loaves on Tuesday that lasted 'til Thursday, then a dry crust found the previous day, and not a crumb for the last thirty-six hours, a real dance in front of the cupboard! What she knew, though, what she felt in her bones, was the shitty weather, a black cold, a sky as dark as the bottom of a frying pan, heavy with snow that just would not fall. When you feel winter and hunger in yours guts, you can tighten your belt all you want, it won't feed you.)

74 Political Stylistics

After several other paragraphs similar to this one, there is an indication that what follows, and, probably, what preceded, is a representation of Gervaise's thoughts: *elle remuait des idées pas drôles, ce jour là* (she was turning over unamusing thoughts, that day, p. 604) introduces four further pages of internal monologue, the most clear case of internal focalization. As the following passage shows, the representation of popular language increases in intensity:

> Que d'embêtements! A quoi bon se mettre dans tous ses états et se turlupiner la cervelle? Si elle avait pu pioncer au moins! Mais sa pétaudière de cambuse lui trottait par la tête. M. Marescot, le propriétaire, était venu lui-même, la veille, leur dire qu'il les expulserait, s'ils n'avaient pas payé les deux termes arriérés dans les huit jours. Eh bien! il les expulserait, ils ne seraient certainement pas plus mal sur le pavé! Voyez-vous ce sagouin avec son pardessus et ses gants de laine, qui montait leur parler des termes, comme s'ils avaient eu un boursicot caché quelque part! Nom d'un chien! au lieu de se serrer le gaviot, elle aurait commencé par se coller quelque chose dans les badigoinces! Vrai, elle le trouvait trop rossard, cet entripaillé, elle l'avait où vous savez, et profondément encore! C'était comme sa bête brute de Coupeau, qui ne pouvait plus rentrer sans lui tomber sur le casaquin: elle le mettait dans le même endroit que le propriétaire. A cette heure, son endroit devait être bigrement large, car elle y envoyait tout le monde, tant elle aurait voulu se débarrasser du monde et de la vie. (p. 905)

(What a nuisance! What was the point of getting all worked up? If only she could get some sleep! But thoughts of her pigsty of a dump rattled on in her head. M. Marescot, the owner, had come himself, the day before, to tell them he would throw them out if they didn't pay up the late rent within a week. So what? He would throw them out, they wouldn't be any worse off on the streets. There he was, that old gorilla, with his overcoat and woolen gloves, coming up to talk to them about rent, as if they had a nest-egg hidden somewhere! Damn it! Instead of tightening her belt, she'd be putting something in her own stomach! Really, he was too much of a pain, that old fart, a pain in the you know where, and deep up there too! Just like that savage brute Coupeau, who couldn't come home without giving her a tanning: she stuck him in the same place as she put the owner. Right then that place must have been pretty wide, for she was sending all and sundry there, she wanted so much to get rid of the world and of life.)

Along with the many popular expressions, the standard syntactical markers are also present: phatic elements, unfinished sentences and numerous exclamations. In this chapter, which Zola had initially conceived of as the last, and which, in the final text, precedes the one in which Gervaise dies, the complete disintegration of her life is signaled stylistically. A disintegration is also emphasized by situations such as her last encounter with Goujet, and the death of *la petite Lalie*. However, contrary to Zola's prescription in the preparatory dossier, the effect is not continuous. Several passages in *écriture artiste* are to be found here. The first follows Gervaise's decision to prostitute herself:

> Entre voler et faire ça elle aimait mieux faire ça, parce qu'au moins elle ne causerait du tort à personne. Elle n'allait jamais disposer que de son bien. Sans doute, ce n'était guère propre; mais le propre et le pas propre se brouillaient dans sa caboche, à cette heure; quand on crève de faim, on ne cause pas tant philosophie, on mange le pain qui se présente. Elle était remontée jusqu'à la chaussée Clignancourt. La nuit n'en finissait plus d'arriver. Alors, en attendant, elle suivit les boulevards, comme une dame qui prend l'air avant de rentrer pour la soupe.
>
> Ce quartier où elle éprouvait une honte, tant il embellissait, s'ouvrait maintenant de toutes parts au grand air. Le boulevard Magenta, montant du coeur de Paris, et le boulevard Ornano, s'en allant dans la campagne, l'avaient troué à l'ancienne barrière, un fier abattis de maisons, deux vastes avenues encore blanches de plâtre, qui gardaient à leurs flancs les rues du Faubourg-Poissonnière et des Poissonniers, dont les bouts s'enfonçaient, écornés, mutilés, tordus comme des boyaux sombres. Depuis longtemps, la démolition du mur de l'octroi avait déjà élargi les boulevards extérieurs, avec les chaussées latérales et le terre-plein au milieu pour les piétons, planté de quatres rangées de petits platanes. C'était un carrefour immense débouchant au loin sur l'horizon, par des voies sans fin, grouillantes de foule, se noyant dans le chaos perdu des constructions. Mais, parmi les hautes maisons neuves, bien des masures branlantes restaient debout; entre les façades sculptées, des enfoncements noirs se creusaient, des chenils bâillaient, étalant les loques de leurs fenêtres. Sous le luxe montant de Paris, la misère du faubourg crevait et salissait ce chantier d'une ville nouvelle, si hativement bâtie. (p. 915)

76 Political Stylistics

(Between stealing and doing that, she preferred doing that, because at least she would be doing no one harm. She was only going to dispose of what was her own. Granted, it was not too proper. But proper and not proper were blurred in her brains at the moment; when you're starving, you don't talk philosophy much, you eat whatever bread you can get your hands on. She had walked as far as the Chaussée Clignancourt. Night was taking a while to fall. So, to pass the time, she walked the boulevards, like a lady who is out for some fresh air before dinner.

This district where she felt such shame, because it was becoming so grand, was now opening itself up in all directions. The boulevard Magenta, coming up from the heart of Paris, and the boulevard Ornano, going off towards the countryside, had torn a gap in the old barrier, a huge demolition of houses, two great avenues still white with plaster, with, on either side of them, the rue du Faubourg-Poissonnière and des Poissonniers whose ends sank in the distance, jagged, mutilated, twisted like dark guts. For a long time, the demolition of the octroi wall had widened the outer boulevards, with footpaths at the side, and a central alley for pedestrians, planted with four rows of small trees. It was an immense crossroads, stretching out to the horizon, with endless streets swarming with people, drowning in the lost chaos of constructions. But, among the high, new houses, many old rickety shacks remained; between sculpted façades sank dark recesses, gaping kennels spreading their shabby windows. Under the rising wealth of Paris, the poverty of the faubourg was bursting to the surface, befouling the site of this newly built city, so rapidly put together.)

After the transitory sentence that opens the second paragraph, the syntax is typical of *phrase tableau*, with a series of verbal clauses separated by commas or semi-colons and an accumulation of details pertaining to this urban landscape, which is presented as a comprehensive, aerial view, obviously not seen through Gervaise's eyes. There are also instances of verb–subject disjunctions such as *Le boulevard Magenta, montant du coeur de Paris, et le boulevard Ornano, s'en allant dans la campagne, l'avaient troué* (The boulevard Magenta, going off towards the countryside, had torn a gap). There are numerous adjectives, juxtaposed in *écornés, mutilés* and *tordus*, and past participles abound, as in *un carrefour immense débouchant au loin sur l'horizon, par des voies sans fin, grouillantes de foule, se noyant* . . . (an immense crossroads stretching out to the horizon, with endless streets swarming with people, drowning . . .). It appears, without insisting any further on the characteristic features of this paragraph, that it contrasts sharply with the one that precedes it, and that it is clearly an instance of *écriture artiste*, a far cry from the pages that precede it. Such descriptions appear five times in this chapter, and function in a manner similar to the one discussed earlier – the sky as seen from the top of the Colonne Vendôme. The reader, completely accustomed to the high density of spoken markers, no longer reacts to their presence. On the contrary, it is the passages in *écriture artiste* that are striking, and the reader's attention is captured by the world-view they present, which, in this twelfth chapter, is crucial to the understanding of the novel as a whole.

The passage quoted above describes Haussmann's modernization of Paris under the Second Empire. This gigantic project of renovation, where old buildings, sometimes entire areas, were pulled down, and new, wider streets were mapped out, is described here according to an orderly movement of both horizontal and vertical expansion: *s'ouvraient, vastes, élargi, latérales, milieu, rangées, immense, hautes* (opening up, great, widened, sides, central, rows, immense, high). However, encroaching on the aseptic landscape, in an almost organic confusion, are the working-class streets, the *rue du Faubourg-Poissonnière . . . dont les bouts s'enfonçaient, écornés, mutilés, tordus comme des boyaux sombres* (the rue du Faubourg-Poissonnière . . . whose ends sank in the distance, jagged . . .). And, beneath the new city, there remains a *misère*, that in a subterranean, uncontrolled and disorderly movement – *creusait, baillait, étalait* (sunk in, gaping, spreading) – might contaminate the new. It is precisely when Gervaise reaches the lowest point in her story, when, starving, she decides to resort to prostitution, that this description of order and renewal appears, and, with it, the mention of a potential threat that will only cease when the old, the poor, and the unclean also undergo this sanitizing transformation, or disappear altogether. Paris has not yet achieved the situation of Manchester, where, as Engels describes it, "a person may live for years and go out daily without coming into contact with the working people's quarters and even with workers."[35] Later, still during her final walk through the city, Gervaise wanders past two familiar buildings:

Elle leva de nouveau les yeux. Elle se trouvait en face des abattoirs qu'on démolissait; la façade éventrée montrait des cours sombres, puantes, encore humides de sang. Et, lorsqu'elle eut redescendu le boulevard, elle vit aussi l'hôpital Lariboisière, avec son grand mur gris, au-dessus duquel se dépliaient en éventail les ailes mornes, percées de fenêtres régulières; une porte, dans la muraille, terrifiait le quartier, la porte des morts, dont le chêne solide, sans une fissure, avait la sévérité et le silence d'une pierre tombale. (p. 918)

(She looked up again. She was standing in front of the slaughter-house which was being demolished; the ripped-open façade showed dark, reeking yards, still moist with blood. And when she had walked down the boulevard, she also saw the Lariboisière hospital, with its great grey wall, above which dismal wings fanned out, regularly pierced with windows; a door, in the wall, terrified the neighbourhood, the door of the dead, of which the solid oak, without a fissure, was as forbidding and silent as a tombstone.)

The slaughterhouse and the hospital are the two places that Gervaise had anxiously observed when, in the opening pages of the first chapter, she awaited Lantier:

Elle regardait à droite, du côté du boulevard de Rochechouart, où des groupes de bouchers, devant les abattoirs, stationnaient en tabliers sanglants; et le vent frais apportait une puanteur par moments, une odeur fauve de bêtes massacrées. Elle regardait à gauche, enfilant un long ruban d'avenue, s'arrêtant, presque en face d'elle, à la masse blanche de l'hôpital de Lariboisière, alors en construction. Lentement, d'un bout à l'autre de l'horizon, elle suivait le mur de l'octroi, derrière lequel, la nuit, elle entendait parfois des cris d'assassinés; et elle fouillait les angles écartés, les coins sombres, noirs d'humidité et d'ordure, avec la peur d'y découvrir le corps de Lantier, le ventre troué de coups de couteau. (p. 602)

(She looked to her right, towards the boulevard Rochechouart, where butchers in blood-stained aprons stood in groups, in front of the slaughterhouse; and sometimes the cool wind carried an acrid stench of slaughtered animals. She looked to her left, running her eyes along a stretch of avenue, and stopping them almost opposite her, looked at the white mass of the Lariboisière hospital, then being built. Slowly, from one end of the horizon to the other, she followed the octroi wall, from behind which, at night, she sometimes heard screams of people being murdered, and she scrutinized the isolated angles, the dark corners, black with moisture and filth, afraid of discovering Lantier's body there, his stomach pierced with knife wounds.)

These are strikingly similar passages, both in their style and subject matter. The one in the twelfth chapter is also unusual in that, even though the buildings are seen through Gervaise's eyes, they are not represented in popular language. It seems that, at this point, making these descriptions stand out from their surrounding context is more important than achieving a coherent relationship of focalization to style.

With the years, and modernization, the buildings change. The old slaughterhouse is now being demolished and the new hospital has been built. The recurrence of similar descriptions when Gervaise first arrives in Paris and just before her death, and the mechanisms by which an old building is torn down and a new one constructed, suggest both continuity and change – in fact, a cyclical movement. Before further discussing the significance of these passages in the narrative and stylistic structure of the novel, the other subject which, in the twelfth chapter, is also described in *écriture artiste*, must be examined: the return of the workers.

> Sur les tas de sable, entre les bancs, des gamins jouaient encore, dans la nuit croissante. Le défilé continuait, les ouvrières passaient, trottant, se dépêchant, pour rattraper le temps perdu aux étalages; une grande, arrêtée, laissait sa main dans celle d'un garçon, qui l'accompagnait à trois portes de chez elle; d'autres, en se quittant, se donnaient des rendez-vous pour la nuit, au Grand Salon de la Folie, ou à La Boule Noire. Au milieu des groupes, des ouvriers à façon s'en retournaient, leurs toilettes pliées sous le bras. Un fumiste, attelé à des bricoles, tirant une voiture remplie de gravats, manquait de se faire écrasé par un omnibus. Cependant, parmi la foule plus rare, couraient des femmes en cheveux, redescendues après avoir allumé le feu, et se hâtant pour le diner; elles bousculaient le monde, se jetaient chez les boulangers et les charcutiers, repartaient sans trainer, avec des provisions dans les mains. Il y avait des petites filles de huit ans, envoyées en commission, qui s'en allaient le long des boutiques, serrant sur leur poitrine de grands pains de quatres livres aussi hauts qu'elles, pareils à de belles poupées jaunes, et qui s'oubliaient pendant cinq minutes devant des images, la joue appuyée contre leurs grands pains. Puis, le flot s'épuisait, les groupes s'espaçaient, le travail était rentré; et, dans les flamboiements du gaz après la journée finie, montait la sourde revanche des paresses et des noces qui s'éveillaient. (p. 917)

(On sand heaps, between benches, children were still playing, in the falling darkness. The procession went on, women returning from work, trotting along, hurrying, to make up for time wasted looking at shop windows; a tall one, standing still, let her hand linger in a young boy's, who had walked her to three doors away from her home; others, as they left one another, made plans to meet that evening at the Grand Salon de la Folie, or at the Boule Noire. Among the groups, tailoring hands, on their way home, held their folded work under their arm. A chimney sweep, harnessed with straps, pulling a cart full of gravel, was almost run over by an omnibus. Meanwhile, among the thinned-out crowd, bare-headed women hurried by, who had come back out after having lit the fire, and were now hurrying for dinner. They hustled people out of their way, threw themselves in and out of bakers and pork-butchers, without losing a minute, their provisions in their hands. Little girls of eight, sent out on errands, walked near the shops, holding to their chests four-pound loaves, as big as themselves, resembling big yellow dolls, and who lost themselves in dreams in front of pictures, their cheek resting against the big loaves. Then the flow quieted, groups thinned out, everyone had gone home; and, in the glare of the gaslight, now that the day's work was over, the dull rumbling of awakened sloth and dissipation broke to the surface.)

A typical feature of this style is the disjunction (subject–verb or verb–complement) often caused by the presence of an adverb indicating the manner of the action. There are numerous instances of this form here:

- Les ouvrières passaient, trottant, se dépêchant, pour rattraper . . . (Women returned from work, trotting along, hurrying, to make up . . .)
- Une grande, arrêtée, laissait sa main . . . (A tall one, standing still, let her hand linger . . .)
- D'autres, en se quittant, se donnaient . . . (Others, as they left one another, made appointments . . .)
- Un fumiste, attelé à des bricoles, tirant une voiture remplie de gravats, manquait . . . (A chimney-sweep, harnessed with straps, pulling a cart . . .)

Another characteristic of *écriture artiste* is that, often, a sentence begins with one or several complements of circumstance, indicating time or manner:

- Sur les tas de sable, entre les bancs, les gamins jouaient . . . (On heaps of sand, between benches, children were playing . . .)
- Cependant, parmi la foule plus rare, couraient les femmes . . . (Meanwhile, among the thinned-out crowd, women ran . . .)
- Et, dans le flamboiement du gaz, après la journée finie, montait la sourde revanche . . . (And, in the glare of gaslight, now that the work-day was over, the dull rumbling rose . . .)

A precious tone is conveyed by the (untranslatable) subject–verb inversion of *couraient les femmes*, and *montait la sourde revanche*, a construction that, unlike those mentioned above, is also present in the description of the Paris sky. So too is the type of sentence that displays a long conglomeration of subordinate clauses and complements, also found here. Furthermore, as is the case with the descriptions of the city's renovation, the description of workers in the twelfth chapter often echoes similar ones in the first. As Gervaise awaits Lantier in the morning, she watches the workers begin their day:

A la barrière, le piétinement du troupeau continuait, dans le froid du matin. On reconnaissait les serruriers à leur bourgerons bleus, les maçons à leurs cottes blanches, les peintres à leurs paletots, sous lesquels de longues blouses passaient. Cette foule, de loin, gardait un effacement platreux, un ton neutre, où le bleu déteint et le gris sale dominaient. Par moments, un ouvrier s'arrêtait court, rallumait sa pipe, tandis qu'autour de lui les autres marchaient toujours, sans un rire, sans une parole dite à un camarade, les joues terreuses, la face tendue vers Paris, qui, un à un, les dévorait, par la rue béante du Faubourg-Poissonnière. (pp. 603–4)

(At the barrier, the herd went trampling past, in the chilly morning. You could tell the locksmiths by their blue overalls, masons by their white jackets, painters by their coats with long smocks showing underneath. This crowd, from a distance, seemed of a nondescript, plaster-like tone, a neutral color, where washed-out blue and dirty grey predominated. At times, a worker suddenly stopped, lit up his pipe again, while around him the others still walked, without a laugh, without a word said to a workmate, their cheeks pale, their face turned towards Paris, which, one by one, swallowed them up, down the gaping hole of the Faubourg-Poissonière.)

82 Political Stylistics

Thirty years later, they return from work in the evening, walking down the same street, the rue du Faubourg-Poissonnière:

> Le boulevard Magenta et la rue du Faubourg-Poissonnière en lâchaient des bandes, essoufflées de la montée. Dans le roulement plus assourdi des omnibus et des fiacres, parmi les haquets, les tapissières, les fardiers, qui rentraient vides et au galop, un pullulement toujours croissant de blouses et de bourgerons couvrait la chaussée. Les commissionnaires revenaient, leurs crochets sur les épaules. Deux ouvriers, allongeant le pas, faisaient côte à côte de grandes enjambées, en parlant très fort, avec des gestes, sans se regarder; d'autres, seuls, en paletot et en casquette, marchaient au bord du trottoir, le nez baissés; d'autres venaient par cinq ou six, se suivant et n'échangeant pas une parole, les mains dans les poches, les yeux pâles. (p. 916)

(The boulevard Magenta and the rue du Faubourg-Poissonnière propelled forth hordes of them, breathless from the upward climb. Amid the duller rumbling of omnibuses and coaches, the hand carts, delivery carts, the trolleys, galloping home empty, an ever-increasing swarm of smocks and jackets covered the sidewalk. The porters were returning, their porters' hooks on their shoulders. Two workmen strode along, walking faster, taking long strides side by side, talking very loud, gesturing, without looking at each other; others, alone, in coats and caps, walked on the curb, noses down; others were in groups of five or six, following each other and not exchanging a word, their hands in their pockets, their eyes pale.)

One thing that does not change in this city is the routine of the workers who, day after day, year after year, go to their workplace in the morning and return home at night. Like the style that describes it, this activity is invested with a constancy, a reassuring solidity and stability. The repetition, in the twelfth chapter, of descriptions that had initially appeared in the first, underscores the sense of continuity and reliability. The effect was intentional, already devised in the preparatory dossier, where Zola had written: "le retour du travail, *pendant au premier chapitre*, très large, par grands morceaux, coupé des sensations de Gervaise" ("the return home from work, *reminiscent of the first chapter*, very large, in great segments, cut through with Gervaise's sensations' – fol. 80, my emphasis). These scenes, as they rise above the dislocation of Gervaise's and Coupeau's lives, show that the misfortune of an individual is quite separate from and does not affect the routine movement, the circular productive motion of the masses. As Naomi Schor points out in *Zola's Crowds*, one aspect of the crowd's – here, the crowd of workers – underlying unity is an unvarying opposition to the individual protagonist.[36] Stability, rather than disruption, is emphasized. Even though Gervaise's life deteriorates, it ends with the day, at the same place, with the same scene that she awoke to at the outset of the novel, and with the same sense of isolation. Another characteristic of Zola's representation of the crowd that Schor mentions is its unvarying temporal cycle. Even though thirty years have passed, herds of workers return home in the evening, as they had left, on what could very well be the same day. And the necessity of their labor, the daily production of the workforce and the workers' apparently inflexible endurance of their lot, is unimpaired by the downfall of a few. The description in *écriture artiste* of the new architecture of the city is also invested with a particular movement: that of a stable and dependable progress. Faith in material improvement and an admiration for the new topography of Paris is conveyed by the depiction of its clean geometry, its wide and straight avenues, its immense squares, its rows of trees. Only the fear of working-class encroachments blemishes the optimism. Again, repetition underscores the suggestion of a world that runs its solid course independently of the characters' itineraries. The old, sordid slaughterhouse that worried Gervaise at the beginning of the novel is being torn down, while the construction of a new hospital is being completed. Progress is shown to be achieved in continuity, through sustained effort, without sharp ruptures.

This textual analysis builds on Bakhtin's model of novelistic style as an interaction of stylistic unities, on Riffaterre's model of a stylistic effect that first disrupts, then later establishes the internal norm, and, finally, on Iser's notion of an implied reader, an anticipated but undefined recipient. The implied reader is not historically situated, and the reactions to the textual structures described are created by the work only, rather than by its interaction with an external horizon of expectations. For the (hypothetical) historically situated reader who holds no specific political position, and can thus be considered purely a "literary" reader, popular language (as the representation of the people in general) outside of directly reported conversations contradicts his or her expectations. In the exchange between Gervaise and Virginie during their fight at the washhouse, such a reader might have noticed the higher than usual incidence of popular markers. These are unexpected and, unlike in previous novels, their otherness is not emphasized with italics, translations in parentheses, or footnotes. However, at this early point, the popular markers are maintained within the conventional boundaries of directly reported speech. And the reader might be reassured by the context: two working-class women in an undignified, somewhat farcical, situation. The fact that Zola made use of this situation for the introduction of popular markers indicates a highly conscious and cautious utilization of popular language. But, within the boundaries of the acceptable, the intention was none the less to shock: in the preparatory dossier Zola had planned this scene as "something very energetic and very dramatic – outrageously so" (fol. 42). Zola's caution is also suggested by the fact that he transformed the popular language of one of his sources, Poulot's *Le Sublime*, by bringing it closer to correct usage. Such a transformation is, to a large extent, inevitable, so unsuited is written language to represent the spoken. But a comparison of the conversations in *L'Assommoir* with those in *Le Sublime* shows that Zola could have retained the presence of many more syntactical forms than he did, rather than restrict himself to the use of primarily lexical ones. In the second and third chapters of *L'Assommoir*, with the increasing use of indirect and free indirect style (syntactical forms that permit – but, it is important to remember, do not require – the retention of the characteristics of individual expression) popular language extends beyond the clearly marked representation of directly reported speech. The boundaries between characters' utterances and the narrative are eroded, and a certain ambiguity as to who speaks sets in. Even though popular markers clash with an external norm, they do so gradually; and they do not oppose – in fact they partake in – the norm internal to the text. This, again, would suggest an intention not to challenge the reader aggressively, not to draw his or her attention suddenly to this stylistic peculiarity. Preparatory documents show that Zola, once he had begun to write the novel, had envisaged the use of popular markers to convey the characters' vision of the world. The text supports this suggestion. The fact that popular markers appear with greater intensity when Gervaise's and Coupeau's lives deteriorate, particularly in the long internal monologues of the twelfth chapter, suggests that Zola uses them to signal the characters' downfall. Furthermore, Goujet, the token "good worker," differs from the others not only with his actions, but with his speech.

However, the characters' vision of the world is not the only one put forth in the novel. What disrupt the reader's expectations, and call attention to themselves with sudden breaches in register, are the passages in "elevated" style. Whether it is by reinstating the order and hierarchy symbolized by the Colonne Vendôme, showing the unalterable and stable cyclic movement of the labor force, or celebrating the sanitizing effect of Haussmann's renovations, they represent a dominant world-view that emerges in opposition to the surrounding context. The ahistorical reader's attention is drawn to the passages in *écriture artiste* because they are juxtaposed to and clash with a stylistic context in which popular language predominates. As for the reader of the time, the historically situated reader, not only do these passages draw attention to themselves, but an act of recognition also takes place: for the *écriture artiste*, in accordance with external norms, is the style of major, honorific novels of the time, such as the Goncourts' and Huysman's, and is thus invested with authority and legitimacy. The *écriture artiste* achieves a double valorization, internal and external, as it interrupts, controls and resists the flow of popular language.

All such passages are descriptive. It is interesting to bring Lukács' essay "Narrate or Describe?" to bear on this fact.[37] Lukács constructs his arguments around a set of oppositions, the most general one being between the epic and naturalistic novel. He favors the epic, which shows "the poetry of men in struggle, the poetry of the turbulent, active interaction of men" and which provides an account of the relationship of human beings to the world, of "man and his social practice – not as an artificial product of the artist's virtuosity, but as something that grows naturally, as something not invented but simply discovered."[38] Naturalism, in which descriptions rather than narration, the typically dominant mode in the epic, prevails, excludes the representation of social practice, and shows only the outcome of power structures. "The decisive ideological weakness of the writers of the descriptive method," Lukács argues, "is their passive capitulation to the consequences [of capitalism] and in their seeing the results but not the struggles of the opposed forces."[39] For example, Lukács contrasts the representation of horse races in *Nana* and *Anna Karenina*. In Tolstoy's novel, the race is narrated from the point of view of a character and is essential to subsequent events, whereas in Zola's it is seen by an outside observer, and only loosely related to the plot, forming a static, background tableau. As Lukács notes elsewhere in his work, human beings and their social surroundings are always sharply divided in Zola's novels:

> Perhaps no one has painted more carefully and suggestively the outer trappings of modern life. But only the outer trappings. They form the gigantic backdrop in front of which tiny haphazard people moved to and fro in their haphazard lives.[40]

In *L'Assommoir*, the passages in *écriture artiste* do indeed form such sweeping backgrounds: the description of the Paris sky dominates the characters when they themselves felt subjugated by the city

– thus suggesting a sense of entrapment; the new architecture of the boulevards along which Gervaise wanders aimlessly, awaiting nightfall; the routine movement of the workers going to and from their place of work. This latter description is one of the more central dynamics of modern life. Yet, as Lukács notes, what Zola shows is a consequence of relations of production, dissociated from more specific mechanisms of social domination. Also true is the fact that many descriptions are unrelated to the characters' lives (as Schor demonstrates in the specific case of crowds). Rather, they emphasize that dissociation: the hospital is built despite Coupeau's accident, and the routine of the workers is unaffected by the characters' demise.

I have argued that those passages convey dominant discourse by way of the lexical and syntactical features of their style on the one hand, and the world-view they convey on the other. Lukács identifies an added political function in the very nature of descriptions. They are a consequence of the development of capitalism and become a means by which these consequences are reinforced:

> The domination of capitalist prose over the inner poetry of human experience, the continuous dehumanization of social life, the general debasement of humanity – all these are objective facts of the development of capitalism. *The descriptive method is the inevitable product of this development.* Once established this method is taken up by leading writers dedicated in their own way, and then in turn it affects the literary representation of reality. The poetic level of life decays – and *literature intensifies the decay*.[41] (my emphasis)

L'Assommoir, however, differs from the general model of naturalism that Lukács proposes, since the descriptions there do not dominate quantitatively. They do not draw the reader's attention because of their frequency of occurrence, but, rather, stand out because they are at once unexpected (according to an internal norm) and recognizable (according to an external norm). What does prevail quantitatively is a representation of the characters' world-view – their speech, their thoughts, their attitudes, which are not described by an outside observer, but narrated from their own point of view. In this respect, something that partakes of Lukács' conception of the epic, which should show the poetry of people in struggle and represent their social activity, is present in *L'Assommoir*. However, in those parts of the text that do indeed narrate the characters' world-view, there is, once more, an internal resistance – although not a stylistic one this time – that, along with the descriptive passages, confines the novel to a conservative outlook. The activities of the workers, as they are represented in *L'Assommoir*, are shown as restricted to their own class; the novel fails to include a representation of their interactions with the bourgeoisie (as in Balzac's *The Peasants* (*Les Paysans*), or even Zola's *Germinal*), and does not, any more than the descriptive passages, show "the relationships of human beings to the world." Even though it is narrated with popular language, the characters' world-vision in *L'Assommoir* is extremely narrow, typically shown to revolve around sex, food and drink – hardly what Lukács would consider "the significant and vital aspects of social practice." The only struggle is short-lived, as Gervaise works hard to open her laundry shop. She attempts to overcome adverse circumstances (the outcome of social structures) rather than question the root of these adverse circumstances (the social structures) themselves. Her success is brief and followed by a downward movement, resulting from a sudden catastrophe that one may consider a micro-economic crisis, an economic crisis within family structures: Coupeau, while working, falls off a roof. He is injured, and so loses his job; he drinks and drives Gervaise to drink. As Lukács points out, Zola diagnoses Coupeau's alcoholism (and hence the family's downfall) as the effect of unemployment, and hence as the result of his accident, whereas in reality alcoholism was endemic to several categories of French workers. In the case of construction workers, it is explained by the fact that they worked only intermittently and spent their free time in the taverns. What Zola presents as a crisis, was in actuality linked to the underlying structure of socio-economic conditions. The novel does not point to these. Yet, *L'Assommoir* gave rise to many contradictory political interpretations in the press; for, the internal resistance notwithstanding, the novel does show the working class as the subject of a serious representation in the literary text, and this without the obvious marks of objectification and distancing that accompanied its presence in earlier works.

INSURRECTION AND PHILOLOGY

L'Assommoir first appeared as a serial in *Le Bien Public*, a daily newspaper founded in 1871. Originally of right-wing sympathies, it was bought in 1876 by the industrialist Menier, and later became more liberal and progressive. Much publicity surrounded the publication of the first episode of the novel on 13 April 1876. Early editions of the newspaper were handed out on the street, and several copies distributed to Paris coaches. However, after the first seven chapters had appeared, a sudden decision to terminate the publication of Zola's novel was announced in *Le Bien Public* on 5 June:

> The first part of the remarkable novel that we have been publishing must end in the early part of June. M. Emile Zola had taken up the burden of finishing, as it was being published, that study so rich in detail and written in such an elaborate language. But he fell behind his schedule, and, wishing to give his full attention to the second part, has requested that we grant him the time to do so, while we fulfill our obligation towards other novelists.

Zola was indeed a little behind schedule, but there were various other reasons why this newspaper suddenly dropped the serial. One was the discontent of readers who, offended by the style, sent letters of outrage to the editors and may have canceled subscriptions (the reference to the "elaborate language" might have been designed indirectly to counteract such criticism). However, Henri Mitterand suggests different causes for its termination, citing a letter that Zola had written to Paul Alexis on 1 July. Apparently, republican readers may have wished for a more flattering picture of the people:

> Even though there is no doubt that the novel surprised the subscribers to the *Bien Public*, it did not provoke cancellations, according to Yves Guyot himself, and contrary to what was said later . . . The reasons that account for the suspension of publication in *Le Bien Public* are political rather than moral or literary. Zola explains it himself in a letter to Paul Alexis on July 1: "*L'Assommoir* did not seem radical enough and was terminated in *Le Bien Public*."[42]

The publication was resumed in July in *La République des lettres*, a periodical headed by Catulle Mendès which, while primarily dedicated to the work of *Parnassiens*, also encouraged naturalist efforts. Mendès, it is interesting to note, had been a notorious anti-Communard; if he agreed to publish *L'Assommoir* it is clearly not because he read it as a celebration of the people.[43] The government, however, was worried. Reflecting its intolerance towards what it considered a morally and politically damaging work, the Procureur de la République threatened to forbid the sale of the paper after the publication of the first installment, should *L'Assommoir* continue to be printed – obviously not because he found the novel too conservative. Only after an intervention by Catulle Mendès did the official opposition subside, but the authorities were never entirely reassured. After the novel's publication in book form, the government forbade its sale in train stations, in order to halt a widespread diffusion. The attempt failed, and the work was a spectacular commercial success: thirty-eight editions appeared in 1877 alone, and a total of ninety-one before 1882. Well-known political figures on the left also denounced the novel: Charles Floquet wrote that it was "a ridiculous pamphlet directed against workers, and that provided ammunition for reactionaries."[44] Arthur Ranc, exiled in Brussels, wrote that "[Zola] has for the people the scorn of a bourgeois, and, at the same time, the scorn of an artist who produces art for art's sake, a Neronian scorn."[45]

The obvious point that emerges from these incidents is that, as the reactions in the political press will further illustrate, *L'Assommoir* was read in widely diverging ways. For example, Albert Wolff in *Le Figaro*, a conservative paper read by a very large audience of the high bourgeoisie, applauds the political implications that he detects in the work:

> M. Zola will remain the most powerful and most intelligent protestation against cabaret braggarts who want to make the bourgeois solely to blame for the misfortune of this population of drunkards, bad workers, horrendous husbands, abominable fathers that swarm in the faubourgs.[46]

However, Dancourt, in *La Gazette de France*, a *légitimiste* paper (supporting a return of the Bourbon branch of kings) begins his article which appeared promptly after the publication of the first episode, with a statement that places the novel in a very different political light: "M. Zola is the leader of the literary Commune."[47] It is not to Zola's beliefs that he refers here, he adds (and rightly so, for Zola did not support the revolt of 1871), but to his "literary methods." He locates revolutionary potential in the style, which he considers "insurrectional" and, of course, "lamentable." Particularly offensive to Dancourt, and central to his arguments, is the "washhouse scene" which became the starting point of a virulent and long-lasting polemic. As I have shown, popular markers appear with some density in this passage, and their presence is sustained over a number of pages. They are, as was the case in earlier works by Hugo and Balzac, restricted to the directly reported speech of characters, but their otherness is not indicated with parentheses or translations. I also mentioned that the violent and farcical character of the fight between Gervaise and Virginie at the washhouse might have, in itself, drawn attention away from the language or served to justify its presence. This is not the reading that Dancourt proposes. He blames the style as much as the subject matter of this passage, for both display "outrageous realism."

Here we have the republican novelist and the royalist journalist occupying radically different positions. Zola, in his assessment of *Germinie Lacerteux*, wrote that there could be no excess of truth: "in principle, there can be no limit to the study of truth."[48] Dancourt judges the first chapter of *L'Assommoir* to be overly and shockingly realistic. What he means by this is clear; some topics and words should simply not be represented. There is a certain knowledge that should not be acquired. Denying the very right to existence of the working class and its language, Dancourt blames Zola for calling things by their crudest names, for using words that, up to then, had been confined to dictionaries and that the most elementary education prevents one from saying. Objectification, in this remark, is taken to its extreme: Dancourt does not consider an argot dictionary as representing popular language, but as being the sole locus of its existence. And he assumes that the most elementary education is universally shared. Popular language, by virtue, it seems, of its mere presence in the novel (and in whatever context, for Dancourt's judgment was passed before the popular language became pervasive and reached beyond directly reported speech), loses its subservient place and character. This is a clear instance of how the word can be perceived as directly linked to the social realm, as carrying within itself traces of social struggle and bringing them, by means of the literary text, into clear focus and legitimacy. Popular language is seen to function in itself as an oppositional sign, operating, when brought into the novel, in an openly and immediately recognizable subversive way. There is, however, a twist in the argument at the end of the article, where an unexpected parallel is drawn between Zola and Voltaire, to Zola's benefit. Even though Voltaire carefully selected the words he used, says Dancourt, the insidious "democratic infiltrations" in his work are far more dangerous, because they are less immediately apparent than they are in the inclusion of slang and vulgar expressions: "M. Zola, at least, has the merit of being frank. He, at least, is not a traitor; he does not disguise what he has to say. Before blushing at the word, begin rather by blushing at the thing." The substance of Voltaire's work was dangerous for the aristocracy, but was couched in an elegant form, and hence was more devious in its operation. However distasteful, Dancourt reads Zola's style on the other hand as being overtly rather than covertly politically subversive.

Dancourt, then, believes that the novel shows unequivocal support for the working class. However, Wolff, also from a conservative point of view, enthusiastically approved both its style and content. In his article in *Le Figaro* he finds *L'Assommoir* highly moral because it demonstrates that no one except the workers themselves can be blamed for their hardship. The novel provides a welcome contrast to all those earlier works that idealized the people:

> The principal merit of the work is that it does away with the conventional worker, such as he had been painted before Zola by novelists, playwrights and vaudevillians. The Parisian worker exploited by men of letters had two faces: either the writer showed us the false worker, vaudeville style, dissipated but with a noble soul, or that other type, falser still, of a worker who lives through corrupt times without the slightest stain on his smock; for both, the faubourgs seemed to be the conservatory of moral righteousness and high sentiments. The upper classes wallowed in orgies, sustained themselves on infamies, while the noble worker was a shining example of virtue and devotion.

For Wolff, popular language supports the realism and guarantees the veracity of the depiction. And what he perceives as the truth of *L'Assommoir*, that the worker is responsible for his own misfortune, is one that urgently needs to be upheld. What makes his reading different from those of the other critics who also note the negative representation of the working class is that he does notice those passages through which Zola elevates himself above his subject. It is appropriate, he says, to have the characters speak their own language: it adds strength to the depiction of their world, especially since a too crude expression is counteracted by passages where "Zola immediately compensates for such fickleness with first rate pages, where the man of letters rises with singular strength, and where the philosopher displays a rare power of observation." Such passages are testimony to Zola's rare insights and to his ability to elevate himself above his subject. For Dancourt, on the other hand, the question is not whether the representation of the working class and its language is sympathetic or not. For him, it is a subject that should not, under any circumstance, be represented. The working class need not be acknowledged, and nothing brings it into more powerful existence than its language. The difference between those two readings may, perhaps, be accounted for in terms of the divergent views of Dancourt, a royalist, and Wolff, a representative of the high bourgeoisie; for the former, the working class does not even enter his social vision; whereas for the latter, it is a force to be toughly reckoned with.

Generally, however, the critics did not address the novel's political implications in such a direct manner. The overwhelmingly negative readings focused on two issues: bad taste and immorality. A fiercely negative appraisal of the novel by Albert Millaud in *Le Figaro* (where Wolff later published his positive assessment) on 1 September 1876, consists, for about two-thirds of its length, of extracts of the latest episode. Millaud begins by claiming that he was, before reading *L'Assommoir*, quite well disposed towards Zola, for even though he did not share the author's political and social positions, he found previous novels of the *Rougon-Macquart* not without qualities: "Those early works allowed one to hope that M. Zola, even though he was too much of a realist, would forge a niche for himself and enjoy a successful career in the difficult art of the contemporary novel."[49] But *L'Assommoir* came as a shock and Millaud considers Zola's talent and potential now to be forsaken. Utterly loathsome, of course, are the events of the episode in which Gervaise, after an outing at the *Café-Concert* with Lantier, returns home to her drunk and sick husband, and yields to her former lover's advances. But above all it is the style that Millaud finds odious and grotesque, filthy rather than realistic, pornographic rather than crude. This does not, however, dissuade him from quoting the novel at greater length than a simple illustration of his views would warrant. And to these passages Millaud adds what Zola had omitted: he underlines the popular expressions. He also flagrantly manipulates the text and grossly exaggerates when he says: "Let us confine ourselves to these extracts, that are among the mildest, the most reasonable, the cleanest of all that has been published of M. Zola's novel up to this point." Zola responds to this attack in a letter published in *Le Figaro* on 7 September:

> *L'Assommoir* is the painting of a certain working class, a primarily literary attempt, where I tried to reconstitute the language of Parisian faubourgs. One must hence view the wrought and elaborate style of the book as a philological study and nothing more.[50]

Zola places the novel in an "art for art's sake" framework ("a primarily literary attempt") and, at the same time, justifies the style in linguistic and historical terms, which is another way to deny any current social implication. The language of *L'Assommoir*, he says, is "wrought" and "elaborate." Artificiality, rather than spontaneity, is stressed, in order to establish scholarly distance from popular language. Finally, Zola protests the fact that isolated extracts are quoted, showing the importance he attaches to the subtle introduction of popular markers and to the organization of the stylistic unities.

In an ongoing polemic, Millaud reacts to Zola's response. He now accepts the presence of "crude language" in the characters' utterances;

however, he still cannot see a justification for its representation outside of these:

> M. Zola claims that he intended to produce a primarily literary work, in which he reconstituted the language of the Parisian faubourgs. Granted, we readily accept that M. Zola's characters speak in their habitual manner, that the dialogues are rendered in crude language in the same way that Balzac's Baron de Nucigen and Remonecq the Auvergnat speak patois. But we do not understand that the narrative, the description, the analysis of personalities – which emanate from M. Zola, which are his own reflections, his own depictions – we do not understand why M. Zola has written these in the vulgar tongue that he has his characters use.[51]

A few days later, on 21 September, the novel is attacked along similar lines in the Bonapartist paper *Le Gaulois*.[52] Contradicting what Zola had claimed in his recent letter, Fourcaud here denies that *L'Assommoir* has any literary value: "Is it really literature, this foul language." He describes the style with a simple phrase – it stinks: "Not a single sentence that does not stink," he writes, and adds, again with a great deal of exaggeration, that the entire novel, from the first to the last line, is written in the most atrocious language. The subject matter, says Fourcaud, requires the moral presence of a narrator who would provide a stylistically defined contrast to the horror and filth represented throughout, "to throw over the filth a bridge from which the reader would be able to see without dirtying himself." The narrator, to satisfy a right-wing reading, should have displayed his authority over and dissociation from his subject in a manner far more obvious than Zola did with the passages in *écriture artiste*. Zola answered these accusations in a letter published along with the critic's comments on 26 September. The core of his arguments is as follows:

> In *L'Assommoir*, which, by the way, belongs to a vast corpus of work, there is a simple question of art, a question of exact representation, along with a question of philology. I myself intended nothing more and I am the first to be astounded by the strange discoveries that the critics claim they make.[53]

Fourcaud is not convinced, and includes an extract of the conversation between Gervaise and Coupeau around Nana's Communion, and, unsurprisingly, finds the passages where a drunk Coupeau mocks the Catholic ceremony "ignoble, nauseating, shameful." The critic considers *L'Assommoir* to be a "fake wart" on the author's talent, a talent present in earlier works, and wonders why Zola felt compelled to dip his pen in "Coupeau's vomit." His tone is indignant:

> The novel, from the first to the last line is written in the crudest of crude languages. The author's voice is careful to avoid discordance from this concert. Is it good, useful, fruitful, this philosophy of aggression and philology of the sewer![54]

Jules Barbey d'Aurevilly, in another Bonapartist paper, *Le Constitutionel* (29 January 1877) shares this disgust: the language of *L'Assommoir* is carved in "human excrements."[55] Zola, he claims, has lost in the most contemptible slang the language that used to be his. He is corrupted by his subject when he himself speaks like the characters in his novel. Trying too hard to paint them, he has molded himself and lost himself in their filth. There is, in this novel, a double abjection: of language and of feeling, and one emerges from it as pigs, those four-legged realists, emerge from a mire: a mire of things, a mire of words, an unbreathable mire. By this time, *L'Assommoir* has been published in book form, and Barbey d'Aurevilly contrasts the preface to the rest of the novel, a preface written, he says, as though Zola had sensed trouble and felt the need to "cleanse" his work. It is indeed a text rich in justifications. Zola regrets the fact that *L'Assommoir* was attacked, denounced, and accused of all possible crimes. This, he says, was because of the style:

> The form alone startled. The words provoked anger. My crime is that I had the literary curiosity to gather and cast in a very elaborate mold the language of the people. Ah! the form, there is the great crime! Dictionaries of that language nevertheless exist, men of letters study it, and delight in its crudity, in the unexpectedness and power of its images. It is a treat for rummaging grammarians. Still, no one realized that my intention was to produce a purely philological work that I judge to be of high historical and social interest. (p. 599)

The term "curiosity" in "literary curiosity" implies a certain innocence, a lack of ulterior motives, a spontaneous interest, and, again, distances Zola from popular language. The textual analysis shows that popular markers do not appear haphazardly but are carefully and consciously organized – this is underlined by his reference to the "very elaborate mold." Zola then goes on to justify his stylistic choice by equating it, once more, with an academic exercise. To draw a comparison to dictionaries, to view *L'Assommoir* as a delight for "rummaging grammarians" and to consider its style as a purely philological endeavor – all these claims are attempts to restore some scholarly respectability to his stylistic choice, and they certainly do not support the promise in Zola's first reference in the preparatory dossier to the "style – full force." The onslaught continued, and the preface did not change the reaction of Armand de Pontmartin, who, in *La Gazette de France* (18 February 1877), said that reading this work was a real torture, for, throughout, the dirtiest image is poisoned by the filthiest word.[56]

As for reactions in the republican press, there were far fewer; among these, however, was a strongly negative one in *Le Journal des débats*. It was written by Henri Houssaye, an historian and member of the Académie Française – which would not, of course, favorably dispose him towards the style of the novel. He declares puerile the innovation that consists in writing a novel on the "faubourgs" in the language of those who live there. According to that logic, Houssaye claims, a history of Germany should be written in German. It must be by an act of defiance, he adds, that Zola places in his work all those words that written language does not authorize, uncaring as to whether the expression fits as long as it is crude. The result is a narrative that seems as though it is written by Coupeau, rather than by Zola, who, as his previous works, especially *Ninon's Tales* show, is in fact a "sensitive man of letters." Houssaye suggests that Zola's motivations were practical and opportunist. Fearing that it would take him too long to conquer a well-earned reputation, he wanted to dazzle and shock the public to achieve notoriety. Particularly offensive to Houssaye, again, is the fact that he perceives the author as having adopted popular language as his own:

> He wanted to use those very expressions that he supposes the working class uses, so that the novel's style be cast in the same mold, with the same characteristics and the same taste as the subject matter and the characters. He is not content with providing the characters with a most trivial and crude language in the dialogue; in the narrative, when he himself speaks, he uses the same language.[57]

Houssaye remarks, however, that Zola himself is not absolutely convinced of the value of his system: his "real" style is sometimes juxtaposed on the same page as the style of "the author of *L'Assommoir*."

Anatole France, in *Le Temps* (27 June 1877), a paper of the Républicains Modérés, offered a favorable judgment. He writes that he admires this powerful book that provides a strong illusion of reality: "*L'Assommoir* is certainly not a pleasant book, but it is a powerful one. Life is represented in an immediate and direct way, there could be no greater illusion of reality." Elements of popular language are used to transmit characters' thoughts or to describe their state of mind, he notes, and he accurately points out that Zola resorts to his own vocabulary for certain descriptions. He concludes perhaps ironically – and this would be the only veiled attack against these passages – that, apparently, popular language lacks the words to describe a sunset:

> The many characters speak the language of the faubourgs. When the author, without having them speak, suggests their thoughts or describes their state of mind, he himself uses their language. For this he has been criticized. I praise him. One cannot faithfully translate a person's thoughts and feelings except in his own language. It is true that, for the descriptions, M. Zola has had to resort to his own vocabulary. The idiom of the working class, it appears, lacks terms to describe a sunset.[58]

Other than Wolff, the critics do not pay much attention to the passages in *écriture artiste*; those who do mention them offer only brief comments, without recognizing the vital role that these passages play in the overall stylistic composition of the novel. For Houssaye, their presence indicates that Zola was not altogether committed to the representation of popular language: his occasional return to a conventional style marks his hesitation and uncertainty. France points out that the language of the novel is more varied than many had claimed, but does not assign a specific signification to these passages. However, his remark "the idiom of the working class, it appears, lacks terms to describe a sunset" could be understood as ironical, and as suggesting a veiled critique of those elevated descriptions.

In general, the critics' attention is overwhelmingly drawn to the new and extensive presence of popular language, which most of them condemn for being extremely offensive and distasteful, for going against what they consider to be the eternal, normative and transcendent category of "good taste." Zola, by dipping his pen in "Coupeau's vomit" and "human excrement" has also debased literature. The fact that popular language extends beyond clear boundaries of characters' discourse is much emphasized, denounced, and taken as further proof that Zola has entirely lost his bearings. Many critics are of the opinion that such a language, if represented at all, requires a stylistically defined moral contrast and they deplore the fact that the narrator's authority is not displayed in any obvious way. Reminding us that Zola does have access to legitimate language, Houssaye distinguishes between and opposes the "language of the author of *L'Assommoir*" to "Zola's language," regretting that the latter no longer exists; in a similar gesture, other critics mention his early works in unusually positive terms. Hence, the only possible motivations for Zola's stylistic choice in his latest novel are childish defiance and the desire to achieve a rapid notoriety. In following this dangerous path, Zola has become contaminated by the popular, corrupted by his subject, and has let himself be dissolved in his characters' low-life. What the critics are suggesting here is not so much that Zola is a defender of the people (many claim, in fact, that the novel implies the opposite) but that the current "liberal" political régime allows the corruption of the bourgeoisie by the working class, and the corruption of the categories of good taste and literature by such distasteful subjects and language.

The negative critics are intent on denying that any aesthetic quality was achieved in *L'Assommoir* for two reasons. First, because as Jan Mukarovsky explains in *Aesthetic Function, Norm and Value as Social Facts*: "Wherever in social intercourse it becomes necessary to emphasize any act, object or person, to focus on it, to free it from undesirable associations, the aesthetic function emerges as an accompanying factor."[59] Inversely, one might conclude, because the aesthetic function is generally held to exist a priori in literary representation, popular language in the novel could be illuminated by this positive perspective. Second, it is "the greater sensitivity towards the aesthetic function, and its more intensive utilization, in the higher levels of society which attempt to distinguish themselves from the other social levels."[60] Bad taste, Mukarovsky notes, is the most acute antithesis to art:

> We only speak of bad taste when we evaluate an object produced by human hands and in which we observe a tendency to fulfill a certain aesthetic norm and which at the same time lacks the ability to fulfill that norm.[61]

Bad taste, then, is a failed attempt at the aesthetic. The literary text is, in the public's horizon of expectations, held to lean towards such norms. But when Zola dedicated *L'Assommoir* to "his great friend Flaubert, in hatred of good taste," his professed motivations do not suggest an aesthetic attempt, but, on the contrary, imply a rejection of the aesthetic – a motivation which later he denied.

This critics' strategy implicitly relegated Zola to the same social level as the class he represented. Yet, in a provocative and manipulative gesture, they delight in quoting numerous passages, then describe them as grotesque, filthy, pornographic. With a great deal of exaggeration, they claim that the entire novel is written in this style and that the passages quoted are among the mildest. Clearly, the novel was not ignored, hence not silenced, by the press. On the contrary, the critics' principal strategy was not to repress but to discredit, and to read *L'Assommoir* as an illustration of the negative effect democracy had on literature and society. The critics suggest that the novel's style, which allows the pervasion of the popular, is the reflection of a too-liberal society. This accounts for their triumphant tone and their eagerness to quote so many passages. From the defensive tone of his counteractions, it appears that Zola was somewhat taken aback by the readings. All of his justifications concerning the novel's style are similar, and one element recurs: philology, with all the scholarly detachment from popular language that this term implies. Zola's many responses to the accusations of bad taste do not at all reflect the bravado of the dedication, "in hatred of good taste." He either flatly denies the accusation, by emphasizing the literary motivations behind *L'Assommoir* ("a primarily literary attempt, a simple question of art") or claims that his concerns were of a scholarly, philological nature – hence implying that the novel could not be in bad taste, since the aesthetic was never intended. Both claims also deny the existence of any political motivation behind the work.

Accusations of immorality were provoked by the depiction of the characters' behavior during their downfall, as the *ménage à trois* between Gervaise, Coupeau and Lantier takes shape under the prying gaze of the young daughter Nana, and within a context of excessive eating and drinking. In *Germinie Lacerteux*, however, the maid's sex life was far more dissolute than Gervaise's, but no such critical reactions ensued. This, again according to Mukarovsky, might be because the artist is allowed to subvert moral norms, if such a violation is accompanied by the aesthetic function – which, in *L'Assommoir*, is not the case. Zola responded to this criticism with two different arguments. The first, which also served on the issue of tastelessness, claimed that the work was purely literary, therefore suggesting that because of its inherent good taste, it was allowed to subvert moral norms. The other was to acknowledge that, if the characters' behavior was indeed immoral, this did not by any means indicate that the novel was. On the contrary, Zola claims in his response to Millaud that *L'Assommoir* is, in fact, highly moral: "Furthermore, *L'Assommoir* has not yet been fully published, and, at this early point, no one can judge the moral content. I promise that the lesson will be terrible, vengeful, and that no author's intentions have ever been more honest."[62] Not unlike Racine who, in the preface to *Phèdre*, responded to similar criticism, Zola draws attention to a lesson that Gervaise will learn – through her death. This suggests that the deterioration and end of her life, then, should be considered punishment for her depraved actions and drinking; if she is punished, she, rather than social conditions, are to be blamed and held responsible for her demise. This is a far cry from the theory of environment that Zola had claimed he would illustrate. The position expressed here is diametrically opposed, and is also present in the dossier: a moralistic view that suggests that the workers' situation is the outcome of free choices, and that nothing could be of greater benefit to them than a self-achieved improvement of their habits and attitudes. In the preface to the book form of the novel, Zola claims that *L'Assommoir* is "the most chaste of my books," and, again, his address of the moral question is not without political consequence and ambiguity. He calls himself a "dignified bourgeois," clearly establishing the side to which he rallies, but says that he does not want to show that the entire working class is bad, only that some workers are ignorant and "corrupted by the environment of hard work in which they live." Elsewhere in the preface, however, he does not clearly adhere to the theory of environment:

> I wanted to paint the fatal downfall of a working-class family in the corrupt environment of our faubourg. After drunkenness and laziness, there is the loosening of family ties, the filth of promiscuity, the progressive oblivion of honest thought, then, as denouement, shame and death. It is moral in action, quite simply. (p. 593)

Although Zola mentions that the workers' downfall takes place "in the corrupt environment of our faubourg," he does not suggest that their misfortune is actually brought on by the environment. In fact, "drunkenness" and "laziness" are the causes to blame, and this implicitly discounts the validity of social determinism. This leads critics to delight in underlining what they saw as a discrepancy between Zola's professed liberalism on the one hand, and his unsympathetic depiction of the working class on the other. Millaud, in the comments which appear alongside Zola's response to the attack he had been subject to the previous week, as well as stating that he could see no justification for the presence of popular language in the speech of characters, also suggests that this novel does not seem to correlate with Zola's political position. Similarly, Pontmartin, even though he attacked the style of the novel as a whole, noted that Zola's unflattering picture of the people served the ruling class by strengthening its domination. When it depended on their cooperation to undertake revolutionary action against a common enemy, the aristocracy, the bourgeoisie glorified and flattered the lower classes, but now that the bourgeoisie rules, it is in the position to tell the people what it really thinks.

Of the two internal resistances, the unflattering representation of those who use popular language, and the tasteful passages in *écriture artiste*, critics seized on the former. One might imagine that, if the characters had been shown in a more appealing light, the novel would have been silenced; if the parts of the novel whereby Wolff perceived that the narrator elevated himself above his subject matter had been more numerous, more conservative critics would have applauded *L'Assommoir*. As it was, the novel remained highly controversial, and gave rise to reactions in the literary field that were as diverse as in the political. From a letter to Ivan Turgenev written in December 1876, it appears that Flaubert, ironically, did not appreciate the work that had been dedicated to him.[63] Like Molière's characters Cathos and Madelon, Flaubert writes, Zola is a "*précieuse*," but an "*inverted précieuse*'; just as those seventeenth-century women believed that some words were, in themselves, elevated, Zola seemed convinced that there is something inherently powerful in popular language. Such abstract principles, Flaubert adds, severely limit the judgment and vision of the author who now appears to have entirely forsaken poetry and style. Mallarmé, on the other hand, expressed much admiration for the novel. It was the style that moved him. In a letter to Zola of 3 February 1877, he calls *L'Assommoir* "a great work," a truly modern work, worthy of a time where truth is the popular form of beauty.[64] He particularly admires the linguistic experiment, the way in which the most popular expression becomes a seductive literary formula that brings tears to the eyes of the most educated, the most learned of readers. Still, however passionate the reactions it provoked, *L'Assommoir* had no direct, visible impact on subsequent novels. Even though it resulted in great financial success, and aroused much interest in his subsequent novels, Zola did not continue his experiment of "the style – full force," nor did other writers take it up. Not until over half a century later, with Céline's *Journey to the End of the Night*, was the literary representation of popular language repeated in a manner that broke similar and further stylistic ground.

3 Céline's *Voyage au bout de la nuit*

> Thinking about Zola, we remain a little bemused before his work; he is still too close to us for us to judge him well, I mean to say in his intentions. He talks about things that are familiar to us . . . It would have been pleasant if they had changed a little.
>
> Allow us a personal recollection. At the Exposition of 1900, we were still young, but the memory remains quite vivid, that it was an enormous brutality. Feet, mostly, feet everywhere and dust in clouds so thick you could touch them. Endless people marching, pounding, crushing the Exposition, and then that moving staircase that grated all the way up to the gallery of machines, full, for the first time, of tortured metals, of colossal threats, of catastrophes in abeyance. Modern life began.
>
> We have done nothing better since. We have done nothing better since *L'Assommoir* either.[1]

In 1933, soon after the publication of his first novel, Céline spoke at a gathering entitled "Homage to Zola." The horror of the world that Zola had depicted, Céline said, remained, in many respects, all too familiar. One would have hoped that it might have improved a little; it had, in fact, become worse. The turn of the century brought to its fullest the dehumanization that *L'Assommoir* had suggested, to the extent that new literary techniques were now required for its representation:

> Today, with our means of information, Zola's naturalism becomes almost impossible. We would not leave prison if we recounted life as we know it, beginning with our own. I mean such as we have come to understand it for the last twenty years. It already required some heroism on Zola's part to show to his contemporaries a few happy scenes from reality. No one is allowed today's reality. Let symbols

and dreams be ours! All the transfers that the law does not reach, does not yet reach![2]

In his reflection on the differences between his times and the 1870s, Céline addresses two issues. The first is related to technological advances in the realm of documentary representation: "Our means of information" no doubt refers to new techniques such as photography and radio, and to the availability of more widespread and effective means of communication. The second point, recurring throughout Céline's speech, concerns the worsened state of reality. Already harsh at the end of the nineteenth century, by the third decade of the twentieth it had become so unbearable that only the imagination offered refuge.

The situation of the working class, it is true, had deteriorated in many ways, and by the turn of the century antagonisms between itself and the bourgeoisie were sharper than ever. Mechanization of the workplace resulted in a standardization of labor, which, since it required no special training, became cheap and easily replaceable. New technologies separated the workers from the product of their work, in an increasingly inhumane environment from which they had little hope of escaping. One of the great ideals of the Third Republic was a secular and state-run educational system, but even though elementary schools were open to all, secondary schools, or lycées, were not. They were costly, hence attended only by the bourgeoisie; in fact, between 1880 and 1930, the number of students enrolled in secondary education remained unchanged. The working class experienced a sense of increased alienation, with little chance of improvement through the existing system. Consequently, political opposition emerged in organized form. The left, both reformist and revolutionary, was gathered in a large party, the SFIO (Section Française de l'Internationale Ouvrière – the French Section of the Workers' International), and the workers were represented by a powerful union still in place today, the CGT (Confédération Générale des Travailleurs – the General Confederation of Workers). At the 1908 congress of the CGT, class hostility was bluntly expressed: one of the workers' most urgent tasks was defined as "to tear away from the bourgeois state the brain of the proletatarian's child."[3] The bourgeois state now exerted legitimate control over children, for elementary education was compulsory until the age of 13 – time enough for the child to recognize legitimate French, but not to acquire its usage; enough for the state to indoctrinate the child, but not to provide tools for class emancipation.

A shattering episode of the period that separated the publication of *L'Assommoir* from that of *Journey* was the First World War and its consequences – 1.4 million dead (10 per cent of the active population of France), and the destruction of much of the country's economy. It was, in fact, this aftermath that catalyzed a further radicalization of the French left. Initially the SFIO and the CGT had not opposed the war, and had participated in the Union Sacrée against the Germans; nationalist feelings overcame class antagonisms. There were some, but not many, protests. However, the effects of the war were so disastrous for many individuals and for the country's economy that the few isolated groups that had earlier opposed it gathered support from the far left. Another highly relevant event of the period that concerns us was, of course, the October Revolution, followed in March 1919 by the Soviet CP's call for the unity of all proletariats and its invitation to all revolutionary organizations to form an International Party. At the Tours Congress of the SFIO in December 1920, a splinter group responded to the exhortation, and became the Section Française de l'Internationale Communiste – in other words, the French Communist Party. At that time, only four of the thirty members of the SFIC's Directing Committee were workers. The Party, already as large as 130,000 members, was anxious for middle-class and intellectual support; soon, however, there was a change of direction. Membership dropped drastically to 55,000 in 1923 and intellectuals were made far less welcome; in 1924, nine-tenths of the Directing Committee were workers. Up until the 1930s and Thorez's "politics of the outstretched hand," the Party underwent what has been called a "bolshevization." Cells were implanted in factories, rigid guidelines were established, and so forth. At any rate, despite its difficult beginnings, an organized revolutionary left was firmly in place, and reformist tendencies were now quite separate from radical ones.

Simultaneously, the extreme right consolidated itself, following what Zeev Sternhell calls its "incubation period" of the 1880s when cultural trends such as the resurgence of irrational values and the cult of instincts were brought to bear on an anti-marxist type of "socialism" characterized by strong nationalist principles that advocated the replacement of the liberal fragmentation of society by the fundamental unity of the country.[4] This ideology had found its early expression in Boulangism (1885–9), the first French political movement to endorse anti-semitism. What subsequently became a major component of fascism was supposedly designed as a strategy to overcome internal oppositions and mobilize energies:

Everywhere in the anti-Semitic literature of the period one finds the same theme: the necessity of uniting all social classes, all good Frenchmen, who, said Drumont, "would be ready to embrace one another if the Jews, paid by Germany, were not always there to promote discord."[5]

Such positions were, of course, heightened during the Dreyfus affair (1897–9), a period that witnessed the growth of the Catholic and royalist Action Française. By the end of the century, there were many such groups (Ligue des Patriotes, Ligue Antisémitique, Mouvement Jaune). In 1911 the Cercle Proudhon, for whose members democracy was the greatest evil, was created: "To conserve and increase the moral, intellectual and material capital of civilization, it is absolutely necessary to destroy institutions."[6] The 1920s saw a rebirth of support for the Action Française, and the formation of new groups, Georges Valois' Le Faisceau, for example. Many of these groups, such as the Croix de Feu, grew out of First World War veterans' organizations. All advocated fervent nationalism (as their names often suggest: Jeunesses Patriotes, Solidarité Française), anti-semitism, military dress, and espoused fascist doctrine, including its populist element. In *Notre Avant-Guerre*, Robert Brasillach calls the upheaval of 6 February 1934 that led 30,000 members of the radical right to demonstrate at the Palais Bourbon "an instinctive and magnificient revolt" that signaled "the hope of a national revolution."[7] There is a revolutionary aspect to a fascist ideology, Sternhell points out, that seeks to replace an old order with radically new political and social structures. However, while fascism offered an alternative to bourgeois society and parliamentary democracy, and, as Jameson remarks, while its initial impulse accommodated populism as well as anti-capitalism, its fundamental enemy was marxism.[8]

Céline, in "Homage to Zola," condemns and explains the existence of these "massive rushes of entire countries towards extreme, aggressive and ecstatic nationalisms" not as the outcome of social factors, but in psychological terms. He attributes their growth to a certain masochism in his contemporaries, or even a suicidal tendency, a "loving impatience, almost irresistible, for death."[9] He felt that the spirit of the times was one of extreme pessimism, imbued with a "desire for nothingness, profoundly rooted in man and especially in the masses." Dictators, whether communist or fascist, want one thing – soldiers – and they know that a display of stupidity and brutality can work wonders to raise a large crowd to a frenetic level of enthusiasm. Zola's times were inhabited by a faith in science, a social optimism; not so in the 1930s:

One can obtain everything from an animal with gentleness and reason, whereas the great enthusiasms of the masses, the lasting frenzies of crowds are almost always stimulated, provoked, maintained by stupidity and brutality. Zola did not have to consider the same social problems in his work, especially not presented in such despotic terms. The faith in science, then quite new, encouraged writers of his time to believe in a certain social faith, in a reason to be optimistic . . . .

Since Zola, the nightmare that surrounded man has not only become more precise, it has become official. As our Gods become more powerful, they also become more fierce, more jealous, more stupid. They are organizing themselves. What can you say to them? There is no more understanding.[10]

"NOT A WORK OF ART, NOT LITERATURE"

Céline often claimed that he was from the working class, but one could argue that he belonged, rather, to a very modest petite bourgeoisie – his father was an insurance clerk and his mother ran a small shop. Unlike Zola, he did not merely pass through but always lived in working-class areas of Paris – first, in the Passage Choiseul, then in proletarian suburbs where he practiced medicine. His education did not benefit from any bourgeois privilege. He left the official system at an early age due to financial difficulties, and made a determined effort to pursue independent study for the baccalauréat. This autodidactic experience, by circumventing what was a guarantee of class division – the access to secondary education – enabled Céline to acquire the legitimate language which otherwise would have been unavailable to him: "There lies the serious hurdle, the official hurdle, set up by the state, which protects against invasions. One can become bourgeois, it is true, but first one must pass the baccalauréat."[11] Céline sought to overcome this barrier by individual means. His acquisition of legitimate language thus evaded an institutionalized and authoritarian framework as well the highly classical and literary indoctrination of the lycée, where great emphasis was placed on the appreciation of canonical texts and on the learning of Latin and Greek. Céline's position *vis à vis* the ruling class, then, was ambivalent: he never entered the official system that guaranteed its perpetuation, yet he sought to acquire a status that only it could guarantee. Similarly, even though Céline often stressed that he belonged to the working class, he was also fond of mentioning that his grandfather held a university diploma. At the conclusion of his medical studies, Céline had acquired sufficient competence and authority to produce an official written discourse: his doctoral thesis. This reveals that his rejection of legitimate language as it appears in *Journey* was not the result of ignorance but follows very conscious efforts to master that language. The process that formed Céline's linguistic horizon, then, was the reverse of Zola's. Because of his social origins, popular language was available to him through informal familiarization; it was his own chosen social trajectory, according to which he studied independently for the baccalauréat and his doctorate, that enabled him to acquire his legitimate French.

Popular language in the nineteenth century attracted a great deal of attention as it became the mode of expression of a new urban working class. By Céline's time, it seemed to have lost its novelty in the eyes of the bourgeoisie, and was a topic of less widespread scrutiny than before. One essential book on the subject, for the early twentieth century, was "Popular Language" (*Le Langage populaire*), by Henri Bauche, which was first published in 1880 but gained popularity with its many revised editions in the early twentieth century, and which was "crowned by the Académie Française" – a testimony to its perceived scholarly value and to the seriousness of its author.[12] The work is described as a "Grammar, syntax, and dictionary of the French spoken by the Parisian working class, with all the customary argot terms." While earlier studies focused on lexical particularities, here the rules of grammar and syntax are described as though they were those of a foreign language. However, from the introduction to his work, it appears that Bauche does not consider popular language with the same alarm or with the delight and surprise that characterized earlier reactions. On the contrary, its existence is generalized, and presented as a universal linguistic fact: "To summarize, in every country the lower class speaks a language that differs not only from the written literary language, but more or less from the one that is usually spoken by the upper classes, among high-society people."[13] Bauche defines popular language as the one currently and "naturally" spoken among the people. While admitting that there are only vague boundaries between popular and familiar language (of everyday informal conversation) or common language (spoken not by the working class but by members of the petite bourgeoisie who lack education), he stresses the undeniable distance that still separates popular language from the "literary, classical, correct, official French." However, languages change, and Bauche foresees a situation wherein popular language might slowly penetrate that of the upper classes:

Hence, far from rejecting, a priori, popular language in its entirety, one should, on the contrary, draw from it all that can enrich, render more precise, develop and reinforce our language. The struggle against the flood must be limited to a resistance against real dangers, such as the destruction of the splendid and always useful monuments of our past.[14]

In the nineteenth century, "contamination" was a recurrent image used to describe the possible effect of popular language. In *Popular Language*, however, Bauche suggests the possibility of an enriching, rather than destructive, infiltration. Popular language, he explains, could act as a "fertilizer" that would help an even stronger and more beautiful language to develop. The duty of writers is not to build an impermeable barrier around legitimate French, for this would surely be overcome, but to control the flow and absorption of the popular. Towards the end of the introduction, popular language is discussed in an increasingly positive light, and Bauche makes a surprising claim: "The true French language, is, in its essence, that which the people speak."[15] Naturally, such a statement did not go unnoticed. In the preface to a later edition (1927), Bauche tells us that he has been called a Bolshevik; he is now intent on reassuring the reader that "I am not, contrary to some accusations, a foolish adorer of the working class and of its language. I do not feel any particular fondness for today's Parisian popular language."[16] Drawing on history to consolidate and legitimize his earlier argument, he points out that when Latin had become a dead language, the living, vulgar idiom of the day took over and acquired a literary existence of its own. Because languages inevitably change, to admit that popular language will eventually affect the legitimate one is not tantamount to granting it undue worth. Finally, Bauche stresses that the real enemies of French, the real linguistic problems that must be erased, are the patois:

> What is of prime importance is that France be a country where one speaks French, the French of the upper or lower classes, but French, that of the capital and the Ile de France, rather than foreign languages or local dialects. Linguistic regionalism is deadly for a nation.[17]

It is likely that this preface was shaped by the impact of the First World War on linguistic attitudes. Bauche's statement that the most important thing is that France be a country where all speak French no doubt contains a reference to the recent recovery of the

Alsace-Lorraine. One of the most lamented effects of its earlier loss was that German would be taught in schools; many a tear-jerking story tells of little French children suddenly made to learn that barbaric language. Another relevant point is that, during the war, people of different social backgrounds fought together in aggressive, all-male environments, that did not encourage an adherence to legitimate French, but, rather, promoted the colloquial. In what no doubt partook in a romantic celebration of the great communal spirit uniting of the soldiers of La Grande Guerre, much attention was paid to the language, *le poilu*, that developed in the trenches, drawing both on popular French and military slang. *Le poilu* was recorded in a number of war chronicles, published either in the press or in book form (for one of which, *Le Feu*, by Henri Barbusse, Céline expressed much admiration). It also gave rise to a number of linguistic studies.[18] Furthermore, at this point in time, the working class was a well-defined social entity, rather than in the process of becoming one, as was the case earlier. Class boundaries were now well defined, and conflicts were played out in a primarily political, rather than cultural, arena. The possibility of linguistic integration whereby popular language could positively enrich legitimate French would have been inconceivable when the establishment of social barriers relied on linguistic difference.

Journey to the End of the Night was not Céline's first work of literary intention. "Church" (*Eglise*), a play written in 1926, was submitted to the Nouvelle Revue Française, but rejected. It was eventually published in 1933, after the success of *Journey*. There are ways in which the novel can be related to this early work: the central character of *Journey*, Bardamu, is already present and scenes that take place in Africa and New York are sketched out. However, "Church" is not stylistically innovative. The structure of the sentence remains untouched; there is no great variety among the popular markers (the contraction of *ils* (they) into *y* and the omission of *ne*), which, unavoidably, occur in the characters' utterances. French negations usually contain two elements: "ne. . . pas," "ne. . . jamais," etc., with the verb occurring between the two. The omission of the first element "ne" is a common occurrence in popular language.

The following year, Céline wrote another play, "Progress" (*Progrès*), composed of satirical scenes that take place first in a petit bourgeois salon and then in a brothel. There are more popular markers than in his previous work, principally omissions of *ne* and *rappels*, such as "De mon temps y avaient que les artistes qui avaient des dettes – mais comme ils les payaient jamais eux, ça les rendaient

Céline's Voyage au bout de la nuit 109

pas tristes." (In my day only artists had debts – but because they never paid them, it never made them sad.)[19] Comic effects are produced when familiar expressions, such as *cocue* (cuckold) occur in the same sentence as the elevated and untranslatable *passé simple*, *fut*: "Maman sait qu'elle a été cocue, ça me rendait assez triste chaque fois, mais ce fut encore plus triste d'être veuve." (Mother knows that she has been made a cuckold, it saddened me enough each time, but it was sadder still to be a widow.)[20] Such effects will recur in later works, and so will a character type, the muscular American dancer who visits the brothel (as a curious observer) and attracts more of the clients' attention than the prostitutes themselves when she shows off her legs: "là . . . celui-là . . . le quadriceps . . . le voyez-vous . . . et l'équilibre . . . là . . . et puis ceci encore . . . rien de facilement obtenu . . . travail . . . fermeté . . . touchez . . . sentez-vous?" (here . . . this one . . . the quadriceps . . . do you see it . . . and that equilibrium . . . there . . . and then this one again . . . nothing easily achieved . . . work . . . firmness . . . touch it . . . do you feel it?)[21] The disjunction of syntactical fragments caused by the ellipses translating the rhythm of the sentence – the woman, as she speaks, is performing dance movements to music – will also be a major stylistic device in Céline's novels.

Though one is retroactively able to trace a few lines of continuity between earlier literary attempts and the novel, to the public, *Journey* seemed to have emerged from nowhere. Céline first sent the manuscript anonymously to Gallimard who rejected it. Some time later, in 1932, Denoël published the work, creating an instant curiosity about the elusive, astonishing and unheard-of Docteur Destouches who practiced medicine in a working-class suburb. Prior to its completion, there are very few statements in which Céline mentions his forthcoming work. One of the available documents (the manuscripts of *Journey* are unavailable) is a letter written to his friend Joseph Garcin:

> It is not a work of art [*oeuvre*] – no pretensions at all and no literature, my God no. But I have inside of me a thousand pages of nightmares in reserve, that of the war naturally leads the way. Those weeks of 1914, under viscous rain, in that atrocious mud and that blood and that shit and that human bullshit too, I will never recover, it is a truth that I offer you once again, that only a few of us share. All is there. The drama, our calamity, is that ease with which men forget.[22]

Céline immediately places *Journey* outside of a traditional literary field where *oeuvres* are erected and pretensions prevail. His statement becomes particularly significant when considered in the light of Barthes' remark about *oeuvres*, a notion that, for him, points to the mercantile aspect of literary production, to the object that circulates on the market.[23] It also implies the work's acquisition of a specific status which necessitates a submission to certain rules and renders the text void of any "seductive energy." An *oeuvre* is a unitary product governed by a reductive framework that hinders the "perpetual production" and "unconditional dispersion" of writing. Céline's claim, then, can be seen as a rejection of both the institutionalized, stilted and classifiable literary product, and of the type of writing that this system demands – in this respect the statement can be taken as an indirect reference to his choice of unconventional style. Nothing is said about the presence of popular language; one can only note the phrase "in that atrocious mud and that blood and that shit and human bullshit too" as an indication of what it is to be. Céline's motives for writing the novel, this passage suggests, are cathartic – a deliverance from haunting nightmares. But it also indicates that *Journey* is to serve a less personal function: it will fix in the collective memory horrors that are not to be forgotten. Not only will the product of such an intention escape the category of *oeuvre*, it will not enter that of literature either, Céline claims, already showing signs of what will become a perpetual bad faith. "Not literature" must also be taken as an expression of the great disdain and disinterest Céline later expressed for his predecessors: "Read? In the old days, perhaps, but it has been a long time since I have had the leisure to read. Remember that I did not attend the lycée: only elementary school. So, no classical influences."[24]

No classical influences, he claims, and no modern ones either. Céline spoke in extremely disparaging and mocking terms of contemporary novels. Only two seem to escape his scorn: "Fire" (*Le Feu*), written by Henri Barbusse, and Eugène Dabit's *Hôtel du Nord*. The subject of "Fire" is the First World War as it was experienced by Barbusse himself. To this extent it has a common thematic element with *Journey*. It also displays a certain number of popular markers, but they remain contained within the directly reported speech of characters; there is always a clear difference between the characters' utterances and the narrative. *Hôtel du Nord* is a first-person narrative that recounts events in the daily lives of a family socially situated between the proletariat and the petite bourgeoisie. Although the vocabulary always remains unsophisticated and the syntax simple, popular markers are only occasional, of a lexical nature, and scarce enough to avoid any significant contrast with the narrative. These works, even though they were quite successful at the time of their publication, were far from achieving the renown of *Journey*. Their style can only be tenuously related to that of Céline's novel, and one cannot in any significant way trace a direct line of influence. Rather, the situation that Céline created for himself, both with his statements and his novels, was one of isolation and difference.

In "Homage to Zola," which appears to be one of his less provocative and more serious reflections on this matter, he argues that naturalism could serve no contemporary purpose, and claims that contemporary literature needs now to rely on symbols and dreams: "for, finally, it is in symbols and dreams that we spend nine-tenths of our existence, since nine-tenths of our existence, that is, of real pleasure, are unknown to us or forbidden."[25] He emphasizes the particularly repressive nature of twentieth-century society, and puts forth an unusual explanation for the passage from naturalism to modernism, claiming that a realistic representation of reality would be repressed by the régime in power:

> Here we have reached twenty centuries of high civilization, but, nevertheless, no political régime would survive two months of truth. I mean marxist societies as well as our bourgeois and fascist societies . . . In such conditions, naturalism, whether one wants it or not, becomes political. It gets shot down.[26]

Although Céline hardly ever mentions it, we should note the existence of a crucial literary movement which was also brought into being by the aftermath of 1918: surrealism. For the surrealists, the traditional modes of representing reality were obsolete, as was a vision of the world founded on Cartesian principles and categories. Reason, logic, causality – all these notions were now to be ignored, and great emphasis was placed on the manifestation of the unconscious. Not only did art no longer serve the cause of representation, but an emancipatory effect was assigned to unstable meaning and destructured form. For the first time, formal innovations were expected to translate into political effects, and serve the cause of revolution, as André Breton stated (more or less clearly, and with, at times, some hesitation) in the manifestos.

For Céline, the Exposition Universelle of 1900 announced a change of times: "modern life began." In the spectacular celebration of technological advances he saw a vision of doom: the triumph of machines and their dehumanizing brutality, the menace of catastrophes to come. He paints no brighter a picture of the 1930s: an entire generation, traumatized by sufferings endured in a war from which it felt dissociated and which it did not comprehend, found relief in an all-pervading masochism, a death wish, and a taste for totalitarian

112 Political Stylistics

oppression. Céline was never given to analytical detachment, but the years he describes were indeed grim. The country was struck by an economic depression, ruled by unstable governments oscillating between conservative and liberal/socialist, and threatened by an extreme right that was encouraged by Hitler's rise to power. Amid such tensions and with the threat of another war in the not so distant future, popular language, no longer a novelty, lost its threatening aspect. One can assume that its presence in the novel would not be taken to be as disturbing as before. Céline took a significant stylistic risk all the same, since his status and authority in the literary field were not by any means established. Furthermore, unlike what was the case for poetry, there had been few formal innovations in novels. Populist writers like Barbusse and Dabit, Catholic ones like Péguy and Mauriac or representatives of the haute bourgeoisie such as Proust and Gide did not shatter any stylistic norms. Céline's statements prior to and following *Journey* show that he did not seek to secure his position as a "man of letters" in any conventional sense. There was no niche in which he wished to settle. He wrote from a position of cultural singularity, a position founded on an ambivalent status *vis à vis* both the bourgeoisie and the working class. His origins were popular, but his medical studies economically and socially distanced him from the class into which he was born. In doing so, however, he circumvented the usual indoctrination of the ruling ideology and language, and acquired legitimate French by individual means, without the traditional literary and classical influences. Céline's situation in both the literary and social field was eccentric, and his purpose, at least as he wished to present it, was oppositional: "not a work of art, not literature."

THE POETIC AND THE POPULAR

In the preface to *L'Assommoir*, Zola adopted a critical distance from his work as, in an academic style, he responded to the attacks it had encountered when published in the press. The short text that precedes *Journey* is very different in its form and function:

> Voyager, c'est bien utile, ça fait travailler l'imagination. Tout le reste n'est que déceptions et fatigues. Notre voyage à nous est entièrement imaginaire. Voilà sa force.
>
> Il va de la vie à la mort. Hommes, bêtes, villes et choses, tout est imaginé. C'est un roman, rien qu'une histoire fictive. Littré le dit, qui ne se trompe jamais.

Et puis d'abord tout le monde peut en faire autant. Il suffit de fermer les yeux. C'est de l'autre côté de la vie.[27]

(To travel, it's very useful, it puts the imagination to work. All the rest is nothing but disappointment and fatigue. Our own journey is entirely imaginary. Therein lies its strength.

It goes from life to death. People, beasts, towns and things, all is imagined. It's a novel, nothing but a fictitious story. Littré said so, who is never mistaken.

And anyway everyone can do the same. All you have to do is close your eyes. It's on the other side of life.)

Popular markers are present in the very first sentences: the *rappel*, whereby *voyage* is twice referred to by pronouns, and the adverb *bien*, which carries colloquial overtones. There are others throughout the passage. For example: *C'est un roman, rien qu'une histoire fictive. Littré le dit, qui ne se trompe jamais*. The use of *rien que*, when not part of a negative construction (*cela n'est rien que*) is popular, and so is the structure of the second sentence, where the *qui* does not immediately follow its antecedent (the correct form would be: *Littré, qui ne se trompe jamais, le dit*). What is also unexpected and paradoxical here is the fact that in these lines the authority of a highly normative work, Littré's dictionary, is upheld. Stylistically and in terms of content, the next two sentences, starting with the colloquial *et puis d'abord*, are in the same prosaic and concrete vein. A highly abstract comment, however, follows: *C'est de l'autre côté de la vie*. There is, clearly, a mix of registers in this short text, ranging from a simple remark on the definition of the word "novel" in a dictionary and the matter-of-fact claim that "everyone can do the same" to the cryptic conclusion "it's on the other side of life"; what "the same" refers to (the novel, the subject of the novel, the writing of the novel?) is unclear, and the meaning of "the other side of life" is, of course, vague. This preface – if it can be called that, prologue might be more accurate – clearly serves to reject realism and to present the novel as a product of the imagination, yet it does so in a manner that includes the mundane.

The opening paragraph of *Journey* confirms the predominance of the popular and the mundane:

Ça a débuté comme ça. Moi, j'avais jamais rien dit. Rien. C'est Arthur Ganate qui m'a fait parler. Arthur, un étudiant, un carabin lui aussi, un camarade. On se rencontre donc place Clichy. C'était après le déjeuner. Il veut me parler. Je l'écoute. "Restons pas dehors! qu'il me dit. Rentrons!' Je rentre avec lui. Voilà. "Cette terrasse, qu'il commence, c'est pour les oeufs à la coque! Viens par ici!" Alors, on remarque encore qu'il n'y avait personne dans les rues, à cause de la chaleur; pas de voitures, rien. Quand il fait très froid, non plus, il n'y a personne dans les rues; c'est lui, même que je m'en souviens, qui m'avait dit à ce propos: "Les gens de Paris ont l'air toujours d'être occupés, mais, en fait, ils se promènent du matin au soir; la preuve, c'est que lorsque il ne fait pas bon à se promener, trop froid ou trop chaud, on ne les voit plus; ils sont tous dedans à prendre des cafés crème et des bocks. C'est ainsi! Siècle de vitesse, qu'ils disent! Où ça? Grands changements! qu'ils racontent. Comment ça? Rien n'est changé en vérité. Ils continuent à s'admirer et c'est tout. Et ça n'est pas nouveau non plus. Des mots, et encore pas beaucoup, même parmi les mots, qui sont changés! Deux ou trois par-ci, par-là, des petits . . ." Bien fiers alors d'avoir fait sonner ces vérités utiles, on est demeuré là assis, ravis, à regarder les dames du café. (p. 7)

(It began like that. Me, I hadn't said a thing. Nothing. It was Arthur Ganate who made me talk. Arthur, a student, a medical student, like me, a pal. So we meet place Clichy. It was after lunch. He wants to talk to me. I listen: "Let's not stay outside," [that] he says to me. "Let's go inside!" I go inside with him. Just like that. "That terrace," [that] he begins, "is for hard-boiled eggs! Come this way!" Then, we notice that there's no one in the streets, because of the heat; no cars, nothing. When it's very cold, none either, the streets are empty; it's him, I even remember, who said about this: "People from Paris always seem very busy, but, in fact, they just walk around from morning 'til night: proof is, when the weather is not good, too cold or too hot, they are nowhere to be seen; they're all inside, drinking white coffee and beer. That's how it is! Age of speed, [is what] they say! Where's that? Great changes! [that] they tell you. How's that? The truth is that nothing has changed. They go on admiring themselves, and that's it. And that's not new either. Some words, and even then not many among words, that have changed! Two or three, here, there, little ones . . ." Nicely proud to have uncovered those useful truths, we stayed there, delighted, watching the ladies of the café.)

A striking and immediately perceptible stylistic feature is the high density of popular markers in the initial lines. In fact, the very first word of the novel, *ça*, already present in the first sentence of the prologue and appearing several times in the passage (*où ça, comment ça, ça n'est pas*), is popular. Contractions and repetitions, standard features of spoken language, occur throughout the passage. In the opening sentences, the indefinite pronoun *rien* and the name Arthur are repeated at close range; elsewhere, the verb *rentrer* appears twice, the (untranslatable) form *qu'ils* four times, and finally the noun *mots* is present twice within the first sentence. These forms are equally distributed between the narrator's relation of events and reported speech; likewise, the omission of *ne* in a negative construction appears both in the narrator's voice (*j'avais jamais rien dit*) and Arthur's utterance (*Restons pas*). In Arthur's reported speech, several negative forms are complete, indicating that there is absolutely no tendency for a reported *parole* to lean any closer to popular language than the narrator's voice. A simple and straightforward stylistic device, the use of the pronoun *on*, in this case, is characteristic of spoken language in general, not specific to that of a particular social group. Of a more colloquial nature is the construction *Moi, j'avais* (Me, I hadn't) a form of *rappel*, where the apposed indirect pronoun *moi* marks an insistence and emphasis on the theme of the sentence – here the first-person subject. It is a typical feature of colloquial, familiar speech, and of the speech of children. More popular is the misuse of *que* in *même que*, and the manner of reporting discourse whereby, instead of having the reported phrase preceded by a verb and *que* (*il dit que*) or followed by a subject–verb inversion (*dit-il*), the name or pronoun referring to the speaker is preceded by *que* (that) and follows the reported utterance: *Restons pas dehors, qu'il me dit; cette terrasse, qu'il commence; Grands changements! qu'ils racontent* (Let's not stay outside, [that] he says to me; That terrace, [that] he begins; great changes, [that] they tell you). Incomplete sentences, in their simplest form, are the single words *rien* and *voilà*, whose function is solely emphatic; verbs are omitted from longer phrases such as *Arthur, un étudiant, un carabin lui aussi, un camarade* (Arthur, a student, a medical student like me, a pal), which is broken up by commas into the theme, *Arthur*, on which the rheme, the group of nouns that follows, provides information. Similarly, *Deux ou trois, par-ci, par-là, des petits* ("Two or three, here, there, little ones"), refers to *mots* (words) but does not include the theme which is present only in the previous sentence. This feature is typical of Céline's writing: syntactical links are broken, and syntagms, translating the linear and additive flow of spoken discourse, are joined by juxtaposition rather than subordination. On a lexical level, the only unexpected element is the word *carabin*, slang for medical student. The vocabulary of this passage is certainly not elevated; there is, in fact, only a small amount of argot in *Journey*. A study conducted on this topic reveals that most of the unexpected lexical forms in this novel are what standard dictionaries would label *familier* or *populaire*: only twelve expressions do not appear in *Le Petit Robert* (1968 edition).[28] This is due to the fact that, as we will see in some detail in the next chapter, argot continues to lose its specificity during the twentieth century and becomes increasingly integrated in less marginal French; furthermore, Céline relied far more on syntax than on vocabulary to represent popular language.

Another major difference from *L'Assommoir* is the presence in *Journey* of a first-person narrator, Bardamu. It is through his eyes that the novel is focused. For the purpose of this textual analysis a distinction will have to be established between the narrator/Bardamu's (narrative) voice; the narrator/Bardamu's utterances, and other characters' utterances, reported in a variety of ways. From what we gather from the first sentence, it is his own story that Bardamu will tell. *Ca a débuté comme ça* (It began like that): there is something elliptical in the manner in which he refers to the forthcoming tale of his adventures in the army during the war, to the time he spent in Africa and New York, and, finally, to his medical practice in the suburbs of Paris. It is as though the narrator assumes that the reader already has some idea of what the text is going to be about – maybe suggested by the title. At any rate, an intimacy is established, and, in the sentence that follows, *Moi, j'avais jamais rien dit* (Me, I hadn't said a thing), a certain defensiveness. Speed and haste, and a sense of urgency are conveyed by the quick succession of short sentences that open the novel. It is as though Bardamu cannot wait to tell his story, about the content of which, however, he gives no preliminary information. He begins in a fairly roundabout manner, with an unusual mix of statements, ranging from trivial remarks, *ils sont tous dedans à prendre des cafés crème et des bocks* (they're all inside, drinking white coffee and beers), to sweeping generalizations, *Rien n'est changé en vérité* (The truth is nothing has changed), to curious linguistic observations, *Des mots et encore pas beaucoup, même parmi les mots, qui sont changés* (Some words, and even then not many among words, that have changed). Bardamu, we are told, is a medical student. The probable (but not certain, as Céline's own case demonstrates) bourgeois origin that this suggests is contradicted by the language he uses. Still, and again unlike *L'Assommoir*, the working class is not a theme of this novel, or even referred to in any direct way.

The following passage, taken from near the end of the novel, will serve to illustrate two features: a constancy in the nature of

Céline's Voyage au bout de la nuit   117

popular markers, and the introduction of a new stylistic device, the ellipsis:

> – "Va pas croire Léon, qu'elle m'a dit alors, que je tiens à toi, à cause des affaires du caveau! . . . L'argent tu sais moi ça m'est bien égal au fond . . . Ce que je voudrais Léon c'est rester avec toi . . . C'est être heureuse . . . Voilà tout. . . C'est bien naturel . . . Je veux pas que tu me quittes . . . C'est trop de se quitter quand on s'est aimé comme on s'aimait tous les deux . . . Jure-moi au moins Léon que tu ne t'en iras pas pour longtemps? . . .
>
> Et ainsi de suite que ça a duré sa crise pendant des semaines. On peut dire qu'elle était amoureuse et bien emmerdante . . . Elle y revenait chaque soir à sa folie d'amour. En fin de compte, elle à tout de même bien voulu qu'on laisse le caveau à sa mère en garde, à condition qu'on partirait tous les deux chercher ensemble du travail à Paris . . . Toujours ensemble! . . . Tu parles d'un numéro! Elle voulait bien comprendre n'importe quoi sauf que moi je m'en aille seul de mon côté et elle du sien . . . Pour ça rien à faire . . . Alors plus elle avait l'air d'y tenir et plus elle me rendait malade moi, forcément! (pp. 455-6)

> (– "Don't go thinking Léon, is what she said to me, that I want to keep you because of the crypt business! . . . Money you know me it really leaves me cold in fact . . . What I would want Léon is to stay with you . . . Is to be happy . . . that's all . . . it's only natural . . . I don't want you to leave me . . . it's too much to leave each other when we've loved each other like we loved each other us two . . . Swear to me at least Léon that you won't go for long? . . .
>
> And on and on [that] it went, her craziness, for weeks. You could certainly say that she was in love and a real pain in the ass . . . She started it up again each evening, her love madness. Finally, she agreed that she would leave her mother in charge of the crypt, on the condition that both of us go to find work in Paris together . . . Always together! . . . Talk about a scene! She was willing to understand anything except that I go my way and she go hers . . . Nothing doing, as far as that went . . . So, the more she seemed stuck on that, the more sick she was making me, naturally.)

All the standard popular markers are present here: the contraction of *cela* into *ça*, several repetitions (*c'est, quitter, aime, amour, ensemble*). *Ne* is omitted on two occasions, and *on* is used consistently. The verb *partir* is in the conditional mode, although *à condition que* calls for the subjunctive (*parte*). As in the previous passage, there are a number of syntactical markers. Of the same type as those discussed earlier is the expression *qu'elle m'a dit* and *ainsi de suite que ça a duré sa crise*. In "*L'argent tu sais moi ça m'est bien égal au fond*" (Money you know me it really leaves me cold in fact) there is a double *rappel*, of the subject (*argent*) and indirect object (*moi*). It is interesting to look at the production of the sentence, which is made up of many grammatically and semantically superfluous elements that indicate a lack of confidence on the part of a speaking subject who relies, for affirmation, on linguistic repetition and emphasis. The semantic nucleus, *l'argent m'est égal* (money leaves me cold), is twice reinforced by the adverbs *au fond* (in fact) and *bien* (really). *Tu sais* (you know), a phatic element, then separates the theme, *l'argent* (money), from the rheme, *ça m'est égal au fond* (it leaves me cold in fact). The theme, usually the first constituent, is the "topic" of the sentence; the rheme is the "comment" on the theme and carries additional information. Finally, *rappels* are constructed: the reflexive pronoun *me* is repeated by the preposed *moi*, and *argent* is repeated at the beginning of the rheme by *cela* contracted into *ça*.

Punctuation is a code inherent to written language, primarily used to indicate grammatical relationships, and, as a secondary function, the rhythm of the voice: a short break at commas, complete stops at periods, rising intonations at exclamation marks. Céline does not apply it in the conventional manner, to clarify the syntax; only the secondary function is present here. Commas are very scarce, non-existent in *L'argent tu sais moi ça m'est bien égal au fond* and *Et ainsi de suite que ça a duré sa crise pendant des semaines* (And on and on [that] it went her craziness for weeks). In these sentences the lack of punctuation does not render the syntax ambiguous, as, we will see, it does elsewhere, but, rather, indicates a rapid rhythm of speech. There are, as usual, many exclamation marks to convey intonation, and a new device, the ellipsis. Rather than the artificial and definite break suggested by a period, they indicate the modulation of a voice that slows down, lowers itself and then picks up again, in a delivery that, affected by feelings of frustration and irritation, oscillates between speed and hesitation, whether in the woman's utterance or here, in the long monologue of Bardamu's friend, Léon. The ellipsis, in this passage, occurs either between complete sentences, or to isolate syntagms that contain little information and are used in oral discourse for emphasis and to stimulate the listener's attention – *voilà tout, c'est bien naturel, tu parles d'un numéro* (that's all, it's only natural, talk about a scene). Elsewhere, they affect the syntax in a harsher manner:

> En remuant les souvenirs on se demandait ce qui pouvait bien exister encore de tout ça . . . Qu'on avait connu ensemble . . . On se demandait ce qu'elle avait pu devenir Molly, notre gentille Molly . . . Lola, elle, je voulais bien l'oublier, mais après tout j'aurais bien aimé avoir des nouvelles de toutes quand même, de la petite Musyne aussi tant qu'à faire . . . Qui ne devait pas demeurer bien loin dans Paris à présent. (p. 330)

> (In mulling over memories one wondered what could still remain of all that . . . That which we lived through together . . . One wondered what she might have become Molly, our sweet Molly . . . Lola, her, I was quite willing to forget her, but after all I'd have liked to have news of them all even so, of the little Musyne also why not . . . Who must have been living not too far away in Paris as the moment.)

The voice here is the narrator's. A striking feature of this passage is the manner in which, on two occasions, ellipses disrupt what would be the internal syntax of a sentence, disconnecting subordinate clauses that cannot ordinarily stand alone from their antecedent: *Qu'on avait connu ensemble* (That which we lived through together), and *Qui ne devait pas demeurer bien loin dans Paris à présent* (Who must have been living not too far away in Paris at the moment). In the earlier passage, the ellipsis replaced commas or periods, isolating fragments that could stand as autonomous units, and did not actually subvert the syntax. Here, they occur when no punctuation is necessary, cutting off a constituent from the main clause and upsetting the unity of the sentence. Conventionally, ellipses are used to suggest unspoken implications. In *Journey*, they function in two ways: they confer certain oral characteristics on a written text by suggesting intonations and a fluid yet disorderly output, and/or they violate grammatical rules and disrupt syntax. In Céline's subsequent novels, there are no longer sentences but a succession of syntagms, with the ellipses replacing all other punctuation and conjunctions.

From the first line of *Journey* onwards, the reader is immersed in a language that displays a high density of popular markers. They are continuously present throughout the novel, with an added element towards the end, the ellipsis. However, the style never becomes monotonous, for it repeatedly produces a number of different effects, which I defined earlier in Riffaterrian terms (see p. 39): a deviation from and contrast with a model implied by the surrounding text itself, the internal context. For example, in the first chapter of the novel one comes across the sentences *Enfin nous nous réconciliâmes avec Arthur pour finir, tout à fait. On était du même avis sur presque tout* (Finally we reconciled with Arthur, at the end, completely. We agreed on almost everything – p. 9). The *avec Arthur* (with Arthur) in *nous nous réconciliâmes avec Arthur* (we reconciled with Arthur) is redundant and actually implies that more than two people are involved here. The emphatic function and the position of the adverb *tout à fait* at the end of the sentence and the pronoun *on* that opens the next one also tend towards spoken or popular language. However, the verb *réconciliâmes* conjugated in the *passé simple* and, furthermore, in the first-person plural (a lesser used and more pedantic sounding form) belongs to a different register altogether. Such an element is perceived as incongruous in the context (which calls for *on s'est réconcilié*), stands out, and attracts the reader's attention. In *Writing Degree Zero*, Barthes remarks that one of the hallmarks of a conventional literary language, what one might call belletristic language, is, precisely, the *passé simple*: "Obsolete in spoken French, the preterite, which is the cornerstone of of narration, always signals the presence of Art: it is part of a ritual of letters."[29] This tense is only very rarely used in the first hundred pages of the novel, but appears with a high density soon afterwards, according to Gunter Holtus, who performed a detailed statistical study of these occurrences.[30] There is one other instance of its presence in the first chapter:

> Mais voilà-t-y pas que juste devant le café où nous étions attablés un régiment se met à passer, et avec le colonel par-devant sur son cheval, et même qu'il avait l'air bien gentil et richement gaillard, le colonel! Moi, je ne fis qu'un bon d'enthousiasme. (p. 10)

> (But would you believe that right in front of the café where we were sitting a regiment passed by, and with the colonel in front on his horse, and what's more he seemed rather nice and in fine form, the colonel! Me, I just gave a leap of enthusiasm.)

Even though the context in which *je ne fis* appears is, predominantly, one of popular markers, this less obtrusive and more usual form does not draw as much attention as does the verb *réconciliâmes*, in *passé simple* in the previous passage. Like the ellipsis that may or may not disrupt the syntax, elements of the belletristic style do not have a fixed function in *Journey*. Depending on the surrounding context and on how unusual the conjugation, they sometimes blend with the popular context in an unnoticeable manner, and sometimes blatantly stand out as parody of themselves. Other examples of "discreet" *passé simple* are:

> Ce que furent les dix jours de remontée de ce fleuve, je m'en souviendrai longtemps . . . (p. 162) (What those ten days of following the river upstream were like, I will remember for a long time.)

> Après ce temps là, les convois d'artillerie prirent toutes les routes dans un sens et les civils qui se sauvaient, dans l'autre. (p. 30) (After that time, the artillery convoys followed the road in one direction, and the civilians who were fleeing, in the other.)

Forms of the third-person plural such as *furent* and *prirent* are more common than those in the second-person plural, such as *demeurâmes* and *prîmes* in the following passage. The adjacent context, however, displays few popular markers, so there is no immediate dissonance, as there will be in other cases:

> Et nous demeurâmes tous là en observation pendant des semaines et des semaines, si bien que nous y prîmes des habitudes. (p. 185) (And we remained there in observation for weeks and weeks, so much so that we formed habits.)

The verbs do not display a parodic function, because, despite a certain affectation, they do not clash with surrounding forms. However, such is not the case for *Nous trinquâmes à sa santé sur le comptoir au milieu des clients noirs qui en bavaient d'envie* (We drank to his health at the counter among clients who were drooling with envy – p. 136). Here, not only is a verb that is rarely used in the *passé simple*, *trinquer*, conjugated in that tense, but the context contains lexical popular markers: *à sa santé, bavaient d'envie*. Clearly, the precious, pompous tone that the belletristic *passé simple* adds to an unceremonious context is mocked; the discrepant forms function as self-parody. Often an even more conspicuous and ceremonial feature of belletristic style, the past subjunctive, is incorporated against a backdrop of spoken markers:

> Il me fit sans que je l'en priasse, de Grappa, un portrait express au caca fumant.(p. 155) (He painted, without me having to beg him, of Grappa, a quick sketch steaming with shit.)

> Les douzes miliciens de Topo ressentaient, c'était visible, envers Alcide une véritable sympathie et cela malgré qu'il les engueulât sans limites et leur bottât le derrière assez injustement. (p. 151) (The twelve militiamen from Topo felt, it was visible, a real sympathy towards Alcide, and this even though he endlessly yelled at them and quite unfairly kicked their asses.)

In the first case, the subjunctive imperfect *priâsse*, an extremely rare form, stands out because the reader is unaccustomed to its presence in any kind of context, and this incongruity is strengthened by the vulgar expression *un portrait express au caca fumant* (a quick sketch steaming with shit). In the second example, the verbs themselves, *engueuler* and *botter le derrière*, belong to popular language and do not lend themselves to the subjunctive mode, thus creating an effect similar to the one encountered in the verb in *passé simple*, *trinquâmes*, in the previous passage. Furthermore, they are introduced by the conjunction *malgré que*, which is absolutely incorrect in legitimate language. Finally, the next two examples of pluperfect subjunctive show that this type of construction is a recurrent and significant feature of *Journey*:

> Si les gendarmes ainsi, m'avaient pincé en vadrouille je crois bien que mon compte eût été bon. (p. 19) (Had the gendarmes caught me out on the loose, I am quite certain that my number would have been up.)

> Ils attendaient que nous eussions fini, nous, de bouffer, pour venir s'attabler à leur tour. (p. 207) (They waited for us to finish eating, before taking their turn to come to the table.)

Eût été and *eussions fini* – such expressions do not harmonize with *bouffer, vadrouille, se faire pincer*. Similarly to the past participles and the imperfect subjunctive, pluperfect subjunctive is an element of "high" literary language, highlighted here against a clashing stylistic context. Such elevated forms match the external norm based on the reader's preconceptions of a traditional literary text but, in this case, their role within the text itself serves to undermine this norm. These are examples of hybrid constructions which Bakhtin, in *The Dialogic Imagination*, describes as follows:

> an utterance that belongs, by its grammatical (syntactic) and compositional markers, to a single speaker but that actually contains mixed within it two utterances, two speech manners, two styles, two "languages," two semantic and axiological belief systems.[31]

Céline's Voyage au bout de la nuit   123

Often, within a single paragraph of *Journey*, more than two stylistic unities interact and hybridize. The following extract provides further examples of the parodic function and introduces another, the poetic function:

> Le jour où on les aurait ainsi bousillés jusqu'aux essieux ces salauds-là, au moins nous foutraient-ils la paix, pensais-je, et même si ça ne serait rien que pendant une nuit toute entière, on pourrait dormir au moins une fois tout entier corps at âme.
>
> Ce ravitaillement, un cauchemar en surcroît, petit monstre tracassier sur le gros de la guerre. Brutes devant, à côté et derrière. Ils en avaient mis partout. Condamnés à mort différés on ne sortait plus de l'envie de roupiller énorme, et tout devenait souffrance en plus d'elle, le temps et l'effort de bouffer. Un bout de ruisseau, un pan de mur par là qu'on croyait avoir reconnus . . . On s'aidait des odeurs pour retrouver la ferme de l'escouade, redevenus chiens dans la nuit de guerre des villages abandonnés. Ce qui guide encore le mieux, c'est l'odeur de la merde. (p. 35)

(The day when we would have smashed them down to the spindles, those swines, at least they would leave us in peace, I was thinking, and even if it would be for only one whole night, we would be able to sleep at least for once, entirely, body and soul.

This provisioning, one more nightmare on top of the others, nagging little monster clinging to the back of the war. Brutes to the fore, at the sides, and at the back. They were everywhere. Condemned to a deferred death, we were besieged by an overwhelming desire to sleep, and all became suffering as well as that, the time and effort to eat. A strip of river, a patch of wall over there that we thought we recognized . . . Smells helped us find our way back to the squad's farms, as we became dogs again, in war's night among abandoned villages. What leads the way best, it's the smell of shit.)

As well as a number of standard popular markers (the contraction of *ça*, the pronoun *on*, the misuse of the conjunction *que* in *rien que*), there is a high number of vulgar expressions here: *bousiller, salaud, foutre* (all in the same sentence), *roupiller, bouffer,* and *merde*. Such popular markers are not unexpected. They appear with a high frequency in those pages concerning the war: in passages just prior to this, one finds *gueule, coltiner, roupiller* and *crever*. The first highly noticeable form here is the expression *foutraient-ils*, because of the contrast between a sophisticated subject–verb inversion in the conditional mode and the vulgar nature of the verb *foutre*. As in the cases of *passé simple* and subjunctive described above, it is the belletristic element of the opposition that draws the reader's attention, and it is this aspect that creates the surprise, whereas the popular element is necessary to the contrast but not unusual in the context. This construction is closely followed by a similar one, *pensais-je*, this time with a perfectly appropriate verb; its presence underscores the inversion but also highlights, by way of opposition, verbs of radically different registers. A breach in registers is also created by the presence of *corps et âme* at the end of the sentence. This elevated and stereotypical expression is separated from the verb to which it refers, *dormir*, by a heavy triad of commonplace locutions, *au moins une fois tout entier*, resulting, again, in a narrowly localized opposition. As I mentioned earlier, the function of the elevated forms is to parody and ridicule the style of *belles lettres*; it therefore works in the same direction as popular markers, to subvert a legitimate literary language. What enables this function is, first of all, the highly codified and instantly recognizable nature of belletristic style, for parody can only operate on such a stable and legitimated code, inscribed here in its most stereotypical aspects: *passé simple*, subjunctive, conditional inversion. These peculiarities are heightened because they are isolated, out of context, and sometimes internally distorted, as when a popular verb is inserted in an elevated construction, or conjugated in a sophisticated mode and/or tense. The function of elements of legitimate style, in *Journey*, is quite different from that of the *écriture artiste* in *L'Assommoir*, which takes the form not of isolated expressions but of independent, whole and unified paragraphs. The strong internal cohesiveness of these sections in Zola's novel is strengthened by the ideological weight of the theme. These passages are juxtaposed against those in popular style, but the two never interact in a close way, as they do in Céline's work.

In the passages discussed up to this point, the syntax is not ambiguous. Even when the sentence is fragmented by the ellipsis, its flow remains linear, the construction paratactic and the semantic content immediately comprehensible. Such is not the case in the paragraph quoted above, as a close analysis of the following sentence will show:

> Condamnés à mort différés on ne sortait plus de l'envie de roupiller énorme et tout devenait souffrance en plus d'elle, le temps et l'effort de bouffer.

(Condemned to a deferred death, we were besieged by an overwhelming desire to sleep, and all became suffering as well as that, the time and effort to eat.)

The sentence's complexity primarily stems from the fact that three word groups are repeated by a preposed or apposed pronoun: *Condamnés à mort différés / on* (Condemned to a deferred death / we); *l'envie de roupiller énorme / elle* (an overwhelming desire to sleep / that); *le temps et l'effort de bouffer / tout* (the time and the effort to eat/all). In the first case, it is clear that *on* refers to *condamnés à mort différés*, a *recherché* circumlocution for soldier. The relationship between *envie de roupiller énorme* and *elle* is less obvious, because of the distance that separates them in the sentence, and because the pronoun *elle* (she), even though it correctly replaces *envie*, adds a strange feminine element; *en plus de ça* is what the reader would have expected. Similarly, because *le temps et l'effort de bouffer* is disjointed from *tout* (the pronoun that in this case precedes it), its semantic and grammatical function is not immediately clear. In the earlier passage, constructions where an item was displaced and repeated by a pronoun in no way hindered immediate comprehension. The non-literary function of such displacements is, in fact, to reinforce comprehension. Here, the effect is the opposite: a certain degree of complexity is added to the sentence by these forms, distorting the construction of the sentence and rendering the understanding of the message difficult. The role of the *rappels* here is not dissimilar to that of the ellipsis that separates a subordinate clause from the principal one: an element characteristic of spoken or popular language is used to disrupt syntax. When the disruption impedes communication, as is the case here, it can be said to assume a poetic function. Furthermore, this construction confers a very specific rhythm upon the sentence, which can be divided into four units, the first and last of which are identical in their syllabic count: *condamnés à mort différés / le temps et l'effort de bouffer*. These two groups are also linked by assonance (*différés / bouffer*) reinforced by the third (middle) syllable of each: (*condamn*)*és / et*. Also very much removed from spoken language is *la nuit de guerre des villages abandonnés* (in war's night among abandonned villages). Grammatically, *nuit* (night) partakes of two unusual associations: *nuit des villages* and *nuit de guerre*, neither of which is current. *Nuit de guerre*, however, strongly recalls, phonetically and semantically, *nuit d'enfer*, a standard expression. The transformation of one of the terms of a current syntagm into a word that it phonetically or semantically resembles (*enfer–guerre* in this case) is what André Guyaux calls a *glissement*, a poetic process characteristic of Rimbaud.[32] But the text does not remain in the poetic sphere: the last sentence, *Ce qui guide encore le mieux, c'est l'odeur de la merde* (What leads the way best, it's the smell of shit), with its form and meaning, brings the tone down to the grossly unrefined.

The extract analyzed above reveals an interplay between popular language on the one hand, and on the other, a complex, ambiguous syntax that creates a particular rhythm and rhyme as well as expressions of unstable meaning. These linguistic structures, because they deform and defamiliarize legitimate language in a manner which opposes direct communication, partake in a poetic function. Furthermore, and even more extraordinary than this interplay is the manner in which a poetic function can be assumed by forms inherent to spoken/popular language, like the *rappel* which usually clarifies communication but here impedes it, or by a slightly transformed idiomatic expression. Such compelling effects also occur in the following passage:

> Les crépuscules dans cet enfer africain se révélaient fameux. On n'y coupait pas. Tragiques chaque fois comme d'énormes assassinats du soleil. Un immense chiqué. Seulement c'était beaucoup d'admiration pour un seul homme. Le ciel pendant une heure paradait tout giclé d'un bout à l'autre d'écarlate en délire, et puis le vert éclatait au milieu des arbres et montait du sol en traînées tremblantes jusqu'aux premières étoiles. Après ça le gris reprenait tout l'horizon et puis le rouge encore, mais alors fatigué le rouge et pas pour longtemps. Ça se terminait ainsi. Toutes les couleurs retombaient en lambeaux, avachies sur la forêt comme des oripeaux après la centième. Chaque jour sur les six heures exactement que ça se passait.
>
> Et la nuit avec tous ses monstres entrait alors dans la danse parmi ses mille et mille bruits de gueules de crapauds. (p. 168)

(The sunsets in this African hell revealed themselves to be amazing. There was no avoiding it. Tragic each time like enormous assassinations of the sun. An immense fakery. Except that it was a lot of admiration for just one man. The sky for one hour paraded all splashed from one end to another with delirious scarlet, and then the green exploded in the middle of the trees and rose from the ground in shivering trails reaching the early stars. After that the grey took over the entire horizon again, then the red once more, but tired, the red, and not for long. That's how it ended. All the colours fell in threads, sprawled over the forest like rags after the final battle. Every day at six o'clock sharp [that] it happened.

And the night with all its monsters then chimed in, among its thousands and thousands croaks of the toads.)

As in the previous extract, there are numerous popular markers of a lexical nature: *ne pas y couper, un chiqué, mais alors, ça se passait, entrer dans la danse, gueule, la centième* (meaning *la centième bataille*). At the same time, also on a lexical level, words like *crépuscule, révéler, tragique* and the metaphor *assassinat du soleil* (assassination of the sun) indicate the presence of a thread that escapes the prosaic. At first, this thread is woven into the text with a certain reticence and held down by sentences such as *on n'y coupait pas* and *un immense chiqué*. Creating a dynamic tension between two very different registers, these expressions seem to undercut a poetic intention that is only fully realized in the sixth sentence of the passage:

Le ciel pendant une heure paradait tout giclé d'un bout à l'autre d'écarlate en délire, et puis le vert éclatait au milieu des arbres et montait du sol en trainées tremblantes jusqu'aux premières étoiles.

(The sky for one hour paraded all splashed from one end to another with delirious scarlet, and then the green exploded in the middle of the trees and rose from the ground in shivering trails reaching the early stars.)

The description relies on standard poetic techniques, such as prosopopoeia, in *le ciel paradait, l'écarlate en délire; le vert éclatait* (the sky paraded, delirious scarlet, the green exploded) and very clear alliterations in *trainées tremblantes* and *écarlate en délire*; the verb *gicler* implies movement, and its past participle is not usually used as an adjective, *le ciel tout giclé* (the sky all splashed). Prosopopoeia – *le gris reprenait, fatigué le rouge* (the grey took over again, tired the red) is also present in the next sentence, which is, however, interspersed with heavy and dull expressions: *après ça, et puis, mais alors, pas pour longtemps*. In fact, fluctuations between the poetic and the prosaic animates the entire passage. Factual, somewhat curt statements such as *un immense chiqué ça se terminait ainsi* and *chaque jour sur les six heures exactement que ça se passait* (an immense fakery, that's how it ended at six o'clock sharp [that] it happened) arrest the poetic current – as in, earlier, *ce qui guide encore le mieux c'est l'odeur de la merde* (What leads the way best, it's the smell of shit), strike a vivid contrast, and highlight both poles. Rather than being neutralized by each other, the poetic and the popular operate by way of mutual

128 Political Stylistics

mise en valeur with their underlying presence felt throughout. A certain amount of tension is built in by their co-presence, and the poetic thread reappears forcefully in the final sentence:

> Et la nuit avec tous ses monstres entrait dans la danse parmi ses mille et mille bruits de gueules de crapauds. (And the night with all its monsters chimed in among the thousands and thousands croaks of the toads.)

The expression *entrer dans la danse* (literally: enter into the dance) is a figure of speech that would usually be judged colloquial. It means to become involved in, to join something, to take part in something (which I translate as "to chime in") and the idea of a dance is never taken literally. Here, however, the prosaic is undone, and this expression takes on a more unstable and subtle meaning, the unusual aspect of which stems from the subject *nuit*: the night indicates a poetic function. At the same time, *danse* can be taken more literally than is the case in its idiomatic use – but literally within a poetic sphere – because of the somewhat operatic movements in the description of the sky, and because of a link one could establish with a *danse de sorcière* (a witch's dance), suggested by the references to toads and monsters. This shift, from the idiomatic to the poetic (a shift attained by a passage through the literal) is created by the context rather than by a mutation in the expression itself, such as the *glissement* of *nuit d'enfer* into *nuit de guerre*. There is a form similar to the latter in this text, *mille et mille* (thousands and thousands). Here, a process of amplification, of multiplication, is applied to the standard expression *mille et une* (a thousand and one). As I noted earlier, this *glissement* recalls Rimbaud; so does Céline's ambiguous use of the word *gueule* in *bruits de gueules de crapauds*, where, syntactically, *gueule* can be attached to *crapauds* or to *bruits*, meaning either "face" in the first instance, or the verb *gueuler*, to yell, in the second. Both are popular. Rimbaud made use of this double meaning in "Les Pauvres à l'église" in the line "Aux vingt gueules gueulant les cantiques pieux" (Out of twenty mouths bellowed the pious canticles).[33] Here, *bruit de gueule* would refer to the sound made (like *gueulant* in Rimbaud) and is probably, but not necessarily, used as such, whereas *gueule de crapaud* (toadface) is a standard and insulting physical description. In the passage discussed above, unlike what was the case for the forms belonging to a belletristic style, the poetic elements do not stand out in an incongruous, self-parodic manner. The analysis reveals a deep fusion of the spoken/popular and the poetic, a fluid and dynamic interrelation. The passage shows how elements such as *on n'y coupait pas* and *un immense chiqué* seem to hold back a poetic current that becomes fully realized a few sentences later. But this resistance does not excise, or even dull the poetic; on the contrary, it creates a tension as a consequence of which, the poetic is more fully realized, more concentrated, heightened, when it finally re-emerges.

Approaching *Journey* for the first time, the reader finds in the prologue a number of indications concerning the novel that is about to be discovered, and is confronted with certain instabilities that foreshadow what is to come. The short text launches two attacks. Praising the imagination that transports one to the other side of life as the only value left in a world where all else is "*déceptions et fatigues*" (disappointments and fatigues), it discredits realism. The other attack, suggested by the use of popular language and the comment that *tout le monde peut en faire autant* (everyone can do the same), is directed against an elitist conception of literature. These two positions which, in themselves, can be viewed as somewhat contradictory, are complicated by the reference to Littré's dictionary and by the presence of popular language whose literary function is to reinforce realism. The relevance of a formal authority in linguistic matters contradicts a praise of the imagination and the directive *il suffit de fermer les yeux* (All you have to do is close your eyes). It also conflicts with the presence of popular language. Such ambiguities and ironies, from the outset, draw the reader into the text, who is then held there by the relationship that the narrator immediately establishes: one of complicity *Ça a débuté comme ça* (It began like that) and defensiveness, *Moi, j'avais jamais rien dit* (Me, I hadn't said a thing). Nothing, in *Journey*, resembles Zola's gradual and hesitant introduction of popular markers. They are present from the beginning, in the prologue and in the first lines of the novel, and occur throughout, both in the *récit de paroles* and the *récit d'événements*. They are equally distributed among the narrator's voice, the narrator's utterance, and the characters' utterances. Among the simpler and more standard forms are the contractions, omissions of *ne*, the pronoun *on*, many colloquial expressions and some argot. Stronger and more unusual ones occur on a syntactical level: different types of *rappel*, including the apposition of a pronoun in front of a subject (*moi, j'avais*), and the misuse of the conjunction *que* (*qu'ils disent, malgré que*). Many repetitions which are superfluous in legitimate written language and many verbless sentences which would be judged incorrect abound, while punctuation is not solely used to indicate grammatical relationships but to confer properly oral characteristics within the text. Exclamation marks and more particularly ellipses translate the fluctuations of a speaking voice, its intonations and pauses; they also break the mold of the sentence, which is no longer delimited by a capital letter and a period.

Popular markers are equally distributed among all parts of the novel, but this is not the case for belletristic and poetic elements, which appear only in the narrative voice. The belletristic style is represented by the *passé simple*, various tenses of the subjunctive, and conditional inversions. Forms of the *passé simple* are sometimes inconspicuous enough not to stand out in the sentence, but many rarely used ones, such as the very noticeable second-person plural, draw attention because they clash with the context and/or because the verb does not lend itself to such a tense. As Barthes puts it, they "signal an art." But, in *Journey*, their incongruity simultaneously subverts that signal. Poetic forms, on the other hand, do not work as parody for a number of reasons. First, as I mentioned earlier, parody relies on the isolation and amplification of fixed characteristics to the point of distortion; the style on which it operates has to be highly codified, stable, immediately identifiable and legitimate. Such is not the case for the poetic, where standard features such as alliteration, for example, are not instantly perceptible, and where defamiliarized syntax is not achieved by a set of standard devices. Furthermore, the incongruous and the discrepant are an inherent part of the poetic. Second, poetic forms in *Journey* are not isolated, but appear in groups, so as to form stylistic unities which, however, often fuse with the popular. The co-presence of poetic style and elements of popular language is, of course, highly unexpected, and even more so when these two stylistic unities do not relate by way of opposition but by mutual enhancement. Unlike the case in *L'Assommoir*, popular language is not dominated by another style; on the contrary, it dominates the belletristic and is vital to the poetic function, showing no signs of being objectified or treated with an emphasis on its otherness. Popular language is not used to represent a specific world-view but it is all-pervasive and quantitatively dominant. Precisely because of the effect it creates in conjunction with the poetic, it never becomes a predictable backdrop. The popular itself assumes an aesthetic function, a function which, as Mukarovsky argues, is not an inherent property but manifests itself only under certain conditions, in a certain context.[34] As we saw in the case of *L'Assommoir* and earlier novels, a literary context does not, in itself, necessarily endow popular language with an aesthetic function. The stylistic organization of *Journey*, on the other hand, does. Yet, there is another side to the question. Mukarovsky also notes that the aesthetic function has an isolating property, dissociating its object from "undesirable associations."³⁵ One might wonder, then, whether popular language in this novel becomes absolutely removed from its original, non-literary function, divorced from its social base and social signification.

The question gains depth and clarity when placed at the juncture of two analyses: Bakhtin's views on poetic discourse in *The Dialogic Imagination* and Terdiman's chapters on the prose poem in *Discourse/Counter-Discourse*. Bakhtin sharply dissociates the two genres that the prose poem brings together; Terdiman examines the significance and effect of their conjunction at the end of the nineteenth century. Reaching beyond Saussure's binary opposition, Bakhtin argues that a word, even when syntactically isolated from others, resonates with its history, "tastes of the context and contexts in which it has lived its socially charged life." Novelistic style retains the internal dialogism of words which remain related to the social realm: it "contains within itself indices that reach outside itself, a correspondence of its own elements and the elements of an alien context." Poetry, on the other hand, does not: presuming nothing beyond its own boundaries, it is self-sufficient and removed from its historicity and social determination:

> The language of the poetic genre is a unitary and singular Ptolemaic world outside of which nothing else exists and nothing else is needed . . . The world of poetry, no matter how many contradictions and insoluble conflicts the poet develops with it, is always illumined by one unitary and indisputable discourse.³⁶

Not only is the poetic word self-sufficient, but the various elements of poetic discourse are bound by an internal solidarity. The genre does not accommodate a variety of social languages – what Bakhtin calls a heteroglossia:

> To take responsibility for the language of the work as a whole at all of its points as *its* language, to assume full solidarity with each of its aspects, tones, nuances . . . such is the fundamental prerequisite for poetic style; style so conceived is fully adequate to a single language and a single linguistic consciousness. . . . The unity and singularity of language are the indispensable prerequisites for a realization of the direct (but not objectively typifying) intentional individuality of poetic style and of its monological steadfastness. (Bakhtin's emphasis)³⁷

Although we do not have a poetic genre in *Journey*, we do have a poetic style that involves more than one language, a style that is deeply dialogical, and hence challenges Bakhtin's assertion that the poetic is necessarily sealed off from "the influence of extraliterary social dialects." It is precisely this type of hybrid poetic discourse that constitutes the uniqueness of Céline's style. The question remains, however, as to whether the strong internal coherence of the style, wherein poetic and popular elements are tightly fused, stifles the historical and social connotations that the popular might otherwise carry. In *Discourse/Counter-Discourse*, Terdiman traces the politicized distinction between the genres of poetry and prose to the second half of the nineteenth century. As prose became dominant and all-pervasive in this era of bourgeois rule, it was seen as Republican, democratic. The literary avant-garde, reacting to what they viewed as the standardization of artistic production and its absorption into mass culture, sought differentiation from the "common," the "vulgar," and refuge in aestheticism:

> What faced the avant-garde as the condition of their crisis was the progressive absorption of the world into the market economy, of all discourse into practical discourse. In response, their fundamental resource for maintaining distinction came to be a transformation of the old aristocratic doctrine that practical work is the attribute of inferiority.[38]

However, a section of the haute bourgeoisie, itself in search of distinction and possibly nostalgic for the lost attributes of aristocracy, displayed an aesthetic disposition that, as Terdiman puts it, served as a "polemical symbol marking distance from the degradation of the social whole," for both poets and industrialists alike.[39] This was, of course, a paradoxical situation, and the literary avant-garde, however economically dependent on the bourgeoisie, did not wish to display an aesthetic complicity with the dominant class. A strategy, from the *poètes maudits* of the nineteenth century to the surrealists of the twentieth, was the cultivation of scandal. The prose poem, which Terdiman considers the outcome of the cultural and political configuration described here, was a highly scandalous production:

> The aesthetic doctrines of the avant-garde, the practices of the prose poem in particular, then appear as reflexes of efforts to maintain differentiation from the "bourgeois" in the face of surreptitious similarity between the two antagonistic systems.[40]

The prose poem negates antinomies, and destablilizes fixed and naturalized forms: traditional verse on the one hand and conventional prose on the other. By demonstrating that such oppositions are not immanent and eternal, it implies that they are socially constructed, thereby restoring their historicity and contingency, Terdiman argues. Even though one of the characteristics of the prose poem is a lack of clear, outward-directed referentiality (at least in the cases that followed Baudelaire, where, already, referentiality is greatly wrought and distorted) the new genre was brought into being by external socio-political and cultural factors: "A hybrid generic status acutely registers the texts' self-consciousness of its process of formation."[41] *Journey* achieves such an effect not on a generic but on a stylistic level only, challenging the cultural norms that had established an incompatibility between popular and poetic language. As in the prose poem, the novel's style is animated by an attack on dominant prose, further supported by parodies of the belletristic style. For the historical reader, *Journey* can be placed in the tradition of the scandalous – the aesthetic or ethical subversion of dominant culture – by the very fact of the interrelations between the poetic and the non-poetic. The tight fusion, then, rather than rendering the text closed, hermetic to the extra-literary, opens it up. The social connotations of the popular cannot but infiltrate the text, and render the repercussions of the scandalous more clearly political than otherwise might have been the case. *Journey* can surely be viewed as a counterdiscursive text.

"AMONG US, AGAINST US, OR NOWHERE"

As was the case with *L'Assommoir*, the publication of *Journey* did not go unnoticed. From October 1932 to March 1933, over one hundred articles concerning Céline's first novel appeared in both the general and the more specialized press. The interest was intensified by the polemic that developed around what became known as "l'Affaire du Goncourt." *Journey* was nominated for this prize and considered by many the most likely laureate. However, after last-minute reconsiderations, the judges finally awarded the Goncourt to Guy Mazeline's *Les Loups* ("The Wolves"), a rather inconsequential work. Several critics were outraged, and the topic was discussed at great length in the press. The incident acted as a catalyst in drawing public attention. But even without this, the publication of *Journey* would have been an event. Céline was not at that time a known figure in the literary or political scene. He had issued no statement, made no gesture that might have signaled the violently anti-semitic and pro-fascist positions he was to hold later. His novel was launched with little information regarding its author. Yet both the left- and right-wing press responded with what seemed like the recognition of a potential: the potential of this literary work to convey the ideology each side advocated.

Although the two sides issued reservations regarding their definitive "adoption" of Céline, each found elements in *Journey* that correlated with and could be used to promote their views and intentions.

Brutal and powerful: these are the two adjectives that occur over and over again to describe *Journey*. All articles also stress that this work is a highly original one. For example, Georges Altman in the Communist journal *Monde* (29 October 1932) writes that this book is like no other book, that its prose is like no other prose; *Journey* does not partake in any literary trend, nor does it set one – unique, "savage," it restores a feeling that the reader has lost: astonishment.[42] In *L'Humanité* (9 December 1932), the official publication of the French Communist Party, Paul Nizan remarks that the novel's vigor and breadth are not something to which the "well trained dogs" and the "prissy dwarfs" of bourgeois literature had accustomed the reader.[43] Admiring the boldness with which Céline uses a language that is not hindered by syntax, that reveals the slightest nuances of thought, and that expresses anger and violence alongside the most profound poetry, the author of an article in the anarchist paper *Le Libertaire* (30 December 1932) says he was entranced by the "powerful breath that animates the book and that prevents the reader's interest from weakening."

Altman, also, notes this liberation from syntax: the power of six hundred breathless pages results from a prose that "grates and moans, sneers wickedly, often escapes by a kind of swift impulse, soon drained and shattered, from the structure of the sentence." Compared to a "dark river" that "pushes the book forward at full speed," the style is described as explosive and violent, like man's anger against life. With its power, sound and strength, it imposes itself on the reader who cannot escape its effects, Nizan remarks. In the left-wing and satirical *Canard enchaîné* (14 December 1932), Pierre Scize wrote that the representation of popular language is viewed as intrinsically contestatory and reveals for whom the novel is written: establishing a complicity, not necessarily with a working-class reader, but with a rebellious reader hostile to the established order, it is destined for those who do not like the world as it is, the society in which they live, or men as they are.[44] The communist press, also, hears the anger that *Journey* conveys. Altman writes that the narrator "tells his story in the tough and angry style of a working class man who tells the outrage done to him," while Nizan admires the "quite extraordinary transposition of spoken language." In the left-wing weekly *Marianne* (16 November 1932), Ramon Fernandez considers the voice in *Journey* to "speak popular very skillfully" but points out that there are, in places, "learned forms that are somewhat bothersome."[45] Similarly, Altman, in the same *Monde* article, though he praises the novel's linguistic dynamism which prevents the style from becoming a predictable system, notes that it sometimes tends towards affectation, with learned linguistic forms that do not belong to popular language:

> The use of this popular language could have easily become a mechanical process; an admirable variety of expression and an evident literary talent easily avoid that, even sometimes transforming this rich explosion of hard and fresh prose into something a little studied and precious. But the true accent soon starts to resonate again.

To critics of all political tendencies, *Journey* suggested an extremely pessimistic world-view and showed man's profound dissatisfaction with society. It is not surprising, therefore, that it is in the anarchist paper *Le Libertaire* (30 December 1932) that one finds a wholehearted approval of this outlook: "how can we not sympathize, we, anarchists, with this man, eternally unsatisfied, with the latent revolt that is inside of him, with his insubmission to the war and to its honors, to the old, deeply rotten bourgeois society."[46] No reservation is expressed here about the narrator's presumed position, and the article from which this quote is taken is enthusiastic throughout. The communist press, however, has some disagreement with the political stance that *Journey* seems to suggest. Even though in *Monde* the narrator's voice is likened to that of a working-class man who tells of the outrage done to him, Altman judges him to be a profoundly nihilist character who kindles no hope. Although the narrator shows contempt for those who suffer life's hideousness, he none the less appears to distrust those who, like himself, denounce it:

> He experiences and refuses evil forces, the war, the moral ugliness, the lowliness, the hypocrisy of the world, he describes and denounces in poignant accents, such as we have not heard in a long time; confronted with the hideousness of life, he cannot believe in those who submit to it. Does he have faith in those who, together, refuse it? He does not say, but it seems that his heart is too full of bitterness to welcome any kind of hope.

Since *L'Humanité* is the official organ of the Communist Party, it expresses similar criticism with some severity. Nizan begins by recognizing the truth of the sinister vision of the world presented in *Journey* and applauds the revolt, the anger and the denunciation of illustrious ghosts (the army, scientists, colonists). By tearing away

136 Political Stylistics

all masks and camouflage, Céline destroys illusions and increases contemporary man's consciousness of his downfall. However, because of his profound anarchy, there is no place for him among communists: "Céline is not among us; impossible to accept his profound anarchy, his disdain, his general repulsion that does not exclude the proletariat." Because the concept of revolution seems foreign to him, Céline is unaware of the true explanation for the misery he denounces; Nizan remarks, with foresight, that "This pure revolt can lead him anywhere: among us, against us, or nowhere." In a later review, also in *L'Humanité* (19 December 1932), Fréville presents a similar argument: if Céline condemns the ruling class and understands that the dominating role of the bourgeoisie is soon coming to an end, he does not, however, see the proletariat as a new force, a revolutionary class, and thus remains quite foreign to what communists seek. *Journey*, then, is seen as a work that denounces the established social order and is thus potentially subversive, but does not draw the necessary conclusions from its apocalyptic vision. The outlook it conveys is not properly marxist; it does not advocate solidarity among the oppressed, or an organized, active class struggle. It is true that the Africans are depicted as harshly as the French colonists; Bardamu's poor medical patients are ridiculed as much as his distinguished colleagues.

The impact of *Journey* on the left was not restricted to France. Trotsky, soon after its publication, wrote an article in which he enthusiastically praises the novel: "Louis-Ferdinand Céline walked into great literature as other men walk into their homes." He realizes that Céline, who "from underneath the veils of decorum exposes the mud and the blood," is not a revolutionary, that he is not concerned with reconstructing the society which he denounces.[47] There is no reprimand, but, rather, a certain empathy in Trotsky's explanation of this attitude:

> Only because there are numerous and well paid priests serving the altars of false altruism does Céline turn away from greatness of mind and heroism, from great projects and hopes, from everything that leads humanity out from the dark night of the circumscribed I.[48]

Even though they were not quite as understanding, Trotsky's French comrades were impressed by the novel, such a far cry was it from the complacency of bourgeois literature. The work raised much interest and many questions about its author. In all articles, Céline was treated as one with the narrator, Bardamu, in whom the critics recognized an as-yet undefined political potential whose realization could lead either towards them or against them. The style was found deeply compelling by all. Even those critics who recognized (and deplored) the presence of learned and precious forms judged the overall effect to be one of violence, anger and opposition to the established order. Altman went so far as to say that the voice was that of a working-class man. Popular language was not viewed by left-wing critics as dissociated from its original, non-literary source, and it was not believed that the social connotations – anger, dissatisfaction and contestation – were minimized by their literary transposition and by their aesthetic function. Even though they found the learned, affected and "recherché" tone (referring either to the poetic elements or to those of the belletristic style that do not appear as clear parody) unnecessary, and to hinder the true accent, they did not consider these forms to jeopardize the authenticity of a working-class voice or to dilute significantly its anger. But those elements were certainly not viewed as a contribution to the subversive strength of the style. The scandalous fusion of the poetic and the popular, for the left-wing critics, was of no political consequence whatsoever. In fact, the admiration expressed for the powerful and compelling qualities of the style does not take this important aspect into account. Solely because of its popular elements was it perceived as a challenge to the ruling class. Strong criticism was directed against the novel's content, for, if the social indictment expressed by the style was considered to be implied there also, it is in a manner far less attuned to the left's purpose: the hostility is directed against all, including the working class, and not only towards the bourgeoisie.

Like the left-wing critics who praise *Journey* for breaking with bourgeois literature, Léon Daudet, in *Candide*, a political weekly of the extreme right whose views were close to those of *L'Action française* but addressed to a slightly more popular public none the less, contrasts Céline with Proust, "the Balzac of gossip," and with Gide, whose work is nothing more than a "young girls' diversion."[49] He does not, however, oppose *Journey* to all that precedes it, but to the literary production of the last thirty years in particular (a period of some significance to him, since it was at the turn of the century that fascist ideology arose in France). In fact, Daudet relates the novel to a tradition, though a distant one: its "boldness" and "truculence" has much in common with the work of Rabelais and Villon. Pierre Loewel, in *Ordre* (3 November 1932), finds *Journey* undeniably original and Merry Bromberger, in *L'Intransigeant* (8 December 1932), finds it disconcerting; in *Gringoire*, another publication of the extreme right with fascist tendencies, Marcel Augagneur calls Céline "the scout of the renewal of French literature."[50] This renewal, he says, is much needed, for French literature has recently stagnated and is not in touch with the "customs of the après-guerre." He also makes the connection with Rabelais; the emphasis is thus on both change and tradition. As in the communist press, the style is described as something to which the reader submits, that captures his attention and from which he cannot escape, all of which occurs with a certain violence. Daudet writes that it takes ten hours to read the novel, ten hours during which the reader receives blows in the chest and after which "one must pause, catch one's breath, think about all that." In *Ordre*, the style is described as a "disarray, proliferation, vociferation" that surprises, amuses and exhausts the reader. The term "disarray" must refer to the twisted syntax, while "vociferation" points to the text's violence and also to its properly oral quality. Augagneur notes that Céline writes with superb disdain for the reader, and describes the style's violence in vivid terms:

> One can compare this text to a torrent that rolls, mingling diamonds and mud, in its waters sometimes pure sometimes murky, and with them the reader who, after the last page, it would throw, dizzy, raw, on a deserted shore, lost in an interior solitude.

The reader of *Journey* undergoes a violent upheaval and is left purified, stripped of all the old values that he had held dear, and, as we will see, open to new ones; in this respect, the novel is considered to encourage the establishment of a new order.

In both the left- and right-wing press, the fluid movement and the quick pace of the style is stressed ("pushes the book forward at full speed," "six hundred breathless pages," "one must pause, catch one's breath," "explosion of fresh and hard prose"), and many critics refer to a common image, that of a river ("dark river," "torrent that rolls"). Also shared is the perception of a certain "sound" that emanates from Céline's writing: "grates and moans," "vociferation." An important difference exists, however, between the reaction on the left and right when it comes to the "recherché moments," which the communists denounce. In the right-wing press, these moments are praised. Loewel acknowledges the novel's originality and strength but discerns Céline's real talent in the more poetic moments of the text where "at brief moments the tone changes and one hears a note rise that suggests a true musician." Fascist ideology, as it manifested itself in France in the 1930s, placed a high value on feelings and instincts, and emphasized the primacy of the spiritual over the rational; at the same time it advocated a strict adherence to a new hierarchy of values. Daudet discerns this model, at least potentially, in Céline's novel: "He is closer to the supernatural, doctor Céline, than he thinks, and I wait for him at that time that comes for all expressive writers, when the need to give a meaning to life will explode in him." The disruption of sentence construction, and the often ambiguous syntax, can be considered to indicate a rejection of the highly structured, rational basis on which Cartesian thought and expression are founded. These elements clearly partake in a poetic function. Another significant difference from left-wing readings is that Daudet most emphatically links the style of *Journey* to the national language as a whole, rather than to a particular social group. He repeatedly stresses that this work is deeply, typically French, and implies that Céline has the ability to use legitimate language if he so chooses: "under the apparent disorderliness of the style hides a deep knowledge of the French language." In fact he judges *Journey* to be so French that it cannot be translated – and this, for Daudet, is a great advantage. He refers to the popular language as a "Parisian slang" a "dialect that has been tossed through time in the *sinuous wrinkles of the old capital*" (Daudet's emphasis – a reference to Baudelaire's "The little old women"), a literary artifice whose use he does not consider innovative. Tradition is called upon to justify the style, and Céline's authority is stressed. It is by choice and for literary rather than social motives that he writes as he does. In an unusually negative article published in *Candide* (8 December 1932), André Rousseaux says that he does not care for the style but recognizes that it does not manage to "stifle gifts for literary expression."[51] A mixed response, also written by Rousseaux, is published in *Le Figaro* (13 December 1932), a deeply conservative, but not fascist, publication.[52] Here, the novel's style is described as repulsive, and the vision of the world it conveys as nihilistic. Rousseaux draws a parallel between *Journey* and surrealism. He sees the similar treatment of language as the result of anarchy: "The depth of anarchy is always the same, and the contempt for intelligible expression is an effect of the dislocation of the human being pushed to his limit." In another *Figaro* article (13 December 1932), positive this time, Georges Bernanos stresses the artificiality of the style.[53] Far from being a sterile reproduction of the language of the working class, it expresses precisely what their language cannot convey: their dark and puerile soul. The anger and violence of the style is in fact directed against the working class itself, he concludes, and because of this he finds *Journey* admirable and extraordinary, even though it is a work that scandalizes and that he would not recommend to his wife and daughter. The ideological difference between a right-wing drawn towards fascism on the one hand, and a traditional, conservative one (exemplified by *Le Figaro*) on the other, is clearly illustrated here. In fact, the *Figaro* articles of Rousseaux and Bernanos recall similarly divergent reactions to *L'Assommoir*. When *Journey*, flaunting things that should not be shown or said, is found repulsive and tasteless, we are reminded of Dancourt's assessment of Zola's novel, whereas like Wolff, Bernanos approves of the fact that it reveals a working class in all its lowliness. Obviously, neither of these readings that posit the working class as the enemy harbors the populism displayed in the articles of the more extreme right.

All critics describe the style of *Journey* as powerful. In publications of the extreme right, *Candide* and *Gringoire*, it is also considered virile. Daudet says that the novel draws its strength from the "masculine and unbridled" aspects of the French language, a welcome change from the work of authors who had become increasingly "pale and sugary sweet." Augagneur warns that this vigorous and ferocious book might shock "righteous thinking souls," referring to the ideology of a more traditional, conservative right that attacks neither basic Republican institutions, as opposed to the revolutionary aspects of fascism, nor the spiritual and moral foundations of society (*Le Figaro* holds such positions). These perceptions of aggressive, virile qualities can be understood in the light of what Pierre Bourdieu considers an ill-founded but widespread belief: the belief that "linguistic conformity entails a sort of recognition and submission, that would cast doubt upon the virility of the men who submit to it."[54] The style of *Journey* very clearly transgresses the norms of legitimate language. Céline consciously disregards the rules that govern good French, and this implies a disregard for the authority which enforces them. It is this attitude of defiance which, in a populist move, is interpreted as typically male in a fascist reading adapted to popular criteria. I mentioned how, in *Gringoire*, Augagneur describes the reader of *Journey* thrown "on a deserted shore, lost in an interior solitude." This, the annihilation of cultural identity, is what all the features of *Journey* described above are made to participate in. It is the outcome that a fascist reading constructs. In his article in *Candide* Daudet describes the phenomenon in the following manner: present times are troubled, he says, even more so than they were under the Revolution, and all values are questioned. He outlines the way in which new ones may be restored:

[The values] must reach the limits of disorder, more exactly the end of the night, so that, still quivering from their emancipation, they be retrieved by hierarchy and the light of day. What is strong, even if it is purulent, tends towards emancipation and fresh air.

This argument leads him to advise Céline now to direct his extraordinary gift "towards the Alps, towards the summit, towards the grandiose"; furthermore, he will soon be gripped by the desire to give meaning to life for "in every blasphemer a moralist lies waiting." Daudet's judgment recalls Habermas' remark in "Modernity – An Incomplete Project" that "The new value placed on the transitory, the elusive and the ephemeral, the very celebration of dynamism, discloses a longing for an undefiled, immaculate and stable present."[55] On a more thematic level, Daudet approves of the fact that the Africans are "not flattered" (failing to mention, however, that the French colonists are not either) and claims that war depicted by a coward like Bardamu is, at least, more entertaining than the tearful tirades of pacifists. Along the same line of thought, Augagneur notes that the novel reflects the understanding of a new order which, in an almost subterranean way, is taking hold of all areas of human activity. *Journey* is seen as a work that, in a Nietzschean manner, overthrows current values and encourages the reconstruction of a new and superior hierarchy, a process that takes place within the specific moral and aesthetic framework that fascism advocates: the cult of instinct and feelings, the demise of reason and materialism, and an anti-intellectualism that exalts energy and strength. Like those on the left, these critics delight in the anti-bourgeois stance suggested by *Journey*, but they do not consider the anger expressed to be that of a specifically working-class voice; for them, the style, in many respects, reflects an essential, non-class-related conception of what is French. They also differ from the communists in that they consider the fusion of the poetic and the popular to be a powerful and positive feature, which adds to Céline's authority and legitimacy; it shows that, if the novel embraces the working class, it does not originate from the working class – an important distinction. Furthermore, drawing on the traditional assessment of prose as democratic and poetry as aristocratic, the fusion is felt to result in a work that partakes in an crucial aspect of fascism: it is both populist and elitist. Finally, the hybrid is scandalous, and here, scandal is taken to be of political consequence. Its effects are considered destabilizing, deeply unsettling, resulting in a rupture, a dissolution of cultural identity, an openness to reconstruction.

When *Journey* first appeared, Céline shunned publicity and was very reluctant to talk about his novel; when he did so, it was in a very laconic manner. In one of his earliest statements (10 November 1932), reiterating the claim made in his letter to Garcin, he declared that *Journey* was not literature, but life as it presented itself.[56] He refers to his work's style for the first time and what he says here he did not repeat later (in fact he often contradicted it): he stresses that he did not consciously attempt to use a "language of the faubourgs," as his interviewer put it, but that he wrote just as he happened to speak, according to his social origins: "I'm from the working class, the real working class." Popular language is his own linguistic instrument, so why not use it, he adds. Here, Céline justifies his novelistic style by denying that it is the outcome of a choice. Rather, he says, it is a necessity, for his linguistic competence is restricted to the use of popular language and legitimate French is unavailable to him – which, of course, is untrue. The position is not one that Céline held for long. A little later, he is reported to have said: "I invented an anti-bourgeois language that also participated in my overall purpose."[57] Here, popular language is not presented as something readily available by virtue of the social class to which he belonged, but as something created by him in a gesture antagonistic to the dominant class. This point will become central to Céline's later arguments. Later, also, he will elaborate upon a claim made here: he wrote in this anti-bourgeois language "because there are feelings that I would not have been able to find without it." The expressive quality of popular language is something that Céline will stress over and over again. In a letter to the critic André Rousseaux published in *Le Figaro* (30 May 1936) he discusses a particular aspect of his stylistic choice: the inclusion of argot.[58] First, he places his style in opposition to a classical one and mocks the latter's pretension to be an "absolute French." All languages die, he writes, and that of his novels will be no exception. But they will have lived, be it for a year, a month, a day, because argot is alive at the time that one uses it – and such is not the case for legitimate language.

After the war, Céline was much more eager to talk about his literary work. He emphasized the importance of its style above all, repeating over and over again: "I am a stylist." This emphasis must be viewed with caution and in the light of the introduction to the 1949 edition of *Journey*, in which Céline claims that the hatred of which he had become the object was due not to the anti-semitic pamphlets he had subsequently written but to the style of *Journey*, a style that no one would accept (which, as the reactions in the press show, was not the case): "You'll tell me: 'But it's not *Journey!* Your crimes that are killing you right now, have nothing to do with it! It's your malediction! Your *Bagatelles!* . . .' But make no mistake! It's for *Journey* that they're after me!" (p. 114) This argument, seeking to shift the politically scandalous on to the literary, is reiterated with astonishing clarity and a *mauvaise-foi* so obvious that it amounts to yet another provocation in July 1961: "Everybody always talks to me about the Jewish question . . . But in fact that's a pretext . . . I think they don't give a damn . . . But the style question, that is unforgiven . . . unforgiven . . . unforgiven."[59]

If, after his return to France in April 1951, Céline claims that literary style is his fundamental concern and if, as we will see later, he mocks "ideas" and "messages" (of which he says there is none in his work), it is clearly to divert the public's attention from the violently anti-semitic positions he took in *Mea Culpa* (1936), *Bagatelles pour un massacre* (1937), *L'Ecole des cadavres* (1938) and *Les Beaux Draps* (1941). These pamphlets led to his retreat to Denmark in 1944, where he spent eleven months in prison. The French authorities demanded his extradition, but it was refused. While still in Copenhagen he was condemned *in absentia* to one year of imprisonment, with a fine of fifty thousand francs, and the confiscation of half his present and future property. Because, ironically, of an earlier proof of patriotism, the judgment was revoked in 1951: an amnesty was granted to those who had been injured in the First World War. Upon his return to France, it is likely that Céline wanted to escape further moral or political blame and he attempted to transform a bitter ideological conflict into a literary one, in which his style became the issue. It is within this framework that his post-war statements must be understood. The two that follow are representative of the positions Céline held until the end of his life:

> I do not pretend to bring a message . . . I invented a style, that's all I can be reproached for . . . I am a technician, a stylist, period.[60]

> I am only a small inventor, a small inventor, that's right! And only of one little thing . . . I invented emotion in written language. Yes, written language had dried out, and I am the one who restored emotion to written language . . . Emotion only lets itself be captured, and with much difficulty, in "the spoken," and reproduced with much time and much patience.[61]

Two elements that did not appear in his earlier justifications are now present. First, the notion of "the spoken," to which he had not previously referred, and, second, emotion. These are to become key terms, and the need to infuse written language with the emotion that is only present in the spoken will become a central argument. It is now extremely common for Céline to attack what he calls "academic French," to which he had referred earlier as "classical style," and which he describes as a conservative, dead language, the language of institutions and of most literary production: "The style of all those things, I find it is the same style as that of the baccalauréat papers, the same style as political speeches, that is to say a verbal style, eloquent maybe, but certainly not emotive."[62]

This argument is repeated in an interview that took place in November 1960:

> We have not gone beyond the style of Jesuits: the sermon! Sermon is everywhere: in schools, in law, in politics, in religion. But there's no emotion. Some say: "At the beginning was the word!" Bullshit! Me, I say: "At the beginning was emotion."[63]

All these claims are accompanied by expressions of disdain and insults addressed to other writers, the Académie Française and the educational system – to name but a few of those whom Céline considers responsible for the perpetuation of an unbearably stilted and arid French.

In many of his statements, Céline refers to the great effort required to capture the emotion inherent in spoken language and to transpose it into written form, a process that depends on a subtle selection of oral elements, an overall reconstruction according to a new architecture which demands extreme delicacy, for an equilibrium has to be attained "in the realm of dreams, between what is true and what is not." This reference points to the presence of another language, the poetic language, which functions in close conjunction with the popular. Céline, in his "Taped interview," notes that his unconventional use of syntax and punctuation does not only serve to represent the rhythm and intonations of a speaking voice, but also introduces a certain ambiguity in the meaning of the sentence: "This style, it comes from a certain way of forcing sentences out of their habitual signification, of unhinging them as it were, of displacing them, and forcing the reader himself to displace the meaning."[64]

In a letter to Milton Hindus (15 May 1947), Céline emphasizes the harmonic quality of his writing, a quality that is not necessarily inherent in the spoken language itself:

The trick is to imprint a certain deformation onto spoken language, so that once it is written, the reader has the impression that someone is talking in his ear. But real spoken language, stenographed, does not give that impression at all (– see speeches!). This distortion is in truth a small harmonic tour de force.[65]

In the same letter, he refers to his style as "the return to a spontaneous and wild poetry," and compares himself to Mallarmé, for both are "colorists of words," but whereas Mallarmé's words are rare, unusual ones, his are of a common, everyday sort.

Finally, Céline justifies his stylistic choice in terms of the effect he wants it to have on the reader. Previously, he had defended the use of slang by opposing it to a dead, academic language. *Conversations with Professor Y*, the fictional interview written by Céline himself, sheds a different light on the issue. Argot, he claims, functions as a literary violence to which the reader wants to be submitted, therefore increasing the hold that the text has over him:

> Argot is a language of hate that'll make your reader perk up . . . destroy him . . . At your mercy! . . . he just sits there flummoxed.
> . . .
> But watch out! careful! I must add: the tingle argot provides is short lived! two . . . three good couplets! two, three good broadsides . . . and your reader pulls himself back together! . . . A book entirely filled with argot is more boring than a court record!
> . . .
> Because the reader is a man of vice! he wants argot in stronger and stronger doses . . . where would you find it for him?[66]

Throughout *Conversations* Céline writes of the presumed effect of the style on the reader in vehement terms which suggest that the readers submit to it independently of their will. Céline conceived of the act of reading as an entirely passive one that does not allow for the implication of the reader's creativity or choice. There is never any hint of his participation in the text: "I ship all my friends on the metro, correction! I take everybody, willy-nilly! . . . charge along!"[67] and "Violently! . . . under the spell! . . . you don't tolerate arrogant intellectuals! dialecticians, for example! no more crossroads, no more yellow lights, no more cops, no more dragass buttocks!"[68]

The analogy that Céline often draws between his style and an "emotive subway" recalls the many references to a fast flowing river that the critics used to describe its effect. In both cases the allusion is to the reader's submission to a constant movement forward. Probably referring to the distorted syntax and the ellipsis, Céline mentions, in the same range of imagery, the "rails specially made, they look straight, but they really aren't."[69] Again emphasizing the text's control over the reader, a control of a persuasive rather than an openly oppressive and violent nature, he mentions that while reading *Journey* one should have the impression that a voice is talking aloud in one's head (this "sound" quality was also something mentioned by the critics). Céline does not think of the reader as a virtual space, a theoretical set of expectations, or an empty vessel to be filled, but as a very material body. Although passive, the reader has a certain physical consistency that has to be overcome by the power of the novel, a power that operates in a manner either violent or seductive.

Much of contemporary criticism claims that it is by virtue of its form that literature contributes most effectively towards subversive ends. Such views are often derived from those of Adorno, who celebrates modernist texts fed on personal rebellion and resistant to social appropriation by virtue, principally, of their style. In his core essay "Commitment," he denies the political validity of a clear message in a work of art – a major point of dissent from classical marxism.[70] Even when the message is politically radical, he argues, by implicitly relying on major assumptions of the dominant ideology it is founded on a certain acceptance of the world as it is. He illustrates his position with a critique of Sartre's literary production, of his plays in particular: they are vehicles for subversive political ideas, but ideas placed in a context that operates nevertheless "with traditional intrigues, exalted by unshaken faith in meanings, which can be transferred from art to reality."[71] The traditional plot undoubtedly indicates an acceptance of current moral values, social situations and concerns. The "unshaken faith in meaning" suggests the lack of a linguistic *mise en cause* and an unquestioned representation of an unquestioned reality. This, according to Adorno, creates two obstacles in the way of the work's revolutionary potential. First, the presence of solid and straightforward ideas in the plays makes them readily available to and easily processed by the culture industry (a consistently negative factor for the Frankfurt School) and from this follows Adorno's somewhat elitist but nevertheless appealing assumption that "the uncalculating autonomy of works of art which avoid popularization and adaptation to the market involuntarily becomes an attack on them."[72] The second obstacle is the fact that those whom Adorno calls "cultural conservatives," whom he equates with political conservatives, are more likely to be attracted to this accessible, clearly relevant type of work that implies a stable reality than to "listen patiently to

Céline's Voyage au bout de la nuit   147

a text where language jolts signification and by its very distance from meaning revolts in advance against a positivist subordination of meaning."[73] It is interesting to note a number of parallels between Adorno's conception of the liberating text and views held by Céline concerning his own work, who, above all, rejects the notion that any ideas or messages might be present: "I have no ideas myself! not one! there's nothing more vulgar, more common, more disgusting than ideas! libraries are loaded with them! and every sidewalk café!"[74]

What Céline privileges above all is style, the main function of which is to convey emotion and to destabilize reality. The reference to a displaced meaning in the statement "This style, it comes from a certain way of forcing sentences out of their habitual signification, of unhinging them as it were, of displacing them, and hence force the reader himself to displace the meaning" distinctly echoes the manner in which Adorno places high value on a text where language jolts signification and establishes a "distance from meaning." Céline's remarks and his actual literary work also reflect Adorno's basic position on the function of art: "It is not the function of art to spotlight alternatives but to resist by its form only the course of the world which permanently puts a pistol to men's heads."[75] Such a resistance, tension or negation Adorno perceives in Beckett's plays and Kafka's prose, which "arouse the fear existentialism merely talks about."[76] These works have a deeply unsettling effect, they shock the reader out of complacency: "The inescapability of their work compels the change of attitude which committed works merely demand." The change of attitude, brought on by the disturbing questioning of the world as it is ordinarily represented, presumably results in a liberated sensibility which could operate as a potential space for a revolutionary conscience to develop. By virtue of its form, *Journey* attacks a traditional, conservative institution: that of the correct French language. The style, oscillating between the tension and fusion of two usually opposed linguistic categories, the poetic and the popular, thus undermines dominant classifications and hierarchies by bringing together opposites. Because of unexpected lexical forms and twisted syntax, the novel represents a destabilized reality. Many important aspects of the novel thus correlate with what Adorno advocates.

The theoretical positions expanded in "Commitment" require examination in the light of what happened in the case of *Journey*. Céline's own appropriation and instrumentalization of his style cannot be ignored. His privileging of form over content was a strategy to deflate the importance of the unambiguous political "message" he expressed in his anti-semitic pamphlets. Furthermore, as the reactions in the press show, the signification of the presence of popular language in *Journey* was open to interpretation. For the communists, though they regretted the highly personal nature of the rebellion and the lack of any suggestion of mass action, the novel's style expressed the anger of a working-class voice that denounced hypocrisy and false values. Critics of the extreme right argued that it conveyed power and virility, while its poetic elements subverted a rational framework. These critics expected that the novel's form, which did not correlate with customary codes and expectations, but transgressed and undermined established norms, would result in a violent impact on the reader. This effect could ultimately be used to restore the fundamental values of hierarchy and order, and *Journey* could hence improve troubled times.

Clearly, his first novel was appropriated by pro-fascist critics, before Céline himself had made any gesture in that direction; this problematizes the theoretical positions expanded in "Commitment." In the light of *Journey*, an obvious shortcoming of Adorno's argument seems to be his linking of the radical right to what he calls "the authoritarian person," which he describes as follows:

> The basic features of this type include conformism, respect for a petrified façade of opinion and society, and resistance to impulses that disturb its order or evoke inner elements of the unconscious that cannot be admitted. This hostility to anything alien or alienating can accommodate itself much more easily to literary realism of any provenance, even if it proclaims itself critical or socialist, than to works that swear allegiance to no political slogans, but whose mere guise is enough to disrupt the whole systems of coordinates that govern authoritarian personalities – to which the latter cling all the more fiercely, the less capable they are of anything not officially approved.[77]

It is clear that this description does not correspond to the most powerful aspects of fascism at work in France in the 1930s, a fascism that advocated a Nietzschean destruction of values, a liberation of sensibility and the celebration of irrational and unconscious forces. Adorno's conception correlates more with the type of right-wing mentality incarnated by what Daudet referred to as "righteous thinking souls." It is this somewhat narrow view of fascism in terms of rigidity and rationality that leads Adorno to his conclusion. Another point worth noting is that, protesting above all against the transformation of works of art into consumer goods, Adorno does not take into account the fact that the political forces involved in their presentation to the public, operating more or less subtly in their attempt to transform literary texts into instruments that would uphold and promote their cause, do so all the more easily when the work in question puts forward no tight thesis, does not convey a monolithic vision of the world, and displays a style that is open to manipulation. The case of *Journey* shows how a specific interpretation is forced upon formal transgression by agents of authoritarian ideologies, all the more forcibly, it seems, at times of ideological and political unrest, when there appears to be much at stake.

Even though the political configuration of the day accommodated vocal and relatively powerful movements of the far left and extreme right, *Journey* emerged from a society no longer in the process of establishing bourgeois rule. By then France had become, as Trotsky put it, the "most bourgeois of nations," a nation "pickled in the consciousness of its bourgeoisdom."[78] The educational system, with compulsory state-run elementary education and costly lycées, was now firmly set in place to preserve linguistic differences, and with such hierarchy secured, popular language was no longer viewed in a threatening light. Céline slipped through the system, circumventing the formal linguistic and ideological indoctrination while acquiring legitimate French all the same. He slipped through the system and, with the poet's license and artist's privilege, he spoke against it. For Trotsky, as for many others, it is from this rejection that Céline draws his force:

> Living creativeness cannot march ahead without repulsion away from official tradition, canonized ideas and feelings, images and expressions covered by the lacquer of use and wont. . . . The richer and more solid is the national cultural tradition, the more abrupt is the repulsion from it. Céline's power lies in that through supreme effort he divests himself of all canons, transgresses all conventions.[79]

Again we are reminded of Habermas' discussion of modernity – a revolt against the normalizing functions of tradition – and, more specifically, of surrealism, of its subversion of conventional language, of its dismissal of a static and dead vision of the world conveyed in a "pure and simple informational style."[80] Contrary to surrealism, however, *Journey* does not question the existence and importance of a central, monolithic subject. The first sentences of the novel make this clear: "It began like that. Me, I hadn't said a thing. Nothing." The immediate suggestion is of an antagonistic relationship between *moi*, the subject, and *ça* (that, referring to the forthcoming story). At the same time, with its first-person pronoun and the highly subjective account, Céline's work sets itself far apart from the clinical detachment and the scientific composition of naturalism. This novel may be a testimony, but it is certainly not a documentary. Popular language is not used for accuracy of representation. Its purpose is, on the one hand, to convey violence and anger: "Argot is a language of hatred." On the other hand, in a letter to Milton Hindus, Céline claimed that "to resensitize language, SUCH WAS MY AIM."[81] One must differentiate between the impact of a vocabulary, argot, which Céline used with much more discretion than Zola, and the oral element, with or without popular overtones, translated by the syntax and the punctuation. "Resensitize" also involves a liberation from a French ideology built on reasoning and logic. It does not depend on popular and oral elements alone, but on their deep fusion with the poetic, bound by fluid and dynamic interrelations. Popular language, however, did not lose its social connotations. It was seized upon and positively viewed in politically motivated readings of the extreme right and far left, two movements that sought the support of the working class as well as that of intellectuals. The communists heard a proletarian voice in *Journey*, while the fascists discerned a violence and a virility that partook in the working class's self-representation, with the parody of the belletristic style reinforcing both these impressions. One cannot say of *Journey*, as Leenhardt does of formally estranging works, that the novel is addressed to "academicians bristling with erudition."[82] *Journey* might have compelled a change of attitude in the reader. Certainly Céline claimed that it was designed to have power over more than just liberals: "I take everybody!"[83] The highly seductive text was meant to reduce the reader's critical distance – a particularly dangerous effect when it came to Céline's pamphlets. For if *Journey*, creating a space, a clearing of consciousness (which the political press immediately occupied), did not determine in what direction the reader would be moved, the anti-semitic pamphlets are explicit in their ideological content and aim. As Julia Kristeva points out in her discussion of these texts, Céline furiously assails freemasons, academics and the Catholic church, as well as Jews and the working class; one might view these reactions as the effects of an all-pervasive and indiscriminate hatred.[84] However, Céline's professed contempt for those whose language he elevates to poetic heights takes on a significance of its own. The style of *L'Assommoir* correlates with Zola's political positions: a humanitarian reformism ultimately aimed at controlling the working class. In *Journey*, the literary and aesthetic value accorded to popular language does not correlate with a sympathetic position *vis à vis* the working class, against which Céline issued venomous and unambiguous invectives:

> The wretched of the earth on one side, the bourgeois on the other, deep down they have one idea, to become rich or to remain it, it's one and the same thing, the outside equals the inside, same currency, same coin, within the hearts no difference at all.[85]

Céline attacks the working class for its lack of ideals, its materialism, and goes so far as to say that fascism is the true friend of the people, that Hitler did more than the Soviet Union for the proletariat.[86] Even though the pamphlets were intended and read as propaganda, and do not by any means partake in literary discourse, they come from a position of linguistic authority and would not have been noticed, probably not published, had Céline not gained fame and status with *Journey* and his second novel, *Death on the Installment Plan* (*Mort à crédit*). Furthermore, the pamphlets are written in a style similar to that of the novels. In these, popular language is relied upon to attack the social class from which it emerges; a style that was initially conceived of as literary, and that displayed potentially liberating and counterdiscursive qualities was used both by the author and critics towards directly repressive ends in the political field.

4 Queneau's *Zazie dans le métro*

When France entered industrial capitalism in the mid- to late-nineteenth century, most factories and businesses were owned and controlled by a single family and remained relatively small. After the First World War, new, larger and more efficient industries developed, sustained by the widespread use of electricity as an energy source, the automation of labor, and the efficiency of assembly lines. In the period that concerns us, the Fourth Republic (following the First World War and up to 1959), bourgeois capitalism gave way to monopoly capitalism. Fredric Jameson, in "Postmodernism and Consumer Society," outlines its particularities:

> non-Marxists and Marxists alike have come around to the general feeling that at some point following World War II a new kind of society began to emerge (variously described as postindustrial society, multinational capitalism, media society and so forth). New types of consumption; planned obsolescence; an ever more rapid rhythm of fashion and styling changes; the penetration of advertising, television and the media generally to a hitherto unparalleled degree throughout society; the replacement of the old tension between city and country, center and province, by the suburb and by universal standardization; the growth of the great network of superhighways and the arrival of automobile culture – these are some of the features which seem to mark a radical break with that older prewar society in which high modernism was still an underground force.[1]

Clearly, a change in society just as radical as the ones that separated *L'Assommoir* from *Journey* separate the latter from *Zazie in the Metro*. The country's economy became dominated by an international market in which the United States (already very much present in France with its contribution to post-war recovery) played an important role. American firms financed many French businesses that became part of a corporation under their control. Small and medium-sized enterprises disappeared through numerous mergers and sales to foreign investors. In large companies, the labor force is governed by "management" (*la direction*) – "management" does not necessarily own capital, but its authority is delegated by those who do. Consequently, as Alain Touraine points out in *The Post-Industrial Society*, the dominant class can no longer be defined by ownership alone: "If property was the criterion of membership in the former dominant classes, the new dominant class is defined by knowledge and a certain level of education."[2] (As we will see later, education remained as much a social barrier as earlier.) An astonishing recovery and expansion of the economy accompanied these structural changes: between 1929 and 1956, industrial production increased by 50 per cent. Along with the social welfare legislation (*allocations familiales, sécurité sociale*) that followed the Liberation, this growth contributed to improved standards of living, the benefits of which, according to Richard Hamilton, who in *Affluence and the French Worker in the Fourth Republic* cites a number of surveys that illustrate this phenomenon, were felt by the working class between 1952 and 1956. One of the surveys shows, for example, that of four "items" – property (house or land), car, radio, and domestic servant – 21 per cent of working-class families enjoyed two or more in 1956, as opposed to 12 per cent in 1952. Since this era of late capitalism, also called consumer society, needed consumers for its products, purchasing was made possible with long-term credit and low interest rates. In 1955, 5 per cent of unskilled and 8 per cent of skilled workers owned a bourgeois status symbol *par excellence*: "a fur coat for the wife."[3]

The new economic structure brought on a political change: a decrease in revolutionary concern among the working class. Even though the Communist Party won a steady 25 per cent of electoral votes throughout the Fourth Republic, membership dropped drastically: 786,000 in 1946; 500,000 in 1951; 203,000 in 1955. Similarly, the circulation of *L'Humanité* fell from 500,000 in 1946 to 179,000 in 1951. A number of surveys cited in *Affluence and the French Worker* suggest that, although many factors (such as international relations and events, the internal politics of the party, and so forth) surely contributed to the situation, the rise of living standards played an essential role in the demise of the Communist Party. For instance, in 1956, 30 per cent of those interviewed who owned two or more of the items mentioned above considered themselves very happy, as opposed to 15 per cent of those who owned only one; and only 25 per cent of the workers who owned a car had a favorable opinion of the Soviet Union, as opposed to 48 per cent of those who did not.[4] These figures suggest that extreme poverty among the working class could no longer be considered a catalyst for revolution. Moreover, Touraine remarks, with the availability of goods and the programed compulsion to consume, social classes came to be differentiated by quantitative rather than qualitative criteria: standards of living rather than lifestyle. Also contributing to the working class's loss of cultural specificity was a relative geographical integration brought on by the development of HLM (government-subsidized housing) in the cities, and, in the suburbs, the opportunity to imitate middle-class life in the new housing developments, the *villes nouvelles*. Another important factor, is, Jameson points out, the ever-increasing means and availability of transport and communication. Furthermore, leisure time became increasingly dominated by the homogenizing discourse of mass-media – radio, TV, magazines – which tended to erase the consciousness of social hierarchies and specific class practices. The outcome of these factors is that, as Touraine remarks:

> Whether it is material or non-material culture, socio-economic groups tend to define themselves more and more by their degree of participation in the activities and products of the culture, and less and less by possession of a subculture different from others.[5]

Not only did monopoly capitalism standardize social practices, it also created a new lower middle class. The increased need for technicians, for example, allowed for promotion within the workplace, and a move away from manual labor. Complex bureaucracies require large numbers of office workers, employees whose social status is markedly different from the one carried by members of the traditional working class – although their income remains low, their work involves no managerial duties whatsoever and requires little educational background. Another new class, the most removed from legitimate language and culture, was created during this period: a sub-proletariat of immigrants. A first influx of workers arrived from Italy and Poland after the heavy death toll of the First World War greatly weakened the French labor force. Their situation in the work place was, already, inferior to that of the French working class. The flow steadily expanded and, in an attempt to organize and control foreign labor, an Office National de l'Immigration was created in 1945. From the 1950s onwards, immigrants from North and Central Africa, came to France in ever-increasing numbers.

Their economic and social situation was far worse than that of workers from European countries. In terms of its social structure, then, post-industrial France is characterized by an abrupt schism separating French and foreign workers on the one hand, while, on the other, the traditional working class, the petite bourgeoisie, and the middle bourgeoisie experience diminishing cultural differences. Pierre Guiraud, in *Le Français populaire*, notes that this phenomenon extends to linguistic matters:

> We are witnessing an integration of social classes. Not that they have disappeared, nor that the signs that mark them are less significant or imperative, but they are less differentiated: today, the vast majority of the population eats, dresses, speaks in a more or less identical way. Hence, linguistic variations (and others), without having lost anything of their reality and importance, are inscribed in a narrower stylistic margin that renders their identification more difficult.[6]

In 1865, the preface to Larousse's *Grand Dictionnaire universel du XIXeme siècle* stated that its purpose was to reproduce the physiognomy of contemporary language which, cultivated and enriched by such writers as Hugo and Balzac, accommodated picturesque words and had become far less rigid and constrained than in the seventeenth century.[7] The *Larousse du XXeme siècle* (1928) defined itself as a "mirror of living French," that included new words, technical terms, and argot, for its aim was not to fix language but to follow its perpetual evolution.[8] Citing Henri Bauche, the *Grand Larousse encyclopédique* of 1960 bears witness to the accentuation of the phenomenon that had begun earlier in the century: "Popular French is changing and slowly penetrates the cultivated classes; it passes from the domestic quarters to the salon, from the factory workshop to the manager's office, from the department store salesgirl to the customer."[9] These statements point to a crucial factor for the period that concerns us, already noted by Guiraud and succinctly put by Désirat and Hordé in *La Langue française au 20eme siècle*: "The hierarchization of vocabulary was much more stable at the end of the nineteenth century than today."[10] The authors illustrate this fact with a striking example: a shift of terms from the category of *populaire* to *familier*. The word *bûcher* (to work hard), for example, was considered *populaire* in the *Larousse du XIXeme siècle*, then became *familier* in *Robert's Dictionnaire de la langue française* of 1960. *Boulonner*, also meaning "to work," did not appear in the *Larousse* of 1867, entered the *Robert* of 1960 under the label *populaire*, and moved to *familier* in the

Robert of 1985. *Chaparder* (to steal) shifted directly from argot in the *Larousse* of 1867 to *familier* in following dictionaries. Similarly, *chiper* (also meaning to steal) switched from *populaire* in 1867 to *familier* in later works.[11]

Even though different dictionaries may differ on the category under which a specific term, at any given time, should fall, the overall linguistic shift, during the period that concerns us, brings certain popular expressions closer to the mainstream. As was the case for cultural practices in general, language itself, Guiraud notes, cannot be relied upon to signify class differences as clearly as it did in the past:

> One will recognize that bourgeois speech, in its familiar usage, shares many traits with vulgar speech. It is notable, furthermore, that the difference between popular French and familiar French (in its cultivated usage) is reduced daily. This is due, on the one hand, to the fact that the popular classes now have access to culture through school and general information; it is a fact, on the other hand, that many bourgeois speakers adopt or accept many more vulgar forms (even slang).[12]

A number of factors account for this evolution: for instance, the development of the new petite bourgeoisie which, even though it strove for correctness, brought into its language expressions that belonged to the class from which it originated. New mass media such as TV and radio, as well as encouraging a loss of class consciousness, disseminated a discourse that, even if it maintained many characteristics of legitimate written French, also relied on forms typical of spoken language. Colloquial expressions often find a place in interviews, spontaneous testimonies and live shows, hence gaining a certain degree of currency and acceptability. Simultaneously, the inverse linguistic shift occurs as the working class is exposed to what remains, overall, the media's fairly correct language. A similar two-way influence is carried out by the educational system. Even if it does not render legitimate French accessible to all, and still ensures the reproduction of a cultural and political elite, the compulsory and free educational system erases certain characteristics of popular language. At the same time, it is likely that some other expressions used by working-class children are appropriated by their bourgeois classmates. This is not to suggest, however, that the educational system failed as a vital mechanism in the maintenance of class hierarchy. An obvious manifestation of this fact is that, until 1967, school was compulsory until the age of 14 only. In the mid 1960s, only 12 per cent of the children in their first year of secondary education came from the working class. In addition, the separation between the lycée, which trained students for the baccalauréat, and the CEG (Collège d'Enseignement Général) which dispensed technical rather than classical knowledge, reinforced social hierarchies. Access to universities was even more sharply restricted to the middle and ruling classes: only 1 per cent of their students was of proletarian background. As for the elitist Grandes Ecoles, they were firmly established bastions of the bourgeoisie. While linguistic differences declined slightly during the second half of the the twentieth century, they were not reduced enough to allow those who did not already benefit from acquiring legitimate linguistic capital through familiarization to gain and convert it into a scholarly value.

The social field, in the transitory period between the Second World War and De Gaulle's Fifth Republic, underwent drastic changes. The literary field, also, evolved during the twenty-three years that separate *Journey to the End of the Night* from *Zazie in the Metro*. Two very different and powerful trends influenced the novel: one is that of *littérature engagée*, an immediate consequence of the war (in contrast to the effect of the First World War, which produced Dadaism and surrealism); the other is the *nouveau roman*. In the first category, although their novels exhibit numerous differences, one might include, for simplicity's sake, the works of Camus (perhaps), Nizan, Malraux and Sartre; Sartre was its theorist. In *What Is Literature?* he highlights the impact of the German occupation on the literary circle to which he belonged:

> The destiny of our works themselves were bound to that of a France in danger. Our elders wrote for idle souls, but for the public which we, in turn were going to address, the vacation was over. It was composed of men of our sort who, like us, were expecting war and death. For these readers without leisure, occupied without respite with a single concern, there was only one fitting subject. It was about their war and their death that we had to write. Brutally reintegrated into history, we had no choice but to produce a literature of historicity.[13]

The outcome of a crisis, a reaction to the occupation, the notion of a "literature of historicity" persisted after the euphoria of the Liberation. The duty of writers continued to be to make history, to abandon a literature of "exis" and embrace one of "praxis." Circumstances had forced them to bring to light the relationship between being and doing, and answer such questions as: "*What* should one do, what ends should one chose *today*? And *how* is it to be done, by what means? What are the relationships between ends and means in a society based on violence?"[14] (Sartre's emphasis). Works concerned with such preoccupations, Sartre adds, cannot aim to please the readers but, rather, to irritate and to worry them: "Fruits of torments and questions, these works cannot be enjoyment for the reader, but, rather, questions and torments."[15] A major premise of this type of literature is that language should be used as a tool that unveils the world, with the intention of changing it: "The 'engaged' reader knows that words are action. He knows that to reveal is to change, and that one can reveal only by planning to change."[16] Style is only a secondary feature. Of utmost importance is the author's choice of what aspect of the world is to be unveiled and what changes are to be brought about. The unveiling, first implemented through linguistic means, must then translate into action: books are "the instruments of a possible action."[17] Unlike what had been the case for the earlier *romans à thèse* of Barrès, Drieu la Rochelle and Brasillach, the change would be towards the left. Equally vital to this literature of praxis is the reader's freedom which the author calls upon and requires to collaborate in the production of the work.

The type of novel called the *nouveau roman*, which came about in the 1950s, radically differs from the one outlined above. In fact, it developed in reaction to the use of instrumental and self-effacing language. The works of Sarraute, Butor and Robbe-Grillet can be included in this category; and Robbe-Grillet, with his *For a New Novel* (1965), can be considered its theorist. The aim was to present an alternative to those novels that, by repeating codes and conventions, naturalize a reality, represented as coherent, immutable, entirely given and easily readable:

> All the technical elements of the narrative – systematic use of the past tense and the third person, unconditional adoption of chronological development, linear plots, regular trajectory of the passions, impulse of each episode towards a conclusion, etc – everything tends to impose the image of a stable, coherent, continuous, unequivocal, entirely decipherable universe.[18]

By challenging and subverting these codes, the fundamental assertion of the new novel is that language, rather than mirror reality, should produce it. At the same time, what Stephen Heath in *The Nouveau Roman* outlines as its main features – the emphasis on the practice of writing, the dramatization of its possibilities and the *mise-en-scène* of forms – reveals the high self-consciousness of the text as text.[19] The primacy of the linguistic is unambiguously stated in *For a New Novel*:

> Let us, then, restore to the notion of commitment the only meaning it can have for us. Instead of being of a political nature, commitment is, for the writer, the full awareness of the present problems of his own language, the conviction of their extreme importance, the desire to solve them from within. Here, for him, is the only chance of remaining an artist and, doubtless too, by means of an obscure and remote consequence, of some day serving something – perhaps even the revolution.[20]

Clearly, the two trends that, one after the other, typified the post-Second World War literary field are diametrically opposed. In one case, language is considered a tool for effects outside of the literary field, whereas in the other, commitment is of a linguistic nature.

TOWARDS A NEW FRENCH

Even though linguistic issues are central to Queneau's theoretical and literary work, he does not address the specific aims of the *nouveau roman*, nor those of any other school. Early in his career (1924) he had been attracted to surrealism, although his involvement did not last long. He was not a pivotal member of the group, and according to Michel Leiris, lacked real faith in the movement: "Granted, [Queneau] was a conscientious and even scrupulous surrealist, but probably because of his personality more than because of real conviction."[21] Queneau broke with Breton in 1929, quite violently it seems, judging by his novel *Odile*, a scathing satire of surrealism, which he published some time later. With Bataille, he participated for a short while in the Cercle Communiste Démocratique, but, again according to Leiris, with no great enthusiasm: "As at the time of the Révolution Surréaliste, Queneau was rather withdrawn: it is probable that no group activity really suited him."[22] However, because of these literary connections and activities, Queneau was not unknown when he published his first novel, *Le Chiendent* (*The Bark-Tree*) (1933), and his position in the literary field was well established and carried a significant degree of authority by the time he wrote *Zazie in the Metro*. In 1938, he worked as a reader for Gallimard, and became Secrétaire Général in 1941. He also directed the literary programs of the RTF (Radio et Télévision Française) and was elected member of the Goncourt Academy in 1951. Even though, through his early involvement with surrealism, Queneau was familiar with drastically innovative literary practices it seems unlikely that he continued to advocate a primarily oppositional function in literature, when he was employed by the prestigious and powerful publishing firm – one can hardly imagine Breton as a reader for Gallimard. In fact, soon after his rejection of surrealism, Queneau turned to activities that were anathemas to the group's practices. For example, he resumed his studies in philosophy, attended Alexandre Kojève's classes on Hegel at the Ecole des Hautes Etudes, and later edited the lectures for Gallimard. This philosophical interest occurs in Queneau's own work. In 1952, Kojève published an article in *Critique* in which he discusses the presence of a concept drawn from his work on Hegel, the concept of wisdom, in three of Queneau's novels: *Pierrot mon ami* ("Pierrot my Friend"), *Le Dimanche de la vie* (*The Sunday of Life*) and *Loin de Rueil* ("Far from Rueil").

As well as being conversant in philosophy, Queneau was an adept mathematician, and wrote a number of articles on the subject: "La Dialectique des mathématiques chez Engels" ("The Dialectics of Mathematics in Engels"), published in *La Critique sociale* in 1938; "Sur la Cinématique des jeux" ("On the Cinematography of Games"), published in *Le Sphynx* in 1955; and "La Place des mathématiques dans la classification des sciences" ("The Place of Mathematics in the Classification of the Sciences"), published in *Cahiers du Sud* in 1948. Again, this interest extends to his literary work, which, as he tells us on p. 17 of "Technique du roman" ("Technique of the Novel"), is affected by numerical patterns: "It would have been unbearable for me to leave to chance the number of chapters in these novels . . . Hence *The Bark-Tree* is composed of 91 (7 times 3) sections, 91 being the sum of the first 13 numbers, and its 'sum' being 1." Other complex configurations involve the number of letters in Queneau's name, his date of birth, and so forth. Also subject to such systems, Queneau explains, are the number and organization of characters which could only be explained with complex diagrams. In the early 1950s he became a member of the Collège de Pataphysique, a term coined in 1911 by Alfred Jarry to mean the science of imaginary solutions. The group advocated pure speculation, of an often skeptical and parodic kind, with no intention to act or have effect outside of itself. It was during that period that Queneau undertook yet another scholarly project, as he began work as an editor of Gallimard's *Encyclopédie de la Pléiade*.

In an unusual work published in 1947, *Exercises in Style*, Queneau demonstrates a linguistic virtuosity that will be central to *Zazie*. Seizing on a variety of stylistic idiosyncrasies and mannerisms, he recounts a single anecdote in 99 different and clearly defined ways. For example:

Précieux
Un autobus à la livrée verte et blanche, blasonné d'un énigmatique S, vint recueillir du côté du Parc Monceau un petit lot favorisé de candidats voyageurs . . .

Philosophique
Le philosophe qui monte parfois dans l'inexistantialité futile et outilitaire d'un autobus S y peut apercevoir avec la lucidité de son oeil pinéal les apparences fugitives et décolorées d'une conscience . . .[23]

(Precious
A bus in green and white livery, emblazoned with an enigmatic S, came to gather from the neighbourhood of the Parc Monceau a small and favored batch of postulant passengers . . .

Philosophical
The philosopher who sometimes ascends in the futile and utilitarian inexistentiality of an S bus can perceive therein with the lucidity of his pineal eye the transitory and faced appearance of a profane consciousness . . .[24])

Many of the styles in *Exercises* are recognizable types and, with such a high concentration of their most salient features, tend towards parody, especially when the trivial subject matter (a bus ride) is treated in an elevated register; others are the outcome of Queneau's imagination, such as the "Arc-en-Ciel" ("Rainbow") which includes as many colors as possible, or the "Auditif" ("Auditory") rendered through sounds: "Coinquant et pétaradant, l'S vint crisser le long du trottoir silencieux" (Quacking and letting off, the S came rasping to a halt alongside the silent pavement). The passage called "Vulgaire," with its contractions and colloquial expressions, is the one that comes closest to the representation of popular language which occurs, to varying degrees, in many of Queneau's earlier novels and which culminates in *Zazie*. In *The Bark-Tree*, for example, it occurs primarily in characters' utterances: "Un autobus lui a passé sur le corps à ce pauv" Meussieu . . . Ah alors non, sûr qu'il n'a pas eu vot' chance, Meussieu? Messieu?" (A bus ran over that poor man . . . But no, sure that he didn't have your luck, Sir, Sir?) What is particular to Queneau, in this example and elsewhere in his work, is not only the transcription of popular diction (the dropping of final letters in pauv" and vot") but also a spelling of *Monsieur* that is closer to the manner in which it is pronounced. In the narrative, colloquial expressions such as *le bouffer* (grub), *le gosse* (the kid), *pioncer* (to sleep) are present, but only occasionally. Queneau also provides a large amount of theoretical material concerning this aspect of his stylistic choice in the form of a series of articles and interviews published in 1950 as a volume entitled "Sticks, Numbers and Letters" (*Bâtons, chiffres et lettres*).[25]

In this work, the foundation of Queneau's arguments on linguistic issues is that the gap between spoken and written language has reached extreme proportions, and that written French, by not reflecting the reality of oral discourse, has become stilted. He describes this vast difference in emphatic terms: the distance between oral discourse and legitimate, written French, which he calls "Voltaire's French" is as great as the distance which separates the latter from Latin. Both are antiquated, and do not reflect any existing linguistic practice. Illustrating his point with an abbreviated history of the now "dead" French language, a language that emerged during the Renaissance, became fixed in the seventeenth century, and which romanticism only slightly affected, Queneau claims, "one must elaborate a new language" (p. 93). This language, that does not yet exist, but "that is asking to be born," he calls neo-French. Obsolete and belletristic forms such as the imperfect subjunctive and the *passé simple* would disappear. The future tense would be replaced by the present, and interrogative forms would no longer be expressed with inversions. The implementation of neo-French necessitates drastic changes on three levels: vocabulary, syntax and orthography. Concerning the lexical issue, Queneau has little to say, except that argot should be used only sparingly, for, however rich a source of linguistic innovation, it evolves so rapidly that it cannot seriously be relied upon – a somewhat paradoxical statement since one of the aims of neo-French is to overcome the static nature of legitimate French. Concerning the new syntax, he defers to Céline: "As for the second point, the reform or revolution has been achieved: see Céline" (p. 19). He recognizes that *Journey* has a definite influence on his own work, and considers that novel to be "the first important book where, for the first time, an oral style moves ahead (and with few *Goncourdises*) from the first to the last page" [*Goncourdises* are signs of high literary *écriture artiste*] (p. 17). Particularly important is the fact that "spoken French is not limited to the dialogue, but also enters the narrative" (p. 55). Of utmost importance to Queneau is the third area, orthography. It is there that he advocates the most complete change, for he considers French spelling to be "a system of chaotic, absurd and arbitrary rules, an invention of the first printers to make their trade difficult and hence to create for themselves corporate privileges" (p. 79).

A drastic simplification of the spelling system is necessary for two reasons, Queneau explains. The first is of a practical order. School children waste too much time learning the intricate rules and exceptions to the rules as they are forced to memorize and use an unnecessarily complex system: "One wonders why they do not force the children to also learn feudal law, heraldry and falconry" (p. 78). The second point is more theoretical: it is in the disparity between the sound of the word and the manner in which it is transcribed that Queneau locates the greatest divergence between written and spoken language:

> Current orthography is the trap, the stumbling block, that hinders a closer correspondence between the two: A spelling reform, or rather the adoption of a new spelling is imperative, because it will demonstrate an essential point: the pre-eminence of the oral over the written. (p. 25)

To attain this goal, he proposes a system whereby a precise and invariable phonetic value is given to each letter, which is always pronounced in the same way, whatever its position in the word might be, and whatever letters precede and follow it. He illustrates the result with the following (untranslatable) lines:

> Avrédir, sémêm maran. Jérlu toudsuit lé kat lign sidsu, jépapu manpéché de mmaré. Mézifobyindir, sé un pur kestion dabitud. On népa zabitué, sétou. Unfoua kon sra zabitué saira tousel. (p. 22)

This example shows that, in some instances, the boundaries of the word as they are traditionally known are retained: *lé kat lign* for *les quatres lignes* (the four lines), *sé un pur* for *c'est une pure* (it's a pure) in others they are not: *avrédir* for *à vrai dire* (to tell the truth), *mézifobyindir* for *mais il faut bien dire* (but it's quite necessary to say). The criteria that govern this aspect of his transcription are unclear, for the rhythm of oral speech would allow *lékatlign*. In these articles, Queneau also answers the objections that such a reform would be likely to provoke. For instance, some people might argue that correct spelling indicates the etymology of the word and thus provides semantic information. But this reasoning is not always reliable, Queneau remarks, for *poids* (weight) originates from the latin *pensum*, in which there is no *d*; *dompter* (to tame) from *dominare*, in which there is no *p*; *legs* from *lais* (legacy) in which there is no *g*. Another objection could be that differences in spelling indicate different significations (*saut, sceau, sot, seau* – all pronounced the same, but spelled differently and meaning different things) and that a more systematic orthography would erase such information. In that case, asks Queneau, shouldn't there be different spellings attached to each meaning of *son* (which can mean *his*, *sound* or *bran*) for example. Citing the strong reactions that the possibility of spelling reforms have already brought on, Queneau interprets these very negative reactions as a fear of changing deeply rooted habits, and as an indication of how strongly the respect for the authority of legitimate written language is rooted:

> Concerning this reform, a "faithful reader" of the *Figaro Littéraire* spoke of "national danger, of insanity, of ethnic sabotage." (p. 75)

In one of the readers' letters mentioned above, a music professor from Nantes declared that if one wrote *chevaus* instead of *chevaux*, one would contribute to the progressive stultification of the human race. More recently, an editor wrote in the *Figaro Littéraire*: "Spelling mistakes do not make me laugh, they make me cry" (p. 91).

Indeed, French orthography, codified and officialized by the Académie Française, has not changed since the nineteenth century, and is antiquated. As Désirat and Hordé point out, spelling was not, and is not, considered a mere technique associated to the language, but an integral part of it, and is held to reflect not the acquisition of a specific skill, but the individual's general culture.[26] A government memo on the matter (1960) states that a language is known "to the extent that one knows how to spell it correctly." Poor spelling, the memo adds, is not only an immediate criterion for failure in all examinations, it is also an obstacle to employment, however unrelated the work to the practice of writing: "If one does not judge a worker on his writing, one cannot help but be poorly impressed by the incorrect spelling on his letter of application."[27] Queneau's proposed reform, although by far the most drastic, was not the only one. Earlier in the century (1906 and 1926), Ferdinand Brunot and Alfred Dauzat had suggested simplifications. In both cases, one of the principal arguments was that this would facilitate the propagation of French in the colonies. Dauzat argued:

What the reformers have wanted and still want is that the work of purification carried out by the Académie Française since its foundation be continued, that all the necessary complications and bizarre aspects of our orthography be eliminated, along with the parasitical letters that the "great rhetoricians" and the grammarians of the Renaissance had senselessly added to many words . . . Does the Frenchman not realize that these blemishes do not facilitate the propagation of the French language overseas?[28]

Neither of the two proposals was accepted; and, however minor the orthographic alterations suggested by the grammarians Pernot and Bruneau in 1945 as part of a proposal to ameliorate the educational system (simplification of double consonants, suppression of the final x and of Greek letters), these were not adopted either. In 1961, a new argument surfaced: the Commission Beslais expressed concern that French would lose its status as an "international" language of science, and be replaced by one whose spelling was much simpler: "A civilization where science plays a dominant role finds a spelling so complex intolerable."[29] Once again, the attempt failed, and, as in all the other cases, a vocal opposition reacted: French orthography was a dearly held habit, participated in the beauty of the language, was essential to the great literary works of the past, and so forth. Perhaps the underlying concern was expressed by M. Boulenger in 1906: "The necessity for France to remain inimitable is of far greater concern than whether department store salesmen know how to spell correctly or not."[30]

Aside from the practical importance of his orthographic reforms, Queneau was interested in their literary consequence. He advocated:

the creation of a new language, new much more because of its syntax than its vocabulary, new also because of its aspect, a language that, recovering its musical and oral nature, would soon become a poetic language, and the abundant and lively substance of a new literature. (p. 26)

There are historical precedents, Queneau notes, to the direct relationship between a reformed language and a new, vigorous literary production. A new language requires new thoughts and new thoughts require a new language: Dante's writing was dependent upon his use of Italian, it was the neo-French of the Renaissance that produced "the feeling of freedom in Rabelais and Voltaire." The literary use of neo-French, however, should not be reduced to a simple transcription of what Queneau calls "concierge language":

> I specify that I do not mean that literature and poetry must become a simple orthography of what is scornfully known as "concierge language," which in fact is only that of academicians with a few little incorrections. The aim is . . . to give a style to spoken language. We may then witness the birth of a new literature.(p. 40)

As well as stressing that a literary form should shape the raw material of spoken discourse, Queneau denies the existence of a populist impulse in his proposals. He points out that neo-French would gain legitimacy only if it were used in texts that usually call for legitimate French, and should therefore not be tied to a popular subject matter. A philosophical dissertation in neo-French would legitimate this language much more than a popular romance, he explained.

Throughout the essays in "Sticks, Numbers and Letters," it appears that it is not so much the actual institution of legitimate French and its elitist or canonical aspects that Queneau criticizes, but, rather, their inadequate manifestations. As he himself acknowledges, his purpose is far less oppositional than Céline's: "In any case, one must disengage the new French from its past shell. Not that it is bad in itself (as Céline thinks) but they are two realities that have become absolutely different" (p. 20). And, if Queneau feels no particular respect for legitimate language, he does not exalt the popular either:

> I have no respect, or special feelings for the popular, real "life," etc. . . . But precisely because I see nothing truly sacred in our contemporary French, I also see no reason not to elevate popular language to the dignity of a written language, source of a new literature, of a new poetry. (p. 24)

In fact, Queneau unambiguously places the motivations behind his literary representation of popular language outside the social or political fields: "If I try to coordinate the various elements that finally organized themselves in a guiding principle, I am well aware that it is the linguistic principle, exposed in linguistic terms that first fascinated me" (p. 12).

It is through a scholarly work, *Le Langage*, published in 1923 by a professor at the University of Paris, Joseph Vendryes, that Queneau says he became acquainted with linguistic issues, often referring to, and quoting, the text at great length. *Le Langage* is the work of a philologist who approaches his subject in a fairly traditional manner, dividing the first three chapters into considerations on phonetics, grammar and vocabulary. The study tends towards socio-linguistics

Queneau's Zazie dans le métro 167

in that Vendryes does not consider language as an independent system governed by the inner necessity of its laws. Even though he makes no reference to the specific influence of class on linguistic production and practice, he recognizes the play of social forces and the effect of history on language, emphasizing its contingent character, illustrating its development and diversification. Many of Queneau's arguments on orthography and on the difference between spoken and written French appear in this work. For example:

> The gap between written and spoken language is becoming greater and greater. Neither syntax nor vocabulary are the same. Even the morphology is different: the definite past, the imperfect subjunctive are no longer used in spoken language. Above all, the difference in vocabulary is there, blatant, for all to see.[31]

There is, undoubtedly, a very scholarly, bookish aspect to Queneau's interests and concerns. He appears to have been a well-rounded man of letters, which was certainly not the case for either Zola or Céline. His social origin was bourgeois – "I am bourgeois. In fact my childhood was very, very bourgeois." (p. 55) – and he remained settled in the class into which he was born. His education, also, was very conventional (a degree in philosophy) and it is not surprising that, as a child, his acquaintance with popular language was not first hand. It is in written form that he first came to know it: in comic strips (*Les Pieds nickelés*) or satirical newspapers (*Le Canard enchaîné*). Apart from that, he says, "the only argot I knew was that of high school."

PARODIES AND IRONIES

> Doukipudonktan, se demanda Gabriel excédé. Pas possible, ils se nettoient jamais. Dans le journal, on dit qu'il y a pas onze pour cent des appartements à Paris qui ont des salles de bains, ça m'étonne pas, mais on peut se laver sans. Tous ceux là qui m'entourent, ils doivent pas faire de grands efforts. D'un autre côté, c'est tout de même pas un choix parmi les plus crasseux de Paris. Y a pas de raison. C'est le hasard qui les a réunis. On peut pas supposer que les gens qu'attendent à la gare d'Austerlitz sentent plus mauvais que ceux qu'attendent à la gare de Lyon. Non, vraiment, y a pas de raison. Tout de même quelle odeur.
>
> Gabriel extirpa de sa manche une pochette de soie couleur mauve et s'en tamponna le tarin.

168 *Political Stylistics*

– Qu'est-ce qui pue comme ça? dit une bonne femme à haute voix.

Elle pensait pas à elle en disant ça, elle était pas égoïste, elle voulait parler du parfum qui émanait de ce meussieu.

– Ça, ptite mère, répondit Gabriel qui avait de la vitesse dans la répartie, c'est Barbouze, un parfum de chez Fior.³²

(Howcanaystinksotho, wondered Gabriel, exasperated. Ts incredible, they never clean themselves. It says in the paper that not eleven percent of the flats in Paris have bathrooms, doesn't surprise me, but you can wash without. They can't make much of an effort, all this lot around me. On the other hand, it's not as if they've been specially picked from the dosses of Paris. Zno reason. They're only here by accident. You really can't assume that people who meet people at the Gare d'Austerlitz smell worse than people who meet people at the Gare de Lyon. No really, zno reason. All the same, what a smell.

Gabriel extirpated from his sleeve a mauve silk handkerchief and dabbed his boko with it.

"What on earth's that stench?" said a good lady out loud.

She wasn't thinking about herself when she said that, she wasn't so self-centred, she was referring to the perfume that emanated from the meussieu.

"That, dearie," replied Gabriel, who was never at a loss when it came to repartee, "is Barbouze, a perfume from the House of Fior."³³)

At the outset of the the novel's opening paragraph, the reader is confronted with an unexpected element, *Doukipudonktan* (Howcanaystinksotho), which has the appearance of a single word, and is first perceived as such, but arouses no immediate visual recognition. One might assume, initially, that it refers to the unfamiliar name of a person or a place, but the rest of the sentence indicates that it must carry a more complex meaning, so as to complete that of *se demanda Gabriel excédé* (wondered Gabriel, exasperated). The reader, having realized this, must return to the puzzling "word" again, but the eye still does not recognize it. Only when read aloud, or imagined to be read aloud, only when it is phonetically deciphered does it become familiar; the semantic units can be separated in one's mind, the expression makes sense and is recognized as the transcription of *D'où qu'ils puent donc tant* (How can they stink so though). Here, Queneau puts into practice some of the orthographic reforms that he advocated in "Sticks, Numbers and Letters": a type of spelling where silent letters are erased, where boundaries between words disappear or are redistributed, and which would hence correlate much more closely with the sounds that we hear. However, this transformation affects only a short segment of the sentence, and all the new conventions that he has suggested are not respected: the *qu* should be replaced by a *c* (always pronounced in the same way, whether followed by an *i* or not).

Zazie opens with a strong stylistic effect that not only attracts but also requires the reader's attention and holds it for some time: a cryptic form conveying a simplistic message. The strange appearance of the signifier, *Doukipudonktan*, is more likely to draw the reader's attention to its form rather than to its signified. He or she is not at first aware of the words' interrelationship, of what they signify globally or of the popular elements in the expression. The emphasis is on the signifier as it loses its usual accessibility and distances itself from the signified, in a situation that is not dissimilar from one which Jameson describes in "Postmodernism and Consumer Society."

> Again, in normal speech, we try to see through the materiality of words (their strange sounds and printed appearance, my voice timbre and peculiar accent, and so forth) towards their meaning. As meaning is lost, the materiality of words become obsessive, as is the case when children repeat a word over and over again until its sense is lost and it becomes an incomprehensible incantation.[34]

After the initial puzzlement, the cryptic form provokes laughter: a familiar content appears in an unfamiliar form. In *L'Assommoir*, a scene of violent action with burlesque overtones distracted from and perhaps justified the introduction of popular language. Here, even though it is of a primarily linguistic and formal, rather than situational kind, humor accompanies its first occurrence also. In all likelihood, the reader's attention is held by the phonetic representation and the comic effect of *Doukipudonktan*, rather than by the colloquialism of the redundant *que*, the verb *puer*, and the interrogative *donc tant?* However, if the graphic and comic effects distract from the presence of popular language, it is playfully rather than strategically so, for it immediately reappears, undisguised, in the following lines. There, the syntactical markers are of a common sort, already found in the writing of Zola and Céline, and discussed at some length in the preceding chapter: *ne* is systematically dropped in all instances of the negative forms: *ils se nettoient jamais* (they never clean themselves), *ils doivent pas faire de grands efforts* (they can't make much of an effort), *c'est tout de même pas un choix* (it's not as if they've been specially picked), and so forth. There are a number of omissions – of verbs in *Pas possible* (Ts incredible), *tout de même quelle odeur* (All the same, what a smell), and of subject in *non, vraiment, y a pas de raison* (No really, zno reason) –, the usual contractions (*ça, y a pas, qu'attendent*), the use of the pronoun *on* and, on a lexical level, a number of colloquial expressions. The stylistic effects produced here are not dissimilar from the ones in Gervaise's soliloquy, but the impression conveyed is entirely different: this light-hearted passage provokes laughter or, at least, amusement.

Gabriel's internal monologue, as he awaits Zazie, the young girl whose first visit to the capital is recounted in the novel, is an investigation of the problem posed at the outset of the paragraph – who stinks? It consists of speculations, of a number of hypotheses that are put forward then rejected. As he seeks explanations for the surrounding smell, Gabriel first has recourse to information he has read in the press: the lack of bathrooms in Paris. He judges this argument to be inconclusive, however, since a bathroom is not absolutely necessary to wash oneself. Those around him might not have one, but they certainly do not use the kitchen sink either. But people without bathrooms must make up only a small percentage of the Parisian population, and Gabriel finds no rational explanation as to why those unfortunate few are concentrated at the Gare d'Austerlitz (other than, perhaps, that all Parisians stink). With its careful and serious consideration and refutation of various hypotheses, this passage can be viewed as a parody of the form of a high-flown argumentation – but the form only, for the problem investigated, the question asked and the knowledge involved match the language in which it is expressed. As well as the localized comic effect of the phonetic transcription, a broader effect is present here, brought on by the discrepancy between, on the one hand, subject matter and language, both low, and the serious-minded form of argumentation on the other.

A number of spoken markers occur in the narrative that follows the expression of Gabriel's thoughts: on a lexical level the phonetic transcription *meussieu*, on a syntactical level the lack of *ne* in *elle pensait pas* (she wasn't thinking), *elle était pas* (she wasn't). One must note, however, the presence of the *passé simple* in *se demanda, extirpa*, and the precious verb reported in indirect style, *émanait*. Also precious is the expression *soie couleur mauve* (literally: silk of a mauve color) rather than the more ordinary *soie mauve* (mauve silk). There is, in *Zazie*, a mixing of well-defined styles which are not, as in *L'Assommoir*, simply juxtaposed in long passages with the

Queneau's Zazie dans le métro 171

clear domination of one over the other, or, as in *Journey*, deeply hybridized. As we will see later, their relationship can be described as one of multiple ironizations that result in a leveling of hierarchies, a creation of equivalences. In fact, before encountering the first line of the novel, some readers might have noticed its epigram, three Greek words allegedly by Aristotle.[35] Their meaning can be translated as "the one who fabricated it then abolished it" (which, as we will see later, is not without significance), yet it is unlikely that all readers will decipher this immediately. The juxtaposition of the epigram and of *Doukipudonktan* points to a clash between high and low registers. At the same time, an equivalence is established, for both forms look puzzling at first, their meaning is initially concealed. Such juxtapositions and suggestions of equivalences are present throughout the novel, not only linguistically but also in broader terms. For example, what stinks for Gabriel are unwashed bodies, whereas for the good lady, it is "Barbouze, a perfume from the House of Fior." *Fior* is a play on *Dior*, and *Barbouze* is derived from *barbe* (beard), with the popular suffix *-ouze* attached; it also evokes the unfragrant *bouse* (cowshit). Important distinctions are erased later when the Caserne de Reuilly is mistaken for the Invalides, when the Tribunal du Commerce is thought to be the Sainte-Chapelle, and the process extends to several other categories that are brought into equivalence or whose boundaries are eroded. The gender of Marceline, Gabriel's wife, becomes questionable when her name, in the last chapter, suddenly changes to Marcel. Gabriel, at night, slips into a tutu, becomes a dancer and, as someone judiciously remarks: "En tout cas, vous allez pas nier que c'est parce que la mère vous considère comme une tante qu'elle vous a confié l'enfant" (p. 85) (So that's the reason, because you're queer, that the mother asked you to look after this child (p. 7)). One might add that Gabriel, with his high-class perfume and his *pochette de soie couleur mauve*, hardly embodies the stereotypical proletarian. As further references will show, Queneau does not seriously represent the specificity of the working class, and this can be considered as the reflection of a social reality of the time: the erosion of class differences in post-industrial society. Furthermore, many references in *Zazie* point to the characters' eagerness as consumers, not only of food and drink, as in *L'Assommoir*, but of chic, up-market items and American imports. There are, of course, Zazie's precious *bloudjinzes* (phonetic spelling of blue jeans) Gabriel's crocodile manicure set ("It's hard wearing and smart") and Turandot's enthusiasm for American washing machines:

– Vous devriez donner votre linge aux trucs automatiques américains, dit Turandot à Marceline, ça vous ferait du travail en moins, c'est comme ça que je fais moi. (p. 52)

(– You ought to take your laundry to those automatic American whatsits, says Turandot to Marceline, it'd make less work for you, that's what I do. (p. 45))

Another feature of post-industrial society that is reflected in the text is the breakdown of the city/country antinomy, brought on by the expansion of suburbs and the creation of housing developments. Marceline assumes that Zazie's provincialism means that she is accustomed to the primitivism of *une table, une cuvette, un broc* (a table, a wash-basin, a jug). But, on the contrary, *Elle pratiquait le bidet fixe vissé dans le plancher et connaissait, pour en avoir usé, mainte autre merveille de l'art sanitaire* (She was used to a proper bidet screwed on the floor and knew, from experience, many other marvels of sanitary art). We are also told that Gabriel's house includes a *salon-salle à manger* (graphically transcribed by Queneau as a *salonsalamanger* – livingroomdiningroom). This hybrid notion, where the idea of a bourgeois, non-essential *salon* is attached to a functional *salle à manger* indicates a place that is thus designed to serve, by virtue of its new name, more than its pedestrian function: somewhere to eat. The *salon-salle à manger* is indeed a status symbol for those with certain class pretensions, those who cannot afford the luxury of a separate room as a *salon* but want to live with it as a concept nevertheless. Clearly a sign by which members of the working class or petite bourgeoisie seek to upgrade their status, it illustrates yet another feature of post-industrial society: the leveling of social practices.

An analysis of the following passage, still from the first chapter, provides further information on the stylistic characteristics of the text. These traits will pertain not only to this chapter, but to the entire work, and examples found elsewhere in the text will illustrate points highlighted here. For, unlike the style of *L'Assommoir* which evolves throughout the novel (and where spoken markers are very gradually introduced) or that of *Journey* which is in constant motion, a main characteristic of Queneau's work is that the style is set at the very beginning. The effects found in the first chapter regularly reappear throughout the others, without intensification or lessening, or a change in emphasis. The internal norm of the text is constructed at the outset and not challenged later, as it is by passages in *écriture artiste* in Zola's work and by the unexpected resurgence and hybridization of the poetic and the popular in that of Céline. Here, I have emphasized the lexical and graphic spoken markers:

– Tonton, qu'elle crie, on prend le métro?
– Non.
– Comment ça, non?
Elle s'est arrêtée. Gabriel *stoppe* également, se retourne, pose la valoche et se met à *espliquer*.
– Bin oui: non. Aujourd'hui, pas moyen. Y a grève.
– Y a grève?
– *Bin oui, y a grève*. Le métro, ce moyen de transport éminemment parisien, s'est endormi sous terre, car les employés aux pinces perforantes ont cessé tout travail.
– Ah *les salauds*, s'écrie Zazie, ah les *vaches*. Me faire ça à moi.
– Y a pas qu'à toi qu'ils font ça, dit Gabriel parfaitement objectif.
– *Jm'en fous. N'empêche que* c'est à moi que ça arrive, moi qu'étais si heureuse, si contente et tout de m'*aller voiturer* dans *lmétro. Sacrebleu, merde* alors.
– Faut te faire une raison, dit Gabriel dont les propos se nuançaient parfois d'un thomisme légèrement kantien.
Et, passant sur le plan de la cosubjectivité, il ajouta:
– Et puis faut se grouiller: Charles attend. (pp. 13–14)

("Unkoo," she yells, "are we going by metro?"
"No."
"What d'you mean, no?"
She has come to a full stop. Gabriel likewise halts, turns round, puts the suitcase down and starts to iksplain:
"Well yes: no. Today, can't be done. Za strike."
"Za strike?"
"Well yes: za strike. The metro, that eminently parisian means of transport, has fallen asleep under the ground, for the employees with their perforating punches have ceased to work."
"Oo the bastards," cries Zazie, "oo the swine. To do that to me."
"Snot only you they're doing it to," says Gabriel, perfectly objective.
"Don't give a damn. Doesn't alter the fact that it's happening to me, me that was so happy, so pleased and everything to be going to be conveyed by the metro. Blast, bloody hell."
"Have to make the best of it, have to be reasonable," said Gabriel whose remarks were tinged with a slightly Kantian Thomism.
And, passing on to the level of cosubjectivity, he added:

"And anyway we must get a move on. My time and patience may be inexhaustible, but Charley's aren't." (p. 15))

In his representation of popular language, Queneau relies far less on syntactical markers than does Céline. Those present here are standard forms: the *rappel* (*moi qu'étais*) (me that was), the omission of the subject in *faut te faire une raison* (have to make the best of it), the incomplete sentence *Me faire ça à moi* (to do that to me), the contractions *y a grève* (za strike), *j'men fous* (don't give a damn). On a lexical level the text displays expressions such as *voiturer* (to be conveyed), *se grouiller* (to get a move on), and a string of insults and curses in the utterances. In the narrative, there is the argot *valoche* (suitcase) and the popular anglicism *stopper*. Unlike what was the case for *L'Assommoir*, these words are not taken from an argot dictionary: most of the forty non-legitimate expressions in the first chapter of *Zazie*, more or less equally distributed between the characters' utterances and the narrative, can be found in a conventional dictionary under a number of different labels.

The passage displays, however, a number of forms that are specific to Queneau's writing and that, again, translate his concern with orthography, a concern directed at the appearance rather than at the underlying structure of language. The type of contraction present in *y a grève* and *j'men fous* occurs in Queneau's earlier novels, and in those of other writers who attempt to represent characters' utterances with a certain degree of veracity. But there are slightly more unusual forms, such as *lmétro*, where the *e* in the article or pronoun is dropped without being replaced by an apostrophe, according to Queneau's statement in his essays: "The apostrophe remains an attachment to the past, a souvenir that must be left to linguists or philologists" (p. 17). Similar contractions appear throughout the chapter and novel, based either on the elision of *e* (*ptite, jveux*) or of a vowel (*vla*). Two sounds are dropped in *isra* (for *il sera*), *iadessa* (for *il ya de ça*) and *issméfie* (for *il se méfie*). The two latter forms display a double *s*, which is redundant according to the principles put forth in "Sticks, Numbers and Letters". As the letter *k* in the previous examples, they add an incongruous aspect to the transcriptions; this estranging effect is also quite obvious in the double *t* of *autt chose, vott dame*, and *ptètt*. In *Gabriel stoppe également, se retourne, pose la valoche et se met à espliquer*, the *x* of *expliquer* is replaced by an *s*, indicating not only a rapid, familiar pronunciation, but also a more specifically popular one. The same transformation, also in the narrative, is present in *Aussitôt Zazie esprime son désir* (p. 21) and *T'as beau vouloir dit*

Gabriel avec une patience estrême, tu vois bien qu'y en a pas (p. 22). Similarly, the *b* of *obstiné* is dropped in "C'est que c'est un *ostiné*, Charles, malgré tout" (p. 17).

These examples show that only a few of Queneau's graphic representations transcribe spoken and popular diction without tending towards estrangement as well: those based on elision alone, such as *ptite*, *ostiné*: on popular pronunciation alone, such as *espliquer*, or on elision and concatenation, such as *jveux*, *lmétro*. The concatenation of two words and elision of two phonemes in *isra* already tends towards the unfamiliar, and so do forms like *dacor* that rely on concatenation and phonetic transcription. Even more estranging are the representations based on elision, phonetic transcription and concatenation, which, quite often, also display unnecessary presence of certain letters (double consonants, k), resulting in the most cryptic appearance: *iadessa*, *skeutadittaleur* (wottusaidjusnow), *Doukipudonktan* (Howcanaystinksotho). After the initial encounter with *Doukipudonktan* it is likely that the presence of similar phonetic transcriptions still surprise the readers, but no longer provoke disorientation – the readers know what they are confronted with, and how to make sense of the strange word. Such forms appear once or twice in each chapter, and although they are usually restricted to the characters' utterances, they sometimes find a place in the narrative also:

> Elle s'arrêta pile devant un achalandage de surplus. Du coup, a boujplu. A boujpludutou. Le type freine sec, juste derrière elle. (p. 62)
>
> (She stopped dead in front of a display of surplus. What a sight; she doesn't budge. She doesn't budget all. The chap steps on his brakes, just behind her.(p. 53))

Here, in *A boujpludutou* (*elle ne bouge plus du tout*) and *a boujpu*, the *ne* is dropped as is often the case in popular diction; furthermore, *elle* is pronounced and written *a*, initially read as the familiar preposition. Overall, there seems to be no pattern as to which expressions are represented in this manner, nor as to where they occur in the novel, and, as we have seen, many shorter phonetic transcriptions are repeated in different forms at various places in the text. For example, *autre chose* is, on one occasion, transcribed as *ott chose*, on another as *ottchose*; *quelque chose* appears as *quèchose* or *kèchose*; *d'accord* can be *dacor* or *dakor*. On the same page, *voulu me faucher* is reduced to two components (*voulu mfaucher*) or one (*voulumfaucher*). Obviously, there is a move, in *Zazie*, towards free linguistic play and away from the issue of practicality that Queneau, in his theoretical articles, stresses to justify his spelling reforms. The occasional transcriptions, which are isolated enough to remain surprising, vary in an unsystematic manner, do not reflect an increased orthographic rationality and logic, or an increased ease of reading. Should the aim of the novel have been to propagate the use of neo-French and its simplified orthography, Queneau would have been far more consistent in his adhesion to the system that he suggested. Furthermore, his reliance on unnecessary double consonants (*ottchose*, *skeutadittaleur*) and his predilection for a relatively unusual letter in French, *k*, which appears in *Doukipudonktan* and in several other forms like *skalibre*, *a kimieumieu*, and *skeutadittaleur* render the transcriptions even more unfamiliar and disorienting, and work, in fact, in the opposite direction: towards estrangement. If the incongruous aspect of these forms draws attention away from the issue of the presence of popular language in the novel, the transcriptions, by emphasizing to the point of apparent absurdity the particularities of spoken/popular diction (elision, contraction, concatenation), also perform a parodic function. Rather than bridging a gap between such diction and written discourse, they emphasize, with a comic effect, the specificity of spoken French.

The analysis of the opening passage highlighted the presence of words that were non-conventional, either in origin and/or appearance. This feature was present in the paragraph analyzed above in which the other feature discussed earlier, the co-presence of different categories, stylistic or otherwise, also appears. Now, to illustrate the third major characteristic of *Zazie* (abrupt stylistic ruptures, ironies and parodies) I have emphasized the groups of sentences that stand out from the same second passage:

– Tonton, qu'elle crie, on prend le métro?
– Non.
– Comment ça, non?

Elle s'est arrêtée. Gabriel stoppe également, se retourne, pose la valoche et se met à espliquer.

– Bin oui: non. Aujourd'hui, pas moyen. Y a grève.
– Y a grève?
– Bin oui, y a grève. *Le métro, ce moyen de transport éminemment parisien, s'est endormi sous terre, car les employés aux pinces perforantes ont cessé tout travail.*
– Ah! les salauds, s'écrie Zazie, ah les vaches. Me faire ça à moi.

Queneau's Zazie dans le métro   177

– Y a pas qu'à toi qu'ils font ça, dit Gabriel parfaitement objectif.
– Jm'en fous. N'empêche que c'est à moi que ça arrive, moi qu'étais si heureuse, si contente et tout de m'aller voiturer dans le métro. Sacrebleu, merde alors.
– Faut te faire une raison, dit Gabriel *dont les propos se nuançaient parfois d'un thomisme légèrement kantien.*
Et, passant sur le plan de la cosubjectivité, il ajouta:
– Et puis faut se grouiller: Charles attend. (pp.13–14)

("Unkoo," she yells, "are we going by metro?"
"No."
"What d'you mean, no?"
She has come to a full stop. Gabriel likewise halts, turns round, puts the suitcase down and starts to iksplain:
"Well yes: no. Today, can't be done. Za strike."
"Za strike?"
"Well yes: za strike. *The metro, that eminently parisian means of transport, has fallen asleep under the ground, for the employees with their perforating punches have ceased to work.*"
"Oo the bastards," cries Zazie, "oo the swine. To do that to me."
"Snot only you they're doing it to," says Gabriel, perfectly objective.
"Don't give a damn. Doesn't alter the fact that it's happening to me, me that was so happy, so pleased and everything to be going to be conveyed by metro. Blast, bloody hell."
"Have to make the best of it, have to be reasonable," said Gabriel *whose remarks were sometimes tinged with a slightly Kantian Thomism.*
And, passing on to the level of cosubjectivity, he added:
"And anyway we must get a move on. My time and patience may be inexhaustible, but Charley's aren't." (p. 15))

The first rupture in style occurs in Gabriel's statement: *Le métro, ce moyen de transport éminemment parisien, s'est endormi sous terre, car les employés aux pinces perforantes ont cessé tout travail.* (The metro, that eminently parisian means of transportation, has fallen asleep under the ground, for the employees with their perforating punches have ceased to work.) This remark, far different from Gabriel's earlier utterances, is clearly reminiscent of an inflated, sensational and grandiloquent journalistic style, which, here, has undergone a double displacement: appropriated by Gabriel, and represented in a literary text. The unexpected presence of the style of tabloids, the rupture it creates, and Gabriel's attempt to produce, with such words, an impression of authority – all converge into comic effects. Several other references underline the strong influence of the press over the characters. For example:

> – Tu sais, dit Gabriel avec calme, d'après ce que disent les journaux, c'est pas du tout dans ce sens là que s'oriente l'éducation moderne . . . N'est-ce pas, Marceline, qu'on dit ça dans le journal? (p. 30)
>
> – D'ailleurs, dit Gabriel, dans vingt ans, y aura plus d'institutrices: elles seront remplacées par le cinéma, la tévé, l'électronique, des trucs comme ça. C'était aussi écrit dans le journal l'autre jour. N'est-ce pas, Marceline? (p. 30)
>
> ("You know," said Gabriel calmly, "if you go by what the papers say, that isn't at all the direction in which modern education is oriented. It's even quite the opposite. The tendency is more towards gentleness, understanding, kindness. Isn't that right, Marceline, that's what it says in the paper." (p. 27)
>
> "In any case," said Gabriel, "in twenty years, there won't be any more teachers; they'll be replaced by the cinema, the telly, electronics, things like that. That was in the paper the other day too. Wasn't it, Marceline?" (p. 27))

One senses, in Gabriel's words, a veneration for the anticipated age of electronic marvels, a respect for the promised fruit of technology as it is depicted in the daily newspaper. Both Gabriel and Zazie also turn to the tabloids for fascinating information about sex, which they then eagerly quote.

> – Je l'ai lu dans le *Sanctimontronais du dimanche*, un canard à la page même pour la province où y a des amours célèbres, l'astrologie et tout, eh bien on disait que les chauffeurs de taxi izan voyaient sous tous les aspects et dans tous les genres de la sessualité. A commencer par les clientes qui veulent payer en nature. Ça vous est arrivé souvent? (p. 117)
>
> – C'est comme les femmes qui deviennent des hommes à force de faire du sport. On lit ça dans les journaux. (p. 118)
>
> ("I read it in the *Sunday Sanctimontronian*, a rag that's pretty up to date even for the provinces, where they write about famous love-affairs, astrology and everything, well, it said there that taxi-drivers, they see it in all its aspects and of all sorts, sessuality. Starting with the customers who want to pay in kind. Zthat often happened to you?" (pp. 97–8)

"It's like women who turn into men because they're so keen on sport. You read about it in the papers."(p. 99))

There is an absolute trust in the information provided by the media which is a source of not only facts and ideas, but also of language, as revealed by Gabriel's citation and Turandot's remark about Zazie's disappearance: *Elle a ptête fait ce que les journaux appellent une fugue, dit Turandot* ("Maybe it's what the papers call a case of phobia," says Turandot). When she recounts a fantasy of traumatic family drama, Zazie guarantees the truth of her tale by saying: *je vous montrerai un cahier où j'ai collé tous les articles de journaux où il est question de moi* (I'll show you an exercise book where I've stuck all the newspaper articles where there's something about me). The characters' borrowed vision of the world reflects yet another important aspect of society in the late 1950s and early 1960s: the growing power and influence of the media, of mass culture, from which the characters are made to appropriate views, voices, words and styles. After one of her impassioned pleas, Zazie remarks to herself: *Merde, chsuis aussi bonne que Michèle Morgan dans "La Dame aux Camélias'* (Hell, I'm just as good as Michèle Morgan in "Camille"). In these instances, two things are being mocked. First, there is a parody of the type of information that the *presse du dimanche*, the *presse à grand tirage* (the popular press) conveys, as well as of the sensational style in which it is expressed: *les employés aux pinces perforantes* (the employees with their perforating punches). Second, the characters' respect and appetite for the media is mocked. However, there is no hint, in the novel, that they ought to educate themselves with better literature; Zazie does not uphold the value of high culture. It matters little that they cannot distinguish between the Caserne de Reuilly and the Invalides. Again, hierarchies, cultural and linguistic categories of high and low, are brought to the same level.

To return to the passage under scrutiny, the second set of sentences that stand out occur in the following lines (my emphasis):

– Faut te faire une raison, dit Gabriel *dont les propos se nuançaient parfois d'un thomisme légèrement kantien.*
   Et passant sur le plan de la cosubjectivité, il ajouta:
– Et puis faut se grouiller: Charles attend.

("Have to make the best of it, have to be reasonable," said Gabriel *whose remarks were sometimes tinged with a slightly Kantian Thomism.*
   And, passing on to the level of co-subjectivity, he added:

"And anyway we must get a move on. My time and patience may be inexhaustible, but Charley's aren't.")

The italicized comments, which partake in what can be described as a learned style, do not apply to what Gabriel says. On the contrary, there is an enormous discrepancy between his utterances and the judgment passed, which can only be taken as self-consciously false and therefore ironical. The function of these comments is to draw attention to and emphasize the triviality of Gabriel's utterances. Such strategies of irony often rely on hyperbole better to emphasize a contrast which, here as in previous examples, involves the unexpected co-presence of the high and the low, of the familiar and the unfamiliar, of the abstract and the concrete. However, I would argue that, at the same time, the learned style in this instance relies on more than hyperbole – in fact, that it involves parody. The high concentration of philosophical terms (*thomisme*, *kantien*, *cosubjectivité*) and of elegant expressions (*propos*, *nuançaient*, *légèrement*) tends towards mimicry, an imitation that exaggerates, both qualitatively and quantitatively, the most salient features of a particular style. What appears to be at work here are two simultaneous functions, that move in opposite directions and completely destabilize each other: the narrative comments exercise irony against Gabriel's utterances, and parody against themselves. Both statements are undermined, both the learned and the popular styles are mocked. Another example of this process appears in the following lines (my emphasis):

> Le petit type se mit à craindre. *C'était le temps pour lui, c'était le moment de se forger quelque bouclier verbal. Le premier qu'il trouva fut un alexandrin.*
> – D'abord je vous permets pas de me tutoyer. (p. 11)

(The little chap began to get apprehensive. *Now was his time, now was the moment to forge some sort of verbal buckler. The first that came into his head was an alexandrine*:
"And anyway who said that you could call me *tu*?" (p. 12))

The verbose and dramatic tone conveyed by the rhetorical expression *c'était le temps pour lui, c'était le moment* (Now was his time, now was the moment) and by the expressions *forger* (to forge) and *bouclier verbal* (verbal buckler) lead one to expect a response of some impact, hardly realized by what the little chap actually says; and the mere syllabic count of *d'abord je vous permets pas de me tutoyer* (And anyway who said that you could call me *tu*?) certainly does not make it an alexandrine. It is clear that, once more, the comments cannot be taken at face value, and that the contrast between statement and fact points to the presence of irony. And, again, while the high-flown assessment of platitudes mocks the popular, it is complicated by a second emphasis, a parody of the elevated style that it mimics. In the next instance, Turandot's response is mocked by a preciously phrased comment that is ridiculously pompous:

> Turandot s'éponge, se verse un troisième beaujolais.
> – Nondguieu, répète-t-il.
> C'est l'expression qui lui paraît la mieux appropriée à l'émotion qui le trouble. (p. 47)

> (Turandot mops himself up, pours himself a third beaujolais.
> "Jeezers," he repeats.
> It is the expression which seems to him the most appropriate to the emotion which is disquieting him. (p. 41))

Along the same lines, the dramatic comment in the following example undermines both itself and the characters' utterances:

> – Et qu'est-ce que ce serait alors d'après toi?
> La narquoiserie du ton devient presque offensante pour l'interlocuteur qui, d'ailleurs, s'empresse d'avouer sa défaite. (p. 17)

> ("Well what would it be then in your opinion?"
> The craftiness of his tone becomes almost insulting to his interlocutor who, moreover, hastens to admit defeat. (p. 17))

Such instances of the learned style occur in the narrative several times in each chapter to mock the characters' use of popular language and to suggest a situation whereby a narrator knows more than the characters and expresses judgments and opinions. However, since the expression of this privileged knowledge and position involves parody and is a source of comic effects, whatever authority it might be founded on is undermined. It is quite impossible to determine which of the two functions – the parody of the high-flown and inadequate comments or the mocking of the popular – predominates. Furthermore, as we have seen, the narration itself often relies on the popular, whether it describes facts or actions, or, as was the case here, comments on the characters' utterances:

> Gabriel stoppe également, se retourne, pose la valoche et se met à espliquer. (p. 14)

> Elle pensait pas à elle en disant ça elle était pas égoïste, elle voulait parler du parfum qui émanait de ce meussieu. (p. 10)

(Gabriel likewise halts, turns round, puts the suitcase down and starts to iksplain. (p. 14)

She wasn't thinking about herself when she said that, she wasn't so self-centred, she was referring to the perfume that emanated from the meussieu. (p. 11))

Finally, it is important to note that the heterogeneous and unstable stylistic composition is not restricted to the narrative. Even though the popular predominates in the characters' utterances, there are variations there also. For example, a character is first known as *la bourgeoise* because she attempts to express herself with a certain distinction: *La violence, ma petite chérie, doit toujours être évitée dans les rapports humains. Elle est éminemment condamnable* (Violence, my darling, must always be avoided in human relationships. It is eminently to be condemned). Later, as her discourse significantly lowers, she becomes known as *la veuve Mouaque*: *Tordez-y donc les parties viriles, dit la veuve Mouaque, ça lui apprendra à vivre* (Twist his private parts for him, said the widow Mouaque, that'll teach him). Trouscaillon, the *flic* (cop), is also one who can – or tries to – borrow and talk with different registers. Attempting to seduce Marceline, he informs her of his designs in the following straightforward and to-the-point manner:

– Bin voilà, dit le type, j'ai un sacré béguin pour vous. Dès que je vous ai vue, je me suit dit: je pourrais plus vivre sur cette terre si je ne me la farcis pas un jour ou l'autre, alors je me suis ajouté: autant que ça soye le plus vite possible. Je peux pas attendre, moi. Je suis un impatient: c'est mon caractère. (p. 209)

("Well it's like this," said the chap. "I've taken a hell of a fancy to you. The very moment I saw you, I said to myself: I won't be able to go on living on this earth if I don't stuff her sooner or later, so then I said to myself: might just as well be as soon as possible. I can't wait. I'm the impatient type. That's my nature." (p. 172))

Later, when he returns to his official function as cop and interrogates a stranger, he speaks in a strikingly different, convoluted style:

– M'autorisez-vous donc à de nouveau formuler la proposition interrogative qu'il y a quelques instants j'énonça devant vous?
– J'énonçai, dit l'obscur.
– J'énonçais, dit Trouscaillon.
– J'énonçai sans esse.

– J'énonçai, dit enfin Trouscaillon. Ah! la grammaire c'est pas mon fort. Et c'est ça qui m'en a joué des tours. Passons. Alors? (p. 218)

("Do you therefore authorise me to formulate once again the interrogative proposition which a few moments ago I prenounce in your presence?'
"I pronounced," said the Unknown.
"I pronounce," said Trouscaillon.
"I pronounced with a dee."
"I pronounced," said Trouscaillon at last. "Ah! linguistics isn't my strong point. It's certainly played me some dirty tricks. Let's skip it. Well?" (p. 179))

Trouscaillon here refers to the fact that it was while he searched in a dictionary for the imperative form of *dévêtir* (to undress) that Marceline escaped. Now he tries to produce an official discourse that he imagines is best suited to his functions but which he cannot quite master, while the other's interruptions amount to a display of greater linguistic competency and thus an attempt to undermine Trouscaillon's authority. All of this underlines the characters' self-consciousness as to what they say and how, and their ability to use (or attempt to use) a variety of styles. As for Gabriel, it is not only the voice of the media that he appropriates; it is not only with trivial problems that he is concerned. He is, on occasion, able to assume "a majestic air which he effortlessly selects from his repertoire." Lost and alone among a group of tourists, he launches into the following angst-ridden monologue:

– L'être ou le néant, voilà le problème. Monter, descendre, aller, venir, tant fait l'homme qu'à la fin il disparaît. Un taxi l'emmène, un métro l'emporte, la tour n'y prend garde, ni le Panthéon. Paris n'est qu'un songe, Gabriel n'est qu'un rêve (charmant), Zazie le songe d'un rêve (ou d'un cauchemar) et toute cette histoire le songe d'un songe, le rêve d'un rêve, à peine plus qu'un délire tapé à la machine par un romancier idiot (oh! pardon). (p. 120)

(Being or nothingness, that is the question. Ascending, descending, coming, going, a man does so much that in the end he disappears. A taxi bears him off, a metro carries him away, the tower doesn't care, nor the Panthéon. Paris is but a dream, Gabriel is but a reverie (a charming one), Zazie the dream of a reverie (or of a nightmare) and all this story the dream of a dream, the reverie of a reverie, scarcely more than the typewritten delirium of an idiotic novelist (oh! sorry). (p. 100))

Gabriel's poetico-metaphysico laments go on at some length as he reflects on the ephemeral and unreal quality of the world, mixing numerous literary references (from Sartre and Shakespeare among others) and stylistic idiosyncrasies, such as the lyrical repetition *songe, rêve, songe d'un rêve, songe d'un songe* (dream, reverie, dream of a reverie, dream of a dream). The many parentheses belong to written language and do not represent a feature of oral discourse – a breach in the flow of speech is just as accurately suggested by commas. Similarly, Gabriel's reference to himself in the third person is a highly literary device, and, with the reference to *cette histoire* (this story) fiction refers to itself as such, and as more than fiction: *songe, délire* (dream, delirium). In the midst of Gabriel's ravings, *tapé à la machine* (typewritten) is an intrusion of reality (a reality external to the novel) which points to the material quality of the text, the text as object. Furthermore, contrary to the instances discussed earlier where the narrator commented in a disparaging manner on the characters, here, a character disparagingly refers to the novelist: *un romancier idiot*. Categories are blurred with the apology *Oh! pardon* – to whom is it directed? Is a character supposedly addressing the author, or is the author apologizing to the reader for having disrupted novelistic conventions? All of these effects are couched in a style different from what usually appears to be Gabriel's own and in which the literary is strongly signaled and parodied.

As Barthes points out in his essay "Zazie et la littérature" ("Zazie and Literature") Queneau's novel is not without traditional aspects.[36] There is a main character, Zazie, and a central story (her visit to Paris) onto which subplots are grafted (her escapade, the adventures with the stranded tourists, Gabriel's performance). Gabriel, Marceline and Charles play secondary roles, and several background characters occasionally enter the scene. Very much unlike a *nouveau roman* where numerous important foundations are challenged, Queneau's novel remains, as Barthes put it, "a *well-made* novel" (Barthes' emphasis) with an almost classical unity of time (a weekend) and place (Paris). The stability that the traditional narrative structure confers is reinforced by the fact that the stylistic structure, whatever subversive elements it displays, is set at the very beginning of the novel and does not evolve after that. Among its principal features, present in the first few pages of the text, are popular markers of a lexical nature, which occur with the same frequency and which are of the same type in the narrative and the directly reported speech of characters. Some syntactical markers are also present, but do not challenge the structure of the sentence. In fact, the lexical transgressions themselves are relatively mild, for most of the popular, vulgar, familiar or slang expressions that appear in *Zazie* were already authorized in a conventional dictionary. This was due, in part, to the social and linguistic evolution that resulted in a loss of popular language's specificity. Furthermore, the novel, after it was published, encouraged the translation of these non-conventional words from margin to center, since many of them changed labels and entered a more legitimate category in editions of dictionaries by 1977. For example, *foireux* (shitty), first described as *populaire*, became *familier* in the first edition of *Le Petit Robert* which, even though it is not an extensive work, includes all the marginal words that Queneau uses in the first chapter of his novel.[37] Often, his text is chosen to illustrate the legitimacy of their usage. Both *mouflette* (brat) and *déconner* (to bullshit), not found in the earlier edition, are present here, followed by examples taken from Queneau's work.

Barthes notes, however, that even though the deep structure of the novel remains stable, the surface of the text is damaged: "The noble edifice of the written form still stands, but worm-eaten, pricked with a thousand scalings."[38] Undoubtedly, the most striking innovation in *Zazie* is the phonetic transcription of words or groups of words. Although they are linked to Queneau's proposals for orthographic reforms, they do not illustrate them: because they are not systematic, and because they remain isolated. As Jean-Paul Bordufour remarks in "The Linguistic Revolution has Failed":

> If Queneau had followed his own rules, he would have rapidly flooded the market with texts in neo-French, so that the habit would be quickly formed, so that we would all have a good laugh and then become aware of the importance of the innovation. And what does he do instead? he dispenses neo-French drop by drop, for fear of losing its comic effect.[39]

The initial reaction to the phonetic transcriptions, when normal visual recognition is arrested, is puzzlement. Barthes suggests that these forms may even appear aggressive. They jump off the page with their baroque, foreign, barbarous aspect, as unquestioned French orthographic conventions are denaturalized and unusual letters predominate: "But what is pointed out and mocked is not the irrational aspect of the graphic code . . . here it is upon the Frenchness of writing that doubt is cast."[40] Once the transcriptions are decoded, laughter follows the disorientation. The comic effect that these forms produce is experienced by all readers, who, whatever their social and literary background, will recognize the discrepancy between the strange orthography and the legitimate one. Such is not the case for other comic and parodic effects, as we will see. Because the textual analysis itself aimed to provide a description of the textual structures a reader might react to, independently of social and historical situation, this important distinction was not noted earlier.

The relationship of the phonetic transcriptions to popular language is ambiguous for, on the one hand, the effect that the transcription creates (aggression, laughter) are so strong that they draw attention away from the issue of the presence of the popular in the novel. On the other hand, they emphasize the specificity of spoken, popular diction by representing and underlining the typical features such as concatenation, elision and contraction. Yet, these features add to the strange, baroque aspect. If, with these forms, Queneau occasionally undermines a surface manifestation of legitimate language, he does not do so in a manner that affects the social significance and function of conventional orthography, or in a way that helps secure popular language a dominant place among the different styles represented in *Zazie*. The analysis highlighted, for example, the characters' tendency to appropriate and recite what they had read in the press, in a manner that both parodied the sensationalism of tabloids and that mocked the characters' respect and fascination for this source of language and information. These effects are directed at specific readers. Only those who are not fascinated by and who do not routinely quote the tabloids will perceive the mockery. This comic effect, unlike that created by the phonetic transcriptions, is founded on and maintains distance: it is experienced by readers who are, or feel themselves to be, different from the characters and who do not partake in similar practices. At the same time, however, a familiarity with the sensational journalistic style is necessary to recognize the presence of parody, which implies on the part of the author and requires on the part of the reader an awareness of the model parodied. Similarly, a reader must be somewhat "learned" to recognize the parody of styles that all come under the "learned" category – philosophical, precious, dramatic. The absurdity of *Faut te faire une raison, dit Gabriel, dont les propos se nuançaient d'un thomisme légèrement kantien* (Have to make the best of it, have to be reasonable, said Gabriel whose remarks were sometimes tinged with a slightly Kantian Thomism) is apparent to those who are aware (even only vaguely) that Kant was a philosopher, that Thomism refers to the work of Saint Thomas Aquinas and that the understanding these men might have had of "have to be reasonable" radically differs from Gabriel's. Similarly, "Being or nothingness?" must be read with an awareness (again, however vague) of its relationship to Sartre's *Being and Nothingness* and Hamlet's interrogation. By "vaguely aware," I mean able to recognize the connotations of certain key words – names of philosophers, the most famous line of a famous play, titles of well-known books; in other words, a primarily linguistic recognition that addresses the surface manifestations of the learned rather than a knowledge and understanding of its content (as well as a superficial familiarity with the style of tabloids). Because the relationship to the model parodied is one of superficial familiarity rather than deep knowledge, Barthes draws an opposition between Queneau's parodies and those of Giraudoux, for example:

> In Queneau's work, parody takes on a very particular structure. It does not display a *knowledge* of the parodies model; it contains no trace of that complicity with High Culture that marks, for example, Giraudoux's parodies, and that is only a falsely impertinent way to express a profound respect for classico-national values.[41] (Barthes' emphasis)

There is another way in which parody in *Zazie* differs from its traditional form: by tending, in one respect, towards its postmodern counterpart, pastiche, which Jameson describes in "Postmodernism and Consumer Society." Behind all parody there remains the feeling that there is a stylistic norm in contrast to which a certain style is being mocked; not so with pastiche:

> Pastiche is, like parody, the imitation of a peculiar or unique style, the wearing of a stylistic mask, speech in a dead language: but it is a neutral practice of such mimicry, without parody's ulterior motive, without the satirical impulse, without laughter, without that still latent feeling that there exists something *normal* compared to which what is being imitated is rather comic.[42] (Jameson's emphasis)

Zazie, it is true, is not without satirical impulses and comic effects. But Queneau's novel certainly does not suggest the existence of a linguistic norm or privileged style (in this respect, *Zazie* resembles *Exercises in Style*). If a fundamental feature of postmodernism is, as Jameson suggests, a lack of concern for the creation of a unique and individual style, the loss of the high modernist impulse towards stylistic innovation, *Zazie* certainly leans in that direction, with its discontinuous stylistic unities that are not organized in a unified and organic whole, that are not held together by an internal logic and necessity. Parody, in *Journey to the End of the Night*, a high modernist text *par excellence*, is very different, operating as it does with isolated forms that clash with their immediate surroundings, forms that all readers are able to recognize as the obvious stylistic marks of the belletristic, and serving to strengthen the impact of a new, original and privileged style: the hybridization of the poetic and popular. Céline's parody of the stilted belletristic style reveals a deep respect for a healthy and vital manifestation of the literary. Furthermore, drawing on his comparison of Van Gogh's *Peasant Shoes* and Warhol's *Diamond Dust Shoes*, Jameson remarks that a most striking feature of postmodernism is a new kind of depthlessness, "a new kind of superficiality in the most literal sense." The style of *Zazie*, realizing itself in surface manifestations (as Barthes points out, the surface of the novel is "pricked with a thousand scalings") reveals an essential flatness, shuns any assumption or suggestion of depth. And much emphasis is placed on the signifier which, with its graphic peculiarities and cryptic appearance, is distanced from the signified.

Barthes' analysis differs from the one offered here in that he distinguishes Zazie from the other characters and considers that her utterances carry a certain authority; in particular, her recurrent comment *mon cul* (my ass) deflates the speech of others. Her language, says Barthes, is always in direct contact with the real, it is a object-language rather than a meta-language, a parasite-language.[43] The characters' discourse does indeed live off that of others; the recitation of the press, the borrowing of different voices is indeed parasitical. But Zazie is no exception to this. If she avoids the learned, she does appropriate a sensational or dramatic style when she recounts her story of family violence, the alleged assault of the satyr, and when she compares herself to Michèle Morgan. A multitude of different styles are present in the novel, represented, parodied and ironized, but there is no norm, internal or external to the text, in contrast to which this takes place. In *L'Assommoir*, the passages in *écriture artiste* were privileged and dominated the text, because they were unusual within the novel, yet familiar outside of it; they represented a dominant vision, attracting and holding the reader's attention. When this style appeared, it was sustained at some length, carried an autonomous weight, reflected a specific world view and created its own internal norm. Nor does *Zazie* generate a new and original style, such as in *Journey*. Popular language carries no more weight than learned language which, in turn, carries no more value than the journalistic, for example. There is no embedding or hybridization, only a juxtaposition of styles, a switching back and forth from one to the other. Furthermore, it is not only on a stylistic level that opposites are brought together. Immediately following the untranslated Greek epigram, an equally unfamiliar-looking but very trivial sounding expression opens the novel. Also brought into equivalence are the sources of *puer* (to stink): the crowd at the Gare d'Austerlitz for Gabriel, *Barbouze de chez Fior* (Barbouze, a perfume from the House of Fior) for the *ptite mère*. Gabriel's concerns range from the mundane, such as here, to the elevated ("Being or nothingness?"). Historical landmarks of the Parisian landscape lose their referentiality and are confused with less grandiose sites: le Tribunal du Commerce, la Caserne de Reuilly, la Gare de Lyon. This confusion results in another feature which Jameson considers fundamental to postmodernism, the leveling of high and low categories, and illustrates Barthes' comment that *Zazie* is a work that suggests an equivalence between literature and its enemy.

THE GLOBAL SPACE OF POSTMODERNISM

The reactions that followed the publication of *Zazie in the Metro* were less intense and vociferous than those brought on by *L'Assommoir* and *Journey to the End of the Night*. This is not surprising; a variety of factors account for a relatively weak response. Queneau, at that time, was already a well-established novelist, and his name was securely linked to official positions in the literary field. His work, even though it did not belong to a specific school, was presented in a familiar liberal and avant-garde framework. It was less open to speculation about possible motivation, theoretical or political purpose, or future impact than would have been the case for an unknown writer. The representation of lower-class characters was no longer the novelty that it had been in the case of *L'Assommoir*, and most of the familiar, popular, vulgar or argot words that he had used had already been accepted in a dictionary and had appeared in many of Queneau's earlier works. Furthermore, he had already advocated the propagation of neo-French in his theoretical articles, indicating his interest in linguistic innovations and reforms.

The opinions in the press were, nevertheless, divergent. The one that appeared in *Le Figaro* (11 February 1959) is typical of the right-wing readings.[44] The main claim is that *Zazie* proves to be, from the outset, an extremely amusing, entertaining work that opens with a stylistic and comic effect of high impact: "From the first line, the first word of *Zazie*, we are hooked: *Howcanaystinksotho*." Throughout the article, humor is considered the novel's greatest quality. André Billy, the author, believes that Queneau is served above all by his "sense of humor, true gift of the Gods." What he finds particularly funny is the representation of popular language. He describes the novel as: "For the joy of the reader, a story strongly spiced with argot and with fresh language as they say in the milieu through which the author takes us." Underlying this comment is the assumption that the reader does not belong to the milieu represented in the novel. It is also significant that Billy locates the humor of *Zazie* in the simple presence of popular language, when, clearly, this alone is not amusing; its occurrence in *L'Assommoir* certainly was not. The textual analysis revealed a number of comic effects, achieved by a variety of means far more complex than the article suggests. We laugh at the phonetic transcriptions because the familiar appears in an unfamiliar form; we laugh at Gabriel's internal monologue because of the seriousness of the argumentation applied to such a trivial problem; we laugh at his appropriation of a sensational journalistic or high literary style because of a sudden clash of registers and the inflated imagery ("the employees with their perforated punches") and idiosyncrasies ("Paris is but a dream"). When we laugh at the characters' deep interest in and respect for the mundane information conveyed in tabloids, we rely on a perception of difference between their practices and our own – but this has nothing to do with the simple presence of popular language. In general, we laugh at the unexpected equivalences between the high and the low. There are, of course, those instances when popular language is clearly mocked by narrative comments, but because these comments also function as parody, the mocking is neutralized. When Billy mentions the "impression of stupidity and brutishness that pervades the characters' words and actions," he does not take into account the parodic function and he oversimplifies the complex interplay of stylistic unities. Billy also remarks that there is no deliberate harshness in Queneau's portrayals – implying that the author's intentions are not to attack, but to amuse, and that, anyway, his representations are not so far away from the truth. He assures us that even when exaggerations are present, no harm is meant, for Queneau is simply overcome by his poetic and linguistic talent: "He invents some, served by his poetic and linguistic gifts."

Praising light-hearted entertainment, delighting in the picturesque, *Le Figaro* presents *Zazie* as a text that is founded on and maintains distance between the reader and the world that it represents. We are reminded of the attitudes revealed in the literary explorations of the underworld prior to *L'Assommoir* where texts in which popular language appeared contributed to establishing the specificity of the working class and underlining its particularities. A similarity of attitudes emerges at the beginning and end of industrial capitalism. In the late 1950s, as both the bourgeoisie and working class were beginning to lose what had become their traditional attributes, the tendency was to hold on to familiar distance.

The left displayed a similar attitude. Claude Roy, in *Libération*, also concentrates on Queneau's humor, but from a very different perspective. Here, serious doubt is cast upon how funny *Zazie* really is.[45] The laughter it provokes, Roy says, is a *rire jaune*, a bitter, unhealthy laugh which he accounts for in Freudian terms: a defense mechanism of the *moi* that refuses to be affected by the suffering of the outside world, and that transforms a potentially unpleasant experience into a pleasurable occasion. He does not describe the potentially unpleasant experience from which, when reading *Zazie*, our laughter protects us. It is likely to be what he considers the reality of the working class, their hard times, "the suffering of the outside world," which, indeed, is not shown here (the characters in *Zazie* seem to be having a good time). The readers' laugh is unhealthy, and Queneau is described as a politically and morally irresponsible pessimist: "his snickering pessimism has reached a harshness that sends shivers down the spine." The attitude of denial, and the refusal to confront social reality pervades the entire novel. It is likely that the author of this article would have preferred to read about characters who would not manifest such enthusiasm for *bloudjinzes* or American washing machines, characters who would read *Libération* rather than *Le Sanctimontronais du dimanche*. Queneau is judged a pessimist because he does not seem to uphold a marxist utopia. The characters are not shown to encounter undue hardship, and are certainly not united by strong revolutionary concerns and a powerful sense of class identity. Although Roy does not specifically mention the leveling of high and low categories, it is likely that he would find such structures bothersome, for they participate in the invalidation, or at least the questioning, of earlier political models of the left. Unsurprisingly, Roy criticizes Queneau's appropriation of popular language: "What is curious is that, even though Queneau professes (and practices) that one must write as one speaks, I do not have the impression, whenever I meet him, that he speaks like *Zazie*."

The question of Queneau's relation to popular language is central to another publication of the left, *Combat*, where the novel is discussed with a great deal of irony.[46] André Berry illustrates the style with Zazie's favorite expression, "my ass," and, while mocking Queneau's literary credentials and, like Roy in *Libération*, pointing out the difference between what one imagines would be his own language and the one that appears in the novel, he explains: "If I allow myself to cite this somewhat risqué expression, it is because I feel authorized by a member of the Goncourt Academy." Berry judges the representation of popular language to be so repetitive and artificial that he suggests that Queneau, like Zola, used an external source, such as a dictionary (which is most unlikely). He mentions the argot expressions "of which our author, before using them, seems to have made a list." Phonetic transcriptions are criticized, and expressions like *Doukipudonktan* are said to "point to the unawareness, in certain backward or advanced minds, of the logical elements of the sentence." Throughout the article, Berry maintains that Queneau's representation of a language with which he has no real familiarity harbors an attack on those who use it. Berry also notes that Queneau does not appropriate popular language throughout the novel and that, on occasion, a far more classical and scholarly voice is heard. It is not clear whether Berry perceives the parody in such styles where "the usage of Tite-Live or Fénelon pleasantly transpires." The following remark, summarizing Queneau's literary and linguistic enterprise, implies that he does not: "Imagine a Littré of argot, in which the words that prefigure tomorrow's language are gathered by a man of taste and culture." The authority, clearly, remains in the hands of a man of letters who, the conclusion of the article suggests, is also a man of some cruelty: "Read, now, to see to what extent Zazie's father, planting his arrows into the heart of human wretchedness, reaches his cruel and sad aims."

Even though the reactions in the press are far fewer and far less passionate than was the case for Zola's and Céline's novels, they nevertheless illustrate how different ideological belief systems produce different reading systems that determine which aspects of the text are selected and privileged, and which are left unnoticed and unaccounted for. Certain reading strategies are similar to the ones of *L'Assommoir* and *Journey*. These systems also determine different reactions to the elements selected. In both the conservative *Figaro* and the left-wing *Libération*, the issue is the same privileged effect, humor, but the critics differ in their reactions to its presence. For the right, the characters' language and behavior remains a source of pleasant amusement as Queneau leads the reader by the hand through a foreign society. The article places the novel within the safe confines of entertainment and upholds the long-standing tradition of an objectified working class. The other styles, whether they are perceived or not, are not mentioned. For the left, the laughter that the novel provokes is judged to be inappropriate to the representation of lower-class characters. Both *Le Figaro* and *Libération* cling to traditional class models. Even though the characters in *Zazie* arguably belong to a petite bourgeoisie – Gabriel is a cabaret dancer, Charles a taxi driver, Turandot owns a café, Trouscaillon is a policeman – they are regarded as traditional working class. The right applauds a light-hearted portrayal of this class where clownish characters make the bourgeois laugh. The left views the work as pessimistic for it conceals, rather than reveals, a politically active proletariat. In a judgment not dissimilar to the one passed on Céline, Queneau is deemed pessimistic because, even though he showed the hardship of the working class, he did not represent class struggle. Unlike *Le Figaro*, however, *Libération* does not suggest that the characters and their language are subject to ridicule in particular. Rather, the sort of nihilistic humor it detects suggests that all is mocked (which, indeed, is the case). Berry, in *Combat*, is the only critic who mentions the presence of the learned style: "the usage of Tite-Live and Fénelon." He considers this language to be appropriate to Queneau's literary position, whereas popular language is not, and is used in an artificial manner. Predictably, a major concern, for the left, is whether the novel translates a sympathetic and productive position *vis à vis* the working class and *Combat*, like *Libération*, judges it not to be so.

Since the publication of *Zazie* did not cause a violent uproar or polemic, Queneau was not compelled to launch an immediate defensive and to produce explanations or justifications. However, a series of radio interviews that took place in February, March and April 1962 sheds an interesting light on how he perceived his position and production in the literary field, and it illuminates his views on linguistic questions. Even though the interviews, "Conversations with Georges Charbonnier," do not concern *Zazie* in particular, at the outset Queneau is introduced as the one who wrote *Doukipudonktan*.[47] The impact of the first word of this novel, three years after its publication, remains great and seems to be have become the most memorable feature of Queneau's writing, his trademark. Charbonnier, underlining the attention Queneau paid to spoken French and suggesting an inclusive and pluralistic attitude towards language, also describes him as "the only contemporary French writer who took the trouble to listen to each of us speak . . . us without exception, meaning all."[48] Throughout the interviews, Queneau is far less systematic and categorical in his discussion of linguistic issues than he was in "Sticks,

Numbers and Letters." He draws a less sharp distinction between written and spoken French:

> Naturally there's a whole range, there are variants, from an extremely modified French to that spoken on the TV and radio, a French that attempts to be part of "correct" French and that, indeed, exerts a sort of slowing down effect, acts as a brake on the evolution of the language.[49]

The growing influence of radio and television is something that Queneau now sees as a possible restraining factor in the development and propagation of neo-French: "It seems to me that, indeed, the development of purely auditory means of communication adds to the illusion that written French and spoken French are the same language, when they are two different languages."[50] These new means of communication do bridge a gap, it is true, but with a two-way effect: if it is true that in much of the prepared broadcast discourse, typical marks of spoken language are erased, such is not the case for spontaneous interviews and conversations, or for a commentator's appraisal of popular forms of entertainment like sports and games; in these latter contexts, typical spoken and colloquial expressions are often used and legitimated. Concerning the style of his novels, Queneau says that the alternation of spoken and learned language is not systematically and deliberately organized:

> When there is a mixture, the appearance of spoken language is, I think, always spontaneous and involuntary: there always comes a time when I have the impression that that is how it must be, that it must be written in a more or less phonetic writing . . . so, the appearances of neo-French or the phonetic transcriptions, they are completely instinctive; it's because I have the impression that that's the way it must be, at that point.[51]

Queneau disengages his work from a theoretical background; expressions like *spontaneous*, *involuntary* and *instinctive* minimize the importance (even question the existence) of the preparation process and convey a traditional view of artistic inspiration in which explicit intentions and rationales have little place. This is unexpected. Queneau had, earlier, criticized the use of improvisation and chance in surrealism; his *Exercises in Style* are anything but involuntary. Furthermore, in the early 1960s he became an active member of the OULIPO group (Ouvroir de Littérature Potentielle: Workshop of Potential Literature) whose purpose was to invent mechanical processes of literary creation, often relying on mathematical methods.

An example of this is his *One Hundred Million Million Poems*, consisting of ten sonnets with permutable lines and resulting in an enormous number of possible combinations. Another is the rewriting of a literary text in which each noun is replaced by the eighth following one in a dictionary. A similar paradox emerges from the interviews, concerning the category of the literary, which *Zazie in the Metro* parodies in many instances but that Queneau strongly upholds in the interviews. He makes his position very explicit in his answer to the question "How do you recognize literature?" when he suggests the objective existence of a literary quality: "One sees right away that there are people, I mean authors, candidate authors who immediately know what literature is, and who operate on a literary level, even if they are anti-literature."[52] He implies that to be "anti-literature" is an attitude whose surface manifestation does not affect the core of the text – an interesting reflection, perhaps, on his own work. Yet another unexpected statement occurs in an article, "Errata," which Queneau published in 1969 in *La Nouvelle Revue française*, where he denies that, unlike what many critics believed, he ever attempted to rewrite a modern and accessible version of *Le Discours de la méthode* in his novels. He also dismisses the importance of neo-French: "This question of neo-French seems to me less important. Nothing suggests the catastrophic crumbling of French that I believed I foresaw. I realize that the theories that I upheld on the subject have not been confirmed by facts."[53] Ten years after the publication of *Zazie*, Queneau considers his views on and his occasional use of neo-French as unimportant and inconsequential concerns. No external circumstance seems to have prompted this change which does illustrate, however, *Zazie*'s epigram: "The one who fabricated it then abolished it."

The reading of *Zazie in the Metro* offered here suggests that the novel anticipates postmodernism. It appeared before the term was used, defined and analyzed. Except, perhaps, for Queneau's light-hearted insolence and distance towards his work (in place of a vital modernist link), its author displayed none of the postmodern attitudes and stances that have, by now, pervaded the artistic and critical fields. This postmodernism *avant la lettre* can be viewed in terms of a new two-way relationship between the societal and the literary. This relationship informs much of Jameson's fundamental assumptions and conclusions in his analyses of the postmodern, which he considers not as an optional style among others but, rather, as "the cultural dominant of the logic of late capitalism."[54] Because aesthetic production has become integrated into commodity production, the sphere of culture

196 Political Stylistics

has lost the semi-autonomy it previously enjoyed, and the distance that separated the cultural act from the "massive Being of Capital" is lost. Not that the sphere of culture has disappeared, but it now entirely pervades the social realm to form a global space, "the new space of postmodernism." Because of this inseparability, Jameson detects in postmodern art an unavoidable authenticity, an unexpected realism:

> The distorted and unreflexive attempts of newer cultural production to explore and to express this new space must then, also, in their own fashion, be considered as so many approaches to the representation of (a new) reality (to use a more antiquated language). As paradoxical as the term may seem, they may thus, following a classic interpretive option, be read as peculiar new forms of realism (or at least of the mimesis of reality) at the same time that they can equally well be analyzed as so many attempts to distract and to divert us from that reality or to disguise its contradictions and resolve them in the guise of so many formal mystifications.[55]

In ways perhaps more straightforward than the ones that Jameson implies, concrete representations of this new reality abound in the novel. The stylistic profile of *Zazie* reflects a linguistic reality observable outside of the literary: the decline of socially defined linguistic specificity. When Gabriel appropriates the language of the media without quotation marks, thereby incorporating that discourse into his, it is reminiscent of a characteristic of postmodern art: the absorption of mass culture into the literary text. On many other occasions, the characters openly refer to the press: a thematic rather than linguistic illustration, this time, of a feature of post-industrial society, the media's important role in the shaping of opinions and belief. Other aspects of post-industrial society appear in the novel, many of which have to do with the erasure of traditional categories, such as the opposition between the high and the low, city and country, gender differences, and class boundaries. The all-pervading consumerism is also represented, whereas the political is mentioned on only one occasion, and then only to be dismissed immediately:

> – Et quand est-ce qu'elle va finir, cette grève? demande Zazie en gonflant ses mots de férocité.
> – Je sais pas, moi, dit Gabriel, je fais pas de politique.
> – C'est pas de la politique, dit Charles, c'est pour la croûte.
> (p. 19)

("And when's this strike going to be over?" asks Zazie, her words bulging with ferocity.
"How should I know," says Gabriel, "I don't go in for politics."
"Snot politics," says Charles, "it's a question of their daily bread."
(p. 18))

Croûte (daily bread) is opposed to, and overrides, politics; strikes are certainly not seen in the context of class struggle, a notion that many maintain is no longer valid. Neither is, perhaps, the notion of the popular:

> The historically unique tendential effect of late capitalism on all [social] groups has been to dissolve and to fragment or atomize them into agglomerations of isolated and equivalent private individuals, by way of the corrosive action of universal commodification and the market system. Thus, the "popular" as such no longer exists, except under very specific and marginalized conditions (internal and external pockets of so-called underdevelopment within the capitalist world system).[56]

"The popular as such no longer exists." Earlier, I mentioned the various factors that no doubt contributed to a loss of the popular's specificity. It may indeed be the case that, to the delight of the right and dismay of the left, post-industrial society "resists the laws of classical capitalism, namely the primacy of industrial production and the omnipresence of class struggle."[57] Such a possibility, however, need not overshadow the existence and political weight of, in France, a large and hugely exploited sub-proletariat of immigrants and of bewildering unemployment rates in Northern England and in the inner cities of the United States. The economic reality of class oppression has far from disappeared. Jameson ends his essay "Postmodernism and Consumer Society" with the following interrogation:

> We have seen that there is a way in which postmodernism replicates or reproduces – reinforces – the logic of consumer capitalism; the more significant question is whether there is also a way in which it resists that logic. But that is a question that we must leave open.[58]

That question does indeed remain open; but the specific case of *Zazie in the Metro* does not suggest a positive answer.

5 Popular language as literary artifact

Stanley Fish, in "What Is Stylistics and Why Are They Saying Such Terrible Things About It" articulates a convincing critique of methods in stylistics which, even though they claim to be scientifically grounded and to exist in reaction to impressionistic readings of texts, never successfully reach beyond the descriptive stage.[1] Whether they rely on the precise statistical count (often computer aided) of a particular aspect of syntax or vocabulary, or on analyses based on models of transformative grammar, the conclusions drawn from the factual results are merely circular or arbitrary inferences. Such practices do not demonstrate anything, and the relationship they attempt to establish between description and interpretation are as shaky and impressionistic as those that do not claim a scientific basis and the security of an "objective" formalism. Drawing on the distinction between "institutional facts" and "brute facts" (facts that are merely quantifiable) which John Searle establishes in *Speech Acts: An Essay in the Philosophy of Language*,[2] Fish explains:

> In my argument the institutional facts are the events that are constitutive of the specifically human activity of reading, while the brute facts are the observable formal patterns that can be discerned in the traces or residue of that activity. The stylisticians are thus in the position of trying to do what Searle says cannot be done: explain the brute facts without reference to the institutional facts which give them value. They would specify the meaning of the moves in the game without taking into account the game itself.[3]

As a remedy to a process whose sole value resides in labeling decontextualized stylistic constituents, Fish calls for a reader-oriented "affective" stylistics, whereby formal patterns would acquire meaning by virtue of their position in a structure of experience: the experience of "their reception and negotiation by a reader who comes upon them already oriented in the direction of specific concerns and possessed of (or by) certain expectations."[4]

As does the approach that Fish advocates, that which I have established and practiced poses "a direct challenge to the autonomy of the text and to the formalistic assumptions of stylistics."[5] It also views reading as a dynamic and reactive process, and takes into account horizons of expectations, those common to the general public at a given time as well as those specific to certain groups. Not only does a political stylistics move beyond formal description as it looks into the reception of the work, but also, by taking into account the process and context of the text's production it is grounded in a moment prior to its material existence. In this study, what Fish calls the "institutional facts" refer to more than just the experience of reading: "the game itself" includes the rules of linguistic production in general, literary production in particular, linguistic and social stratification, the literary discursive situation, the text's official interpretation and manipulation, and so forth. Attempting both to avoid the shortcomings that Fish outlines in his critique and to expand the framework that he proposes as a solution, this study also moved in a very specific direction, with, as its guiding question, that of the style's subversive possibilities; the question of the return to the social, after its journey through literary mediation, of a potentially politically oppositional language.

As the present chapter will discuss further, a number of resistances, both internal and external to the text, hinder the full realization of this oppositional potential which I defined as "a possible and complexly mediated role in the subversion of relations of production." There is one area, however, in which the representation of popular language in these novels has had a direct and indisputable effect: the *Grand Robert* of 1985 justified its inclusion of a wider vocabulary than previously in the following terms:

> With the nineteenth century and romanticism, one enters "modern" language: the number of words increases with the variety of literary themes and the writer's command of the variety of social usages; the trend intensifies in the twentieth century: without anticipating the question of the representativity of literary discourse – essential for this type of dictionary – one can already note that the reading of Céline or Queneau requires the knowledge of many words described as "popular" or "familiar."[6]

The novels, then, did perform a function of lexical legitimation: the marginal words were authorized when they had appeared in the work of consecrated authors. However, the claim that the dictionary could serve a useful function for those who were not familiar with vocabulary used by Queneau and Céline cannot be taken seriously; neither author relied on expressions whose meaning was not readily available to most readers. The linguistic shift that these works suggest was not brought on by them alone. Rather, *Journey* and *Zazie* (*Zazie* especially) reinforced a trend: during the second half of the twentieth century, social classes came to be less clearly differentiated in terms of their cultural and linguistic practices. Their specificity was at its highest during the mid- to late-nineteenth century, at a time when the new industrial and urban working class built an identity which, simultaneously, was investigated, circumscribed, classified and represented in exaggerated form by the ruling class; at a time, also, when the threatening argot of criminals still resonated in its language. Oppression of a more directly political nature followed the people's first revolutionary attempt, the Commune. At the turn of the century and until the end of the Second World War, evolutions in industrial modes of production increased the workers' alienation. Technological advances and greater productivity did not, by any means, improve the workers' material conditions, nor did they lessen their cultural deprivation. For Céline, the Exposition Universelle of 1900 epitomized those changes: "that moving staircase that grated all the way up to the gallery of machines, full, for the first time, of tortured metals, of colossal threats, of catastrophes in abeyance."[7] Class antagonisms were sharper than ever, and struggle was organized through unions and a relatively powerful Communist Party, which explains, perhaps, why linguistic boundaries were no longer endowed with the same symbolism as earlier. Nevertheless, they maintained their practical function, and the educational system continued to secure linguistically based strategies for the safeguard of bourgeois privilege. The First World War did have the effect of arousing nationalist feelings and of bringing about a wave of enthusiasm for a communal linguistic utopia: *le poilu*, the language spoken in the trenches. However, such reactions were primarily sentimental. It was only after the Second World War and accompanying changes in socio-economic structures that the working class became directed towards complacent consumerism, and popular language lost some, but not all, of its singularity. It appears from a reaction to *Zazie* in *Le Figaro* that the traditional right was not altogether happy with this erosion of boundaries.[8] In a reading very similar to those performed on texts that, one century earlier, pointed out the idiosyncrasies and strangeness of the people, the article attempted to restore cultural distance as it applauded the comic effects derived from the representation of clownish characters. Both cases reveal efforts to circumscribe the working class within the boundaries of a demeaning representation.

In "Postmodernism and the Cultural Logic of Late Capitalism," Jameson describes the linguistic profile of contemporary society:

> Faceless masters continue to inflect the economic strategies which constrain our existences, but no longer need to impose their speech (or are henceforth unable to); and the postliteracy of the late capitalist world reflects, not only the absence of any great collective project, but also the unavailability of the older national language itself.[9]

This description is probably more applicable to the United States than to France, where legitimate language is still imposed as a norm, and continues to exercise its political functions. That popular language has lost some of its specificity does not mean that the inequalities in the competency necessary to its use are no longer class-related. If some differences are, indeed, attenuated, the models of relationships between language and society which I outlined in the first chapter remain valid. Linguistic xenophobia still thrives in France, and recently has also been directed against those English words that, since the end of the Second World War, increasingly infiltrated the national idiom. In fact, several of these appear in *Zazie*. Queneau phonetically transcribed the French pronunciation: *bloudjinzes* (blue jeans), *coboïlle* (cow boy), *baille naïte* (by night) for example. Many of the English words are simply names of products (either generic or trademark) or of practices that come from (or are imagined to come from) the United States: *le shopping*, for example, is a more leisurely, less necessary activity than *les courses*. Some replace expressions that already exist and refer to exactly the same thing, but sound more worldly and sophisticated: "Vous prendrez bien un drink" instead of *un verre* and "on en parlera pendant le break" instead of *la pause*. Numerous others are scientific and technological terms that originated in the United States.

Several interrelated reasons account for the remarkably easy acceptance of English. One is the French fascination for all things American that a professor at the Sorbonne, Henri Etiemble, in his long and alarmist work *Parlez-vous franglais?* traces back to the euphoria that surrounded the triumphant arrival of American troops at the Liberation. Was the victory worth it, he wonders in typically indignant tone, if it brought on the ruin of the French language:

> Two wars in thirty years, in which we were allies with the Anglo-Saxons precipitated our servitude. In order to triumph over Germany, if France must abandon on the battlefield, along with millions of corpses, the corpse of its language, to what good is so much blood, so many ruins, so much foolishness.[10]

Furthermore, after four years of hardship and restrictions, the booming consumerism of the United States in the 1950s was surely appealing, and the perceptions of high standards of living and boundless glamor conveyed by Hollywood movies were not without charm; a fashionable, desirable value became attached to all things American. Along with these subjective appraisals, a material reality was at work: the involvement of the United States in the French economy, with a particularly strong financial presence in the auto and chemical industries. European research in science and technology lagged far behind its American counterpart, and English rapidly became the dominant language in these fields.

So appalled is the author by the pervasion of a foreign syntax and vocabulary that he is willing to accept in its place, as well as provincial expressions, the use of Québecquois, French Caribbean and Belgian words – his conviction that the United States is undertaking a linguistic and cultural invasion, corruption and colonization of France must be particularly strong to bring about such an unexpected position. He is certainly not alone in his outrage. A good number of other purists have issued similar cries, and official action has been taken in the face of this imminent danger. An Office du Vocabulaire Français (Office of French Vocabulary) was created in 1957. One of its tasks was to establish a list of terms to be used in place of the more current English ones: *chef* for *leader*, *parc de stationnement à voiture* for *parking* (meaning car park), *annonceur* for *speaker* (meaning TV announcer), for example. The trend caught on, in theory at least, and in 1963 the numerous existing committees concerned with questions of linguistic purity were grouped together as the Fédération Internationale pour la Sauvegarde et l'Unité de la Langue Française (International Federation for the Safeguard and Unity of the French Language).

The feeling that French might be inadequate and should be supplemented with words taken from other Francophone countries recalls the efforts towards linguistic enrichment during the Renaissance. "The safeguard and unity of the French language" was a central concern during the seventeenth century. The perception that the French language is under siege, contaminated and corrupted by

Popular language as literary artifact 203

a foreign body dates back to the nineteenth century. Then, the foreign body was argot; now, it is primarily English. Then, the threat came from below – the working class's potential disruption of the smooth development of industrial capitalism. In the age of American imperialism and multi-national capitalism, the threat comes from above. "Linguistic oppression" now stems from what, in the perception of many, is an economic and cultural domination. In both cases, the French bourgeoisie, whether it attempts to gain or retain its internal coherence and political privilege, designates and isolates itself against a threatening other. Furthermore, today, as a sub-proletariat of North African immigrants begins to display signs of what appears disturbingly close to a class-consciousness of its own, as well as to voice concerns that are no longer restricted to economic survival, but include political and religious rights, linguistic issues are again at the forefront: the demand for a bilingual (French/Arabic) education in pre-schools and elementary schools met strong outrage. For many, the mere thought of such a possibility wounded their national pride in a manner unparalleled since the German invasion. French language, then, continues to function as a boundary-marker: including some, excluding others, unequally distributing the access to economic and social power. It performs practical functions, and symbolic ones as well, as the guardian and epitome of a highly self-conscious and canonical culture. Such considerations no doubt entered Algeria's recent decision to drop French as its official language.

A number of theoretical possibilities support the hypothesis that the style of the novels reviewed here might carry an oppositional political function that would bring about a decrease in the working class's alienation. One of these derives from an historical perspective: these texts break with earlier instances in which the representation of popular language partook in the profoundly conservative political function of objectification and containment. Hence, a departure from this strategy might suggest a contrary effect. Furthermore, the critique of, or at least the dissociation from legitimate language that the presence of popular language might suggest can be viewed as a critique of its political functions and of the institutions that promote them. It is also conceivable that traces of previous contexts, previous uses, previous functions – including those of antagonisms towards the ruling class – still resonate in popular words, and remain active on the page of the literary text. Another possibility, if one accepts the claim that the novel allows for a re-stratification of languages and hence might overturn existing hierarchies is the construction of a linguistic utopia that would suggest a social one: the popular, in this new organization, might lose the place of subservience in which it is normally held. One or more of these possibilities operate, to varying degrees, in each work. Since *L'Assommoir* is the first novel in which popular language extends beyond the boundaries of directly reported speech, the significance of the rupture with previous practices is greatest in its case. Also innovative in this novel is its subject matter: the working class is depicted as a (falsely) self-enclosed social entity, a cohesive milieu to which the characters and their actions are inextricably linked. The working class had not yet been the unique topic of a "serious" literary representation. Its presence in the work of Hugo and Balzac was far less central than in *L'Assommoir*: there are long theoretical digressions in *Les Misérables* and *Vautrin's Last Avatar* that distract from the plot and in which the narrator posits himself at a critical distance from the characters and events. The emphasis in the Goncourts' *Germinie Lacerteux* is on the deviant psychology of an individual; and Sue only dwells on the most entertaining or scandalous aspects of a highly theatrical underworld. As Barthes put it:

> These picturesque jargons embellished Literature without threatening its structure. Balzac, Süe, Monnier, Hugo found enjoyment in reinstating a few really aberrant forms of pronunciation and vocabulary: thieves' argot, country dialects, German jargon, or the lingo of the concierges. But this social speech, which was a kind of theatrical costume hung on to an essence, never involved the speaker as a total person; the mechanism of the passions went on functioning over and above speech.[11]

Not unlike the often paradoxical readings of *L'Assommoir* (which was denounced by both the political left and right) the literary discursive situation in which it was produced displays ambiguous characteristics. Even though Zola was born bourgeois and undoubtedly enjoyed bourgeois privileges, he did, for a while, come into close enough contact with the working class that it ceased to be an abstraction. His acquaintance with popular language was adequate enough for its representation in *L'Assommoir*, but he relied none the less on dictionaries, in an effort, perhaps, to acquire scientific distance and objectivity. With *The Mysteries of Marseille* and similar works he had earlier addressed a mass audience, whereas with *Les Rougon-Macquart* he sought to place himself in the lineage of Balzac, Hugo and Flaubert. One senses, from his social trajectory, an intention to establish himself firmly as a writer. His relative lack of interest in conventional education, the years of a poverty-stricken artist's life, his work for the Librairie Hachette (which brought him into contact with influential publishing circles) attest to this. When he wrote *L'Assommoir*, Zola was not a newcomer to the literary field, nor had he reached the level of recognition for which he was no doubt striving. The publication of the first few novels of the series did not cause a significant reaction, either positive or negative. The literary discursive situation, then, suggests that a likely strategy would be to strike a difficult balance between producing a highly noticeable work, and not alienating a fairly well-disposed public.

Of the three literary discursive situations, that in which Céline wrote *Journey* seems to allow for most oppositional possibilities. Zola had wandered away from the bourgeoisie only for a while, whereas Céline was born into the lower classes, which he subsequently escaped through perseverent auto-didacticism. His background provided him with a familiarity with popular language; later, he acquired legitimate French without entering the educational system, and hence without being submitted to its ideological inculcation. Unlike Zola, Céline did not depend on writing as his sole means of support; this might have enabled him to take a greater risk, to position his work at a greater distance than otherwise from what he perceived to be the public's horizon of expectations. He had no established readership and thus did not need to be concerned with ensuring its continued support. Furthermore, since he was unknown at the time of the publication of *Journey*, his stylistic choice would have a decisive impact on how he would be viewed and defined in the literary field; this was not the case for Zola, whose *L'Assommoir* the critics often considered an aberration, a "fake wart" so different it was from his earlier works. Although very few documents attest to this, the letter in which Céline claims he wants to produce "not a work of art . . . not literature" indicates that he is animated, from the outset, by the intention to mark his difference.[12] The stylistic risk he took, however, was attenuated by the impact of surrealism, a movement that had accustomed certain readers to the literary ill-treatment of the French language (not, however, in a way that tended towards the popular or that often included the novel). In general, the *entre-deux-guerres* was a period when attitudes of aesthetic negation, iconoclasm even, were very much in vogue. Such reactions, though most forcefully expressed by the surrealists, were not exclusive to their group. The Catholic novelist Georges Bernanos, in "Combat Writings," suggests that this linguistic crisis was very much linked to the war experience: "Whoever held a pen at that time [after the war] felt the obligation to reconstruct his own language, to throw it back into the forge."[13] *Journey* can be situated within a framework constituted, on the one hand, by the populist, post-First World War writing of Barbusse and Dabit, and, on the other, by the oppositional, modernist practices of the period.

Queneau is the author whose social origin and trajectory place him at the greatest distance from the working class. This distance, as far as matters of linguistic competence are concerned, is mediated by the fact that he wrote at a time when popular language was losing its specificity. Because he brought a considerable amount of authority to the literary discursive situation, the stylistic innovations that his work offered carried a certain weight. His authority extended to the intellectual field at large, as his involvement in the production of the Pléiade encyclopedia and his many theoretical articles demonstrate. The fact that Gallimard published the collection of his articles as "Sticks, Numbers and Letters" in 1950, combined with the comfortable success of his previous novels, indicates that the public was ready for him fully to exploit the linguistic innovations that he had sketched out. Unlike what the situation in which Céline wrote *Journey* suggests, Queneau's opposition to legitimate language is devoid of political significance: many remarks in his discussion of linguistic issues show that he advocates the use of a written language that is close to its spoken counterpart for only practical and literary reasons.

One of the subversive possibilities in *L'Assommoir* is suggested in Barthes' introduction to his *Writing Degree Zero*. He comments on *Le Père Duchêne*, a publication that, between 1790 and 1794, expressed the positions of the extreme left (its founder, Hébert, found Robespierre to be too moderate): "Hébert, the revolutionary, never began a number of his news-sheet *Le Père Duchêne* without a sprinkling of obscenities. These improprieties had no real meaning, but they had significance. In what way? In that they expressed a whole revolutionary situation."[14] Outside of what the language of the working class in *L'Assommoir* signifies (which can only be determined in relation to the overall stylistic structure and content of the novel), its mere presence signals, if not an outright revolutionary situation, a revolutionary threat. Such must have been the opinion of the government, which threatened to halt the serial's publication and, later, to intervene in the distribution of the book. One critic, Dancourt, did not hesitate to name the threat: he called the style "insurrectional." Surely, such an extensive representation of popular language (even though it came to the literary page mediated, in part, by documentary works) still rang with the political connotations that threatened the bourgeoisie, as it forcefully brought to attention the existence of the working class, in a far less analytical and objectifying manner than previously.

Another, more specific subversive element in Zola's work is related to the ambiguity, introduced with the indirect style and free indirect style, as to who speaks. The situation is not one in which a fictitious narrator endorses a working-class persona and voice; rather, the pervasion of the popular occurs through a gradual and slow erosion of voice boundaries. Initially at least, a consequence of this strategy is that the readers are less surprised than they would be otherwise by the sudden presence of popular language; yet it subverts all the more forcefully one of its more salient features in earlier representations: the clear demarcation between characters' utterances and narrative voice, a demarcation that was reinforced by the material manner in which popular language was dissociated from the rest of the text, and by the frequent negative comments that accompanied its presence. This infiltration of popular language occurs through what Bakhtin calls character zones:

> These zones are formed from the fragments of character speech, from various forms for hidden transmission of someone else's words, from scattered words and sayings belonging to someone else's speech, from those invasions into authorial speech of others' expressive indicators (ellipses, questions, exclamations). Such a character zone is the field of action for a character's voice, encroaching in one way or another upon the author's voice.[15]

This process is all the more significant in that, elsewhere in *L'Assommoir*, other instances of blurring are presented in an extremely negative light. A particularly striking example is the repulsion suggested by the description of working-class encroachments that, violating the purity of a clean, new, geometrical architecture, survived Haussmann's project of urban renovation: "between sculpted façades sank dark recesses, gaping kennels spreading their shabby windows. Under the rising wealth of Paris, the poverty of the faubourg was bursting to the surface, befouling the site of this newly built city, so rapidly put together."[16]

Many of the conservative critics emphasized and decried the dissolution of linguistic boundaries, deploring the fact that Zola had become "contaminated" by the popular, that he had "lost himself in its filth." The image, rather than suggesting Zola's openness to popular language implies, on the contrary, his engulfment by it, a passive submission to the deteriorating and dangerous effects of a foreign body over which he has no control.

208 Political Stylistics

Journey displays, by far, the most subversive features. Here, the possibility that popular language stands in opposition to legitimate language is reinforced by the fact that isolated belletristic forms are mocked. When the *passé simple*, for example, appears in close proximity to slang expressions, it adds a discrepant, precious note to a less than sophisticated context. On other occasions, verbs that do not usually lend themselves to such tenses are conjugated in *passé simple*, imperfect subjunctive, and pluperfect subjunctive. Many attacks on officialdom (the army, colonists, doctors) and the anger that resonates in the content of these attacks, also reinforce the antagonistic position *vis à vis* the ruling class that is suggested by how it is said. Furthermore, when typical features such as *rappels*, repetitions and ellipses operate in a manner that impedes straightforward communication and renders the meaning ambiguous, or when idiomatic expressions undergo a slight, defamiliarizing transformation, popular language in *Journey* actually participates in a poetic function. Elsewhere, the poetic and the popular, tightly intertwined within one sentence or group of sentences, operate by way of close interaction, mutually reinforcing and highlighting each other. By negating and destabilizing fixed antinomies, these constructions also oppose conventional genre categories and the traditional literary canon that established them. Boundaries are transgressed, hierarchies dislocated: the popular is illuminated by the aristocratic aura of the poetic, the poetic is energized by the living force of the popular, which, clearly, plays a dominant role in the stylistic structure of the novel. Not only is it pervasive and quantitatively dominant from beginning to end, but, also because it is constantly engaged in compelling stylistic effects, it never becomes a monotonous backdrop. Henri Godard, in "Céline's Poetics" (*Poétique de Céline*), notes the great suppleness with which it operates; rather than being confined to one subject matter, to the creation of one type of effect, it participates in many, and remains the most potent stylistic unity:

> It is true that the effect of his use of popular language is, in part, to demystify individuals, acts, or feelings ideologically considered noble, but also to prove that there is no experience that this language cannot express, when one wants it to: distress, nostalgia, or a reverie in the presence of a river or ships, just as well as derision or violence.[17]

Another powerful effect in *Journey* is that of the disconcerting, fluid and dynamic style on the reader, a style that Jean-Pierre Richard, in "Céline's Nausea" (*Nausée de Céline*), describes as one that "imitates, and wonderfully, the movement of inundation and dishevelment."[18] The deeply unsettling reading experience was not lost on critics in the press:

> One can compare this text to a torrent that rolls, mingling diamonds and mud, in its waters sometimes clear sometimes murky, and with them the reader who, after the last page, it would throw, dizzy, raw, on a deserted shore, lost in his interior solitude.[19]

Céline, it appears from later statements, is quite aware of the power his style exerts over the reader who is overcome both by its violent and poetic qualities. However, it becomes clear that to strip the reader of old values and beliefs does not mean that they will be replaced by a sympathetic attitude towards the working class.

Both within and outside of the characters' utterances, popular language is present throughout *Zazie*. On no occasion does it express anger of any kind, nor does it suggest a disconcerting ambiguity of meaning. It does, however, participate in comic effects, and mocks formal literary styles, but these styles themselves mock the popular. There are many other internal resistances that stand in the way of this novel's oppositional potential. One is the graphic peculiarities: the innovative, quasi-phonetic spelling of certain expressions that detract from the presence of popular language and that cause comic effects. If these forms were linked to serious efforts to promote orthographic reforms, and hence tended towards eliminating one of the class-related criteria of selection in the educational system, their function would be very different. Obviously, because of their infrequency, the unsystematic nature of the new "spelling," and the emphasis on their estranging effect, such is not the case. One could even suggest that, with their bizarre appearance they mock non-conventional spelling. Furthermore, within the stylistic structure of the novel, the popular is far from playing a dominant role. It is, in fact, often sharply contrasted with, and even clearly mocked by, a number of other styles, such as the philosophical ("slightly Kantian Thomism"), the dramatic ("verbal buckler"), or the precious ("dream of a dream"). However, since these styles themselves are mocked, they do not dominate either. Throughout the novel, categories of high and low are leveled. It is not as though each is granted similar value, but neither is granted any at all. Popular language is shown to be equal to all the other languages present in the novel, but all are ridiculed.

In *L'Assommoir* and *Journey*, certain oppositional functions are at work; within *L'Assommoir* in particular a number of internal resistances stand in the way of its oppositional potential. The main counteractive feature is the presence of passages in *écriture artiste*, a style typified by the fragmentation of long sentences by commas or semi-colons, the subject–verb disjunction, numerous adjectives, and *recherché* imagery. With a wealth of details, such passages represent vast tableaux, seen from a comprehensive, sweeping, often aerial viewpoint: the Paris sky, the architecture of the city, a stream of workers that fill several long streets. In the same way that their style is in sharp rupture with popular language, these tableaux form backdrops from which the characters are dissociated. Because the *écriture artiste* prevails at the beginning of the novel and becomes more rare as popular language becomes quantitatively dominant, the sudden breach in style that its unexpected appearance creates draws the reader's attention and produces a reassuring effect, particularly when the subject matter of these passages echoes scenes from the early chapters (scenes that occurred before the "invasion" of the popular). Also reassuring to the bourgeois reader is the subject matter of these descriptions, which proposes a familiar, optimistic world-view: one that suggests the stability of a linear progress, achieved smoothly, and without sharp breaks, and the timelessness of the workers' cyclical, daily routine. Interrupting as they do the flow of popular language, these scenes are noticeable to a hypothetical implied reader (a reader who is not historically situated and who does not bring external knowledge, assumptions and expectations to bear on the text) because of the sudden breach in style, and because of the manner in which they stand out from the surrounding context. For the historically situated reader, they are further invested with authority and legitimacy because they correspond to the external literary norms of the time.

The other internal resistance derives from the negative representation of the working class. Already, the preparatory dossier offers a number of ambiguous suggestions as to how Zola viewed the people. On the one hand, when he claims that his aim is to depict their hardship in terms of their living conditions, the workers are represented as passive victims. Calling for greater instruction, more secure employment and so forth, Zola advocates an attitude of humanitarian reformism. However, the inevitability of their "fall" is not always shown to be related to the environment. Zola's reliance on such works as *Le Sublime* suggests the acceptance of a determinism based on moral rather than societal factors. An article from *Le Gaulois* that Zola had collected for the preparatory dossier also tends in the same direction, classifying workers according to moral characteristics and assuring the reader than only self-discipline will ameliorate their condition. As for the presentation of the people in the novel itself, it is equally ambiguous. Living conditions and daily life are indeed depicted throughout the novel, and are depicted as harsh. However, their relation to political structures at large is less than clear. The depiction is solely internal to the class, it is a narrow view that includes, however, graphic scenes that, one imagines, Zola knew would be judged immoral or (independently of the language) extremely offensive: a drunk Coupeau sleeping in his vomit, his alcoholic delirium at the hospital, the young daughter Nana as *voyeuse*, Gervaise's prostitution – such scenes were hardly designed to offer an appealing picture of the characters. Popular language, increasingly used as their lives deteriorate, becomes imbued with, and, in the eyes of many, reinforces, the negativity.

Once a literary work has been launched on the market, a number of external resistances operate to neutralize its oppositional features before it reaches, or as it reaches, the individual reader. Michel Foucault, in his inaugural lecture at the Collège de France, outlined the process: "In any society, the production of discourse is at once controled, selected, organized by a certain number of procedures whose role is to exorcize its powers and dangers."[20] This study has investigated politically motivated readings that were based on specific world-views, experiences, and systems of thought, and that hence operated with particular acts of textual selection and organization. Furthermore, the readings aimed at promoting certain views, and through acts of manipulation, tended to deflate or re-direct political potential. The interpretations and reactions of individual readers were no doubt shaped by these judgments. Another factor that participates in determining the work's reception is the author's intervention in the polemic as he witnesses and perhaps strives to correct the initial reactions to his work.

In the case of *L'Assommoir*, the government itself felt compelled to exercise censorship by seeking to halt the novel's publication and, later, to hinder its distribution. These attempts failed; far more successful was the tactic adopted by many critics who were intent on stressing the negativity of Zola's representation: it certainly is true that the working class, "this population of drunkards, bad workers, horrendous husbands," in Albert Wolff's words, is not shown to be directly oppressed by the ruling class; the critic concludes therefore that the novel proves that "the bourgeois are not to blame" and, in an enthusiastic response, goes so far as to condone the presence of popular language, contending that it upholds the veracity of the descriptions.[21] He is one of the very few who draw attention to another internal resistance, the passages in *écriture artiste* where "the man of letters rises with a singular strength and where the philosopher displays a rare power of observation." Similar strategies are used against the oppositional potential of *Journey* and *Zazie*. Rousseaux, in *Le Figaro*, finds the style of Céline's novel repulsive, but claims that it unveils the dark and puerile soul of working-class people, and applauds the fact that it is hence directed against them.[22] Even though the oppositional tendencies in *Zazie* are extremely weak, a conservative critic none the less found it necessary to stress that the primary virtue of this novel was the representation and mockery of the working class's entertaining idiosyncrasies.[23]

Applauding the realism of a novel that, finally, showed the working class as it really was, the tactic outlined above entirely focuses on the negativity of this representation. So did another strategy that, without even suggesting that the depictions in *L'Assommoir* were unrealistic or biased, judged them far too immoral and distasteful to be shown – a self-righteous position, the hypocrisy of which is revealed by the somewhat triumphant tone and the critics' eagerness to include in their articles many of the less than flattering passages. That these practices were indeed endemic to the people must have been a point that they wished to promote indirectly, while displaying great offense at their representation. As in Wolff's article, nothing is said about the period of time during which Gervaise works hard to open her shop and, before Coupeau's illness, maintains a successful business for a short while. Hand in hand with the accusations of immorality go those of tastelessness which imply, on the part of Zola, a failure: bad taste is not a conscious disregard of aesthetic norms (as the provocative dedication to Flaubert, "in hatred of good taste," suggests) but an unsuccessful attempt at its fulfillment. Hence, the critics remark, *L'Assommoir* does not qualify as literature. The passages in *écriture artiste* were very much silenced by these critics, who deplored the fact that "Zola's language" no longer existed and had been replaced by "the language of the author of *L'Assommoir*,' and that nowhere does the novel offer "a bridge from which the reader can see without dirtying himself."[24] As soon as the polemic developed, Zola attempted to remove *L'Assommoir* from any political function whatsoever. It is true that his motivations were not to celebrate the people; there was certainly nothing to be gained from alienating the vast majority of bourgeois readers, particularly since one of Zola's aims was to have *Les Rougon-Macquart* enter honorific literature. Not surprisingly, then, he stresses the primarily artistic nature of his work: "a very elaborate mold," "a primarily literary attempt."[25] At the same time, and not unlike Hugo, he claimed that the representation of popular language was of practical interest and philosophical value.

However much left-wing critics admired many aspects of *Journey*, they could not entirely endorse the novel because the representation of the proletariat lacked positivity. *Journey*, we have seen, offers a linguistic utopia, which, however, is not supported by its contents. The working class is not represented in utopian terms. There is no suggestion of a unified and cohesive social group; working-class characters are present, but not shown in a flattering light. None of them is motivated by a dedication to political struggle, or even by an interest in political concerns. They are not painted as particularly negative, but they are portrayed as negatively as others. This does not affect the opposition to legitimate language, or the disconcerting effects, but it does lessen the significance of the stylistic restratification whereby the popular plays a dominant role. Certainly, it prevented the communist critics from wholeheartedly supporting the work: "impossible to accept his profound anarchy, his disdain, his general repulsion that does not exclude the proletariat."[26] The same issue reappears in the case of *Zazie*, where the characters who routinely use popular language, even though they are shown with much more sympathy than in Zola's novel, appear to be primarily concerned with quotidian and trivial matters (often revolving, as in *L'Assommoir*, around sex, food and drink).

The political configuration at the time of *Journey* was different from, and far more complex than that in the 1870s when any sign of support for the working class suggested an allegiance with the left; not so in the 1930s when the working class was also courted by the far right. The fascist critics wrote from a position of opposition to the bourgeoisie and expressed quite strong populist attitudes – attitudes that sought to seduce, but not to glorify or liberate, the working class. Their enthusiastic assessment of *Journey* was indeed founded on and reinforced its politically oppositional aspects – oppositional to capitalism, but certainly not favoring its replacement by a social order where the working class would be free from alienation. In popular language, they found – and applauded – anger, violence and virility, but completely dissociated this language from the class from which it originated. Onto the pessimism, the disconcerting effects and the destruction of cultural identity they grafted their own view of a positive consequence: the building of a new order, a fascist order. Later, Céline's own political positions, which the success of *Journey* and *Death on the Installment Plan* gave him the authority to express – to express, again, in a style in which popular language played the dominant role – also belied any benevolence towards or solidarity with the working class. And, in "If That Is What Treason Is," it is for Céline's fascism that Ezra Pound, by no means insensitive to matters of style and poetics, expresses the greatest admiration. Political bonding, here, appears of far greater relevance than literary appreciation. It is the anti-semitic pamphlets, rather than the novels, that he urges the reader to acquire:

> the stock of words remains accessory / the importance of Céline is in his way of seeing clearly / ... / population of 40 million in France in 1938 / 25 million French / soon to become a minority / ... / the active members of the public must BUY their own copy of *L'Ecole des Cadavres*.[27]

Even though we know that the internal properties of texts are not valid criteria to determine their literariness, it is not inappropriate to examine retroactively such properties and their evolution. Barthes, in *Writing Degree Zero*, does precisely this: he traces and underlines the most typical moments in the history of literary language, or, as he puts it, in the history of the signs of literature. The first radical break occurs in the mid-nineteenth century, when form loses its transparency and literary language undergoes a process of "concretization," epitomized in the work of Flaubert:

> Flaubert finally established Literature as an object, through promoting literary labour to the status of value; form became the end product of craftsmanship, like a piece of pottery or a jewel (one must understand that craftsmanship was here made manifest, that is, it was for the first time imposed on the reader as a spectacle).[28]

Literary language then, becomes artifact, a status that popular language in *L'Assommoir* does not escape. Barthes describes Zola's writing, and that of the naturalist school in general, as an unappealing sub-product of Flaubert's "style as craftsmanship." With its "combination of the formal signs of literature (preterite, indirect speech, the rhythm of written language) and of the no less formal signs of realism (incongruous snippets of popular speech, strong language or dialect words, etc.)" nothing is more artificial than this language that claims so accurately to reflect the world.[29] In *L'Assommoir*, popular language is present in more than reported fragments; however, its relationship to traditional literary language in the novel (the "combination") is one wherein the subversive potential is absorbed by an internal resistance.

The second stage in Barthes' sketch of this concretization of the literary is "murder," performed in most splendid form by Mallarmé: "Mallarmé's work, finally, was the crowning achievement of this creation of Literature as Object, and this by the ultimate of all objectifying acts: murder."[30] What Barthes describes as a characteristic of such writing – a dislocation and disintegration of language, a chaos of forms, a syntax of disorder – are clearly present in Céline's. Mallarmé is, in fact, one of the very few writers of whom Céline speaks favorably. In a letter to Milton Hindus, he compares his work to Mallarmé's: like him, he is a "coloriste de mots."[31] But the words he uses, unlike Mallarmé's, are "everyday words," and with these, Céline performs a grammatical denaturalization. Spoken and popular language, in *Journey*, deeply affects the syntax, unlike in *L'Assommoir* where its effects are restricted to a primarily lexical level, and in *Zazie*, to a surface characteristic, orthography. It is here, in this high-modernist text, that the greatest oppositional potential exists. If popular language in *L'Assommoir* ultimately reinforced relations of production, in *Journey* it certainly questioned them, but in a manner that benefited the extreme right. The subversive was diverted from an itinerary that might have benefited the oppressed class by, first, a fascist celebration of the novel, and, later, by the political use to which Céline put his literary legitimacy. It was not only the murder of literature that he advocated.

Queneau typifies the final stage in the trajectory outlined by Barthes, that of absence:

> writing thus passed through all the stages of a progressive solidification; it was first the object of a gaze, then of creative action, finally of murder, and has reached in our time a last metamorphosis, absence: in those neutral modes of writing, called here "the zero degree of writing," we can easily discern a negative momentum . . . Colourless writing like Camus's, like Blanchot's or Cayrol's, for example, or conversational writing like Queneau's represents the last episode of a Passion of writing, which recounts stage by stage the disintegration of bourgeois consciousness.[32]

In "Zazie and Literature," Barthes notes that *Zazie* is a novel that establishes an identity between literature and its enemy. Our analysis viewed the novel as a precursor to postmodernism and Jameson, in "Postmodernism and the Cultural Logic of Late Capitalism" makes the connection: "this new kind of linguistic innovation, which is no longer personal at all, but has its family kinship rather with *what Barthes long ago called 'white writing'*"[33] (my emphasis). Indeed, what is described in *Writing Degree Zero* as a voluntary neglect of ornamentation and elegance, a dismissal of Time and History, and an ideal absence of style corresponds to important features of postmodernism. In 1986, Jameson notes that such works do not merely replicate the logic of late capitalism, they also reinforce and intensify it (*Zazie*, therefore, like *L'Assommoir*, works towards the preservation of the political structures from which it emerged); Barthes, some thirty years earlier, suggested that the search for a "non-style" was a utopic gesture that anticipated an homogeneous state of society:

> Writing therefore is a blind alley, and it is because society itself is a blind alley. The writers of today feel this; for them the search for a non-style or an oral style, for a zero level or a spoken level of writing is, all things considered, the anticipation of a homogeneous social state; most of them understand that there can be no universal language outside a concrete, and no longer mystical or merely nominal, universality of society.[34]

There are ways, indeed, in which contemporary society has achieved a surface homogeneity, through the leveling of cultural practices, the primacy of consumption, the dictatorship of the media. Yet, if political contradictions are better camouflaged and perhaps displaced, we remain far from the ideal of a concrete universality. What the fundamental pessimism of Barthes' utopia suggests, and what the failure of the oppositional qualities of the texts reviewed here confirms, is that, however inseparable the two, a literary resolution of what Barthes calls "the division of languages" did not bring about, or even encourage, a resolution to "the division of classes"; the impasse remains.

Notes

Introduction

1 V. Hugo, *Les Contemplations*, in Vol. 20 of *Victor Hugo's Works*, trans. anonymous, Boston, Estes and Lauriat, 1892, p. 99.
2 V. Hugo, *The Last Day of a Condemned*, trans. Eugenia de B., New York, Fertig, 1977, p. 6.
3 ibid., p. 101.
4 ibid., p. 65.
5 ibid., p. 97.
6 ibid., p. 98.
7 ibid., p. 101.
8 Hugo, *Les Misérables*, in Vol. 4 of *Victor Hugo's Works*, op. cit., p. 213.
9 ibid., p. 213.
10 ibid., p. 214.
11 ibid., p. 213.
12 H. de Balzac, *Vautrin's Last Avatar*, in Vol. 26 of *The Novels of Balzac*, trans. J. Waring, Philadelphia, Gebbic Publishing Co. Ltd, 1899, p. 48.
13 M. L. Pratt, *Towards a Speech Act Theory of Literary Discourse*, Bloomington, Indiana University Press, 1977, p. 122.

1 A political stylistics

1 P. Bourdieu, *Ce que parler veut dire*, Paris, Fayard, 1982, p. 165. It is difficult to translate this title, for it plays on the various meanings of *vouloir dire*: to signify, to mean to say, to want to say.
2 J. Knappert, "Language in a Political Situation," *Linguistics*, 1968, Vol. 39, pp. 59–67.
3 ibid., p. 64.
4 A. Leibnitz, "Language and the Law: The Exercise of Political Power," in *Language and Politics*, W. O'Barr and J. O'Barr (eds), The Hague, Mouton, 1976, p. 451.
5 J. du Bellay, *Défense et illustration de la langue française*, Y. Wendel-Bellenger (ed.), Paris, Larousse, 1971, p. 118.
6 C. F. de Vaugelas, *Remarques sur la langue française*, Paris, Champ Libre, 1981, p. 10.

7 ibid., p. 22.
8 Cited in F. Brunot, *Histoire de la langue française*, Vol. III, Paris, Armand Colin, 1966, p. 34.
9 On this subject, see R. Balibar, *Le Français national: politique et pratique de la langue nationale sous la révolution française*, Paris, Hachette, 1974, and her *L'Institution du français: essai sur le colinguisme des Carolingiens à la République*, Paris, Presses Universitaires de France, 1985.
10 Cited in Brunot, op. cit., Vol. XI, Première partie, p. 11.
11 Note dictated by Napoléon, 21 March 1808. Arch. nat. AF, 909. Cited in Brunot, *Histoire de la langue française*, Vol. XI, Deuxième partie, Paris, Armand Colin, 1979, pp. 29–30.
12 Cited in C. Désirat et T. Hordé, *La Langue française au 20eme siècle*, Paris, Bordas, 1976, p. 94.
13 Bourdieu, op. cit., p. 54.
14 P. Bourdieu and J.-C. Passeron, *La Reproduction: Elements pour une théorie de l'enseignement*, Paris, Minuit, 1970, pp. 144–5.
15 B. Bernstein, "Social Class, Language and Socialization," in *Language and Social Context*, P. P. Giglioli (ed.), Baltimore, Penguin, 1973, p. 167.
16 ibid., p. 163.
17 On this subject, see E. Suleiman, *Elites in French Society: The Politics of Survival*, Princeton, Princeton University Press, 1978.
18 On this subject, see Leibnitz, op. cit.
19 On this subject, see R. Brown and A. Gilman, 'The Pronouns of Power and Solidarity,' in *Language and Social Context*, op. cit., pp. 252–82. This study discusses how, apart from factors related to age, the choice between the pronouns *tu* or *vous* depends not only on the distribution of power, but also on the degree of solidarity, and on whether the exchange is conflictual or not.
20 W. Labov, "Le Changement linguistique," *Actes de la recherche en sciences sociales*, 1983, Vol. 40, p. 69. See also Bourdieu, op. cit., p. 35.
21 Bourdieu, op. cit., p. 85.
22 N. Mailer, *The White Negro*, San Francisco, City Lights Books, 1957.
23 J. Baldwin, "The Black Boy Looks at the White Boy," in *Nobody Knows My Name: More Notes of a Native Son*, New York, Dell, 1961, pp. 171–90.
24 M. L. Pratt, *Towards a Speech Act Theory of Literary Discourse*, Bloomington, Indiana University Press, 1977. W. Labov, *Language in the Inner City: Studies in Black English Vernacular*, Philadelphia, University of Philadelphia Press, 1977.
25 Cited in Brunot, op. cit., Vol. XI, Deuxième partie, p. 864.
26 Vaugelas, op. cit., p. 10.
27 Cited in Brunot, op. cit., Vol. XI, Deuxième partie, p. 870.
28 R. Terdiman, *Discourse/Counter-Discourse*, Ithaca, Cornell University Press, 1985.
29 Bourdieu, op. cit., p. 50.
30 R. Barthes, *Le Degré zéro de l'écriture*, Paris, Seuil, 1972, p. 8.
31 F. Desonay, "Préface de la sixième édition (1955)," in M. Grévisse, *Le Bon Usage*, Gembloux, Duculot, 1975, p. 1.
32 Bourdieu, op. cit., p. 48.

Notes 219

33 Leenhardt points out that those texts that, because of deviant grammar, create unstable configurations of meaning and tend to transform the reader into a producer, contradict the reading codes enforced by the educational system. See his "Towards a Sociology of Reading," in *The Reader in the Text*, I. Crosman and S. Suleiman (eds), Princeton, Princeton University Press, 1980, p. 208.
34 Pratt, op. cit., p. 87.
35 H. R. Jauss, "Literary History as Challenge to Literary Theory," *New Literary History*, 1976, Vol. 2, pp. 7–37.
36 Terdiman, op. cit., p. 48.
37 V. N. Volosinov, *Marxism and the Philosophy of Language*, trans. L. Matejhma and I. R. Titunik, New York, Seminar Press, 1973, p. 19.
38 L. Chevalier, *Classes Laborieuses et classes dangereuses à Paris pendant la première partie du 19eme siècle*, Paris, Plon, 1958, (*Laboring Classes and Dangerous Classes in Paris during the First Half of the Nineteenth Century*, trans. F. Jellinek, New York, Fertig, 1973). Also see C. Nisard, *Histoire des livres populaires et de la littérature de colportage*, Paris, Librairie d'Amyot, 1854.
39 E. Vidocq, *Mémoires de Vidocq, chef de la police de sûreté*, Paris, Tenon, 1828.
40 *Nouveau dictionnaire d'argot, par un ex-chef de brigade sous M. Vidocq*, Paris, Chez les marchands de nouveautés, 1829; M. Froment, *Histoire de Vidocq, écrite d'après lui-même*, Paris, Lerosey, 1829.
41 *Les Mémoires d'un forban philosophe*, Paris, Moutardier, 1829; P. Joigneau, *Les Prisons de Paris par un ancien détenu*, Paris, Chez l'auteur, 1841.
42 *Dictionnaire d'argot ou Guide des gens du monde*, Paris, Chez les marchands de nouveautés, 1827.
43 E. Vidocq, *Les Voleurs, physiologie de leurs moeurs et de leur langage*, Paris, Chez l'auteur, 1837.
44 ibid., p. 2.
45 ibid., p. 4.
46 On this subject, see A. Vitu, *Le Jargon et Jobelin*, Paris, Paul Ollendorf, 1889, and L. Sainéan, *Les Sources de l'argot ancien*, Paris, Champion, 1912.
47 Francisque-Michel, *Etudes de philologie comparée sur l'argot et sur les idiomes parlés en Europe et en Asie*, Paris, Firmin Didot, 1856, p. 31.
48 ibid., p. 31.
49 L. Larchey, *Dictionnaire historique, étymologique et anecdotique de l'argot parisien*, 6th edition, Paris, E. Dentu, 1872.
50 ibid., p. 33.
51 A. Duchesne, "La Langue verte," *Le Figaro*, 29 March 1866.
52 A. Delvau, *Dictionnaire de la langue verte: Argots parisiens comparés*, Paris, E. Dentu, 1866, p. vii.
53 ibid., p. v.
54 A. Delvau, *Les Dessous de Paris*, Paris, Paulet Malarsis et de Broise, 1862.
55 Duchesne, op. cit.
56 D. Poulot, *Le Sublime ou le Travailleur comme il est en 1870 et ce qu'il peut être*, Paris, A. Lacroix, Verboecken and Co., 1872.
57 ibid., p. 390.

58 E. Sue, *Les Mystères de Paris*, Paris, Gosselin, 1843, pp. 2, 12.
59 Sue, ibid., p. 9.
60 V. Hugo, *Les Misérables*, in Vol. 4 of *Victor Hugo's Works*, trans. anonymous, Boston, Estes and Lauriat, 1892, pp. 219, 222, 225.
61 V. Brombert, *Victor Hugo and the Visionary Novel*, Cambridge, Mass., Harvard University Press, 1984, p. 30.
62 Hugo, op. cit., p. 217.
63 ibid., p. 219.
64 ibid., pp. 239, 240.
65 ibid., pp. 240-1.
66 P. Bourdieu, "Vous avez dit populaire?", *Actes de la recherche en sciences sociales*, 1983, Vol. 46, pp. 98–105. Bourdieu adds that, in Nazi Germany, similar implications were carried by the use of the word *Völkisch*; it is interesting to note how, today, the expression *le peuple* often finds a place in the extreme right-wing rhetoric of the National Front, whereas the French Communist Party is more likely to address the *proletariat* or *workers*.
67 Barthes, op. cit., p. 58.
68 G. Lukács, *Writer and Critic*, trans. A. Kahn, New York, Grosset and Dunlap, 1971, p. 126.
69 T. Adorno, "Commitment," in *The Essential Frankfurt School Reader*, A. Arato and E. Gebhardt (eds), New York, Urizen, 1978, p. 304.
70 H. Marcuse, *The Aesthetic Dimension: Towards a Critique of Marxist Aesthetics*, Boston, Beacon Press, 1978, p. 8.
71 Leenhardt, op. cit., p. 209.
72 W. Iser, *The Act of Reading*, Baltimore, The Johns Hopkins University Press, 1978 and T. Eagleton, *Literary Theory: An Introduction*, Oxford, Blackwell, 1983, pp. 78-9.
73 Adorno, op. cit., p. 315.
74 R. Barthes, *The Pleasure of the Text*, trans. R. Miller, New York, Hill and Wang, 1975.
75 Bourdieu, *Ce que parler veut dire*, op. cit., p. 46.
76 M. Bakhtin, *The Dialogic Imagination*, M. Holquist (ed.), and trans. C. Emerson and M. Holquist, Austin, University of Texas Press, 1981, p. 259.
77 ibid., p. 289.
78 Volosinov, op. cit., p. 23.
79 Bakhtin, op. cit., p. 299.
80 ibid., p. 295.
81 Cited in R. Yves-Plessis, *Bibliographie raisonnée de l'argot et de la langue verte*, Paris, Daragon, 1901, pp. 109, 112.
82 J. Goody and I. Watt, "The Consequences of Literacy," in *Language and Social Context*, op. cit., pp. 311–57.
83 ibid., p. 342.
84 Barthes, *Le Degré zéro*, op. cit., p. 18.
85 Bakhtin, op. cit., p. 336.
86 Terdiman, op. cit., p. 36.
87 Bourdieu, "Vous avez dit populaire?" op. cit., p. 99.
88 Bakhtin, op. cit., p. 262.
89 M. Riffaterre, *Essais de stylistique structurale*, Paris, Flammarion, 1972.

90 Bakhtin, op. cit., p. 262.
91 Iser, op. cit., p. 34.
92 Leenhardt, op. cit., pp. 205–24.
93 Terdiman, op. cit., p. 52.

2 Zola's *L'Assommoir*

1 E. Zola, "Préface de la deuxième édition, 1868," *Thérèse Raquin*, in Vol. I of *Oeuvres complètes*, H. Mitterand (ed.), Paris, Cercle du Livre Précieux, 1962, p. 520. *Thérèse Raquin* was first published in 1867.
2 E. Zola, "Balzac," in *Les Romanciers naturalistes*, in Vol. XI of *Oeuvres complètes*, H. Mitterand (ed.), Paris, Cercle du Livre Précieux, 1968, p. 56. *Les Romanciers naturalistes* was first published in 1881.
3 Zola, "Gustave Flaubert," in ibid., p. 98.
4 Cited in F. Hemmings, *Emile Zola*, Oxford, Oxford University Press, 1953, p. 55.
5 ibid., p. 73.
6 Zola, "Gustave Flaubert," op. cit., p. 99.
7 ibid. p. 105.
8 E. Zola, "Germinie Lacerteux," in *Mes Haines*, in Vol. X of *Oeuvres complètes*, H. Mitterand (ed.), Paris, Cercle du Livre Précieux, 1968, p. 70. *Mes Haines* was first published in 1860.
9 ibid., p. 70.
10 ibid., p. 69.
11 ibid., p. 71.
12 E. and J. de Goncourt, Preface, *Germinie Lacerteux*, Paris, Flammarion, 1930, p. 5.
13 Letter to Antony Valabrègue, cited in Hemmings, op. cit., p. 25.
14 Bibliothèque Nationale MS. Nouv. Acq. Françaises 10.271, fol. 1. All further references to this manuscript appear in the text.
15 E. Zola, *Correspondance 1872–1902*, Paris, Bernouard, 1929, p. 435.
16 See H. Massis, *Comment Emile Zola composait ses romans*, Paris, E. Fasquelle, 1966.
17 P. Alexis, *Emile Zola, Notes d'un ami*, Paris, Charpentier, 1895, p. 109.
18 J. Patin, "Du boeuf nature à la table des Beylistes," *Le Figaro*, 7 December 1930.
19 A. Delvau, *Dictionnaire de la langue verte, argots parisiens comparés*, Paris, E. Dentu, 1866.
20 Alexis, op. cit., p. 59.
21 D. Poulot, *Le Sublime ou le Travailleur comme il est en 1870 et ce qu'il peut être*, Paris, A. Lacroix, Verboecken and Co., 1872.
22 ibid., p. 6.
23 On this subject, also see S. Petrey, "Goujet as God and Worker in *L'Assommoir*," *French Forum*, September 1976, no. 1, pp. 239–49.
24 D. Place, "Zola and the Working Class: The Meaning of *L'Assommoir*," *French Studies*, January 1974, no. 28, pp. 39–49.
25 E. Auerbach, *Mimesis*, trans. W. Trask, New York, Doubleday, 1957, p. 438.
26 ibid., p. 446.

27 E. Zola, *L'Assommoir*, in Vol. III of *Oeuvres complètes*, H. Mitterand (ed.), Paris, Cercle du Livre Précieux, 1967, pp. 603, 606, 607. All further references to this work appear in the text.
28 L. Spitzer, "Une Habitude de style, le rappel chez Céline," *Le Français moderne*, June 1936, no. 3, pp. 193–208.
29 On this subject, see R. Niess, "Remarks on the *style indirect libre* in *L'Assommoir*," *Nineteenth Century French Studies*, 1974, Vol. 3, no. 1–2, pp. 124–35.
30 A. Banfield, "Narrative Style and the Grammar of Direct and Indirect Speech," *Foundations of Language*, 1973, no. 10, pp. 1–39.
31 C. Perruchot, "Le Style indirect libre et la question du sujet dans *Madame Bovary*," in *La Production du sens chez Flaubert–Colloque de Cerisy*, Paris, Union Générale d'édition, coll. 10/18, 1974, p. 260.
32 J.-L. Vissière, "L'Art de la phrase dans *L'Assommoir*," *Les Cahiers naturalistes*, 1958, Vol. 4, no. 11, pp. 455–64.
33 M. Cressot, *La Phrase et le vocabulaire de J. K. Huysmans*, Genève, Droz, 1938.
34 K. Ross, *The Emergence of Social Space: Rimbaud and the Paris Commune*, Minneapolis, University of Minnesota Press, 1988, p. 5.
35 F. Engels, *The Condition of the Working Class in England*, in Vol. IX of Marx/Engels, *Collected Works*, London, Laurence and Wishart, 1975, p. 347.
36 N. Schor, *Zola's Crowds*, Baltimore, The Johns Hopkins University Press, 1978.
37 G. Lukács, "Narrate or Describe?" in his *Writer and Critic*, A. Kahn (ed. and trans.), London, Merlin Press, 1970, pp. 110–48.
38 ibid., p. 126.
39 ibid., p. 146.
40 G. Lukács, "The Zola Centenary," in *Studies in European Realism*, trans. E. Bone, London, Hillway, 1950, p. 92.
41 ibid., p. 127.
42 H. Mitterand, "Etude de *L'Assommoir*," in Vol. II of *Les Rougons-Macquart*, Paris, Gallimard, coll. Pléiade, 1961, p. 1556.
43 See C. Mendès, *Les 73 Journées de la Commune*, Paris, E. Lachaud, 1871.
44 Cited in Hemmings, op. cit., p. 123. Charles Floquet was a left-wing député of Paris, best known later for his strong opposition to Boulangisme.
45 Cited in ibid., p. 123. In 1873, the Conseil de Guerre had sentenced Arthur Ranc to death for his support of the Commune. He returned to France in 1879.
46 A. Wolff, "Gazette de Paris," *Le Figaro*, 5 February 1877.
47 Dancourt, "Courrier de Paris," *La Gazette de France*, 20 April 1876.
48 Zola, "Germinie Lacerteux," op. cit., p. 70.
49 A. Millaud, "Lettres fantaisistes sur Paris," *Le Figaro*, 1 September 1876.
50 E. Zola, "Letter to Albert Millaud," *Le Figaro*, 7 September 1876.
51 A. Millaud, "Lettres fantaisistes sur Paris," *Le Figaro*, 7 September 1876.
52 L. de Fourcaud, "*L'Assommoir* de M. Zola," *Le Gaulois*, 21 September 1876.
53 E. Zola, "Letter to Fourcaud," *Le Gaulois*, 26 September 1876.
54 L. de Fourcaud, "Encore *L'Assommoir*," *Le Gaulois*, 26 September 1876.

55 J. Barbey-d'Aurevilly, "*L'Assommoir* par M. Emile Zola," *Le Constitutionel*, 29 January 1877.
56 A. de Pontmartin, "La Semaine littéraire," *La Gazette de France*, 18 February 1877.
57 H. Houssaye, "Le Vin bleu littéraire," *Le Journal des débats*, 14 March 1877.
58 A. France, "Variétés: les romanciers contemporains," *Le Temps*, 27 June 1877.
59 J. Mukarovsky, *Aesthetic Function, Norm and Value as Social Facts*, trans. M. Suino, Ann Arbor, University of Michigan Press, 1970, p. 21.
60 ibid.
61 ibid., p. 34.
62 Zola, "Letter to Fourcaud," op. cit.
63 G. Flaubert/I. Turgenev, *Correspondance*, A. Zviguilsky (ed.), Paris, Flammarion, 1969, p. 191.
64 S. Mallarmé, *Dix-neuf lettres à Emile Zola*, L. Deffoux and J. Royère (eds), Paris, Bernard, 1929, p. 4.

3 Céline's *Voyage au bout de la nuit*

1 L.-F. Céline, "Hommage à Zola," in Vol. II of *Oeuvres de Céline*, F. Vitoux (ed.), Paris, Club de L'Honnête Homme, 1981, p. 23. Also in *Cahiers de L'Herne 3*, D. de Roux (ed.), Paris, L'Herne, 1963, p. 169.
2 ibid., p. 24.
3 Cited in P. Joutard, "L'Ouverture des connaissances et les mutations culturelles, 1871–1914," in *Histoire de la France*, J. Duby (ed.), Paris, Larousse, 1970, p. 503.
4 Z. Sternhell, *La Droite révolutionnaire, 1885–1914: les origines françaises du fascisme*, Paris, Seuil, 1978. Also see his *Ni droite ni gauche: les origines françaises du fascisme*, Paris, Seuil, 1983.
5 Sternhell, *Ni droite ni gauche*, ibid., p. 58.
6 "Déclaration," *Cahiers du Cercle Proudhon*, January–February 1912, p. 1. Cited in Sternhell, ibid., p. 25.
7 R. Brasillach, *Notre Avant-Guerre*, Paris, Plon, 1981, p. 159.
8 F. Jameson, *Fables of Aggression: Wyndham Lewis, the Modernist as Fascist*, Berkeley, University of California Press, 1979, p. 15.
9 Céline, op. cit., p. 25.
10 ibid., pp. 25–6, 27.
11 E. Goblot, *La Barrière et le niveau*, cited in J. Mettas, "L'Entre-Deux-Guerres," in *Histoire de la France*, J. Duby (ed.), Paris, Larousse, 1970, p. 535.
12 H. Bauche, *Le Langage populaire*, Paris, Payot, 1929.
13 ibid., p. 18.
14 ibid., p. 28.
15 ibid., p. 31.
16 ibid., p. 7.
17 ibid., p. 14.
18 See, for example, G. Esnault, *Le Poilu tel qu'il se parle*, Paris, Bossard, 1919.

19 L.-F. Céline, *Progrès*, in *Cahiers Céline 8*, P. Fouché (ed.), Paris, Gallimard, 1988, p. 16. *Progrès* was first published by Mercure de France in 1978.
20 ibid., p. 18.
21 ibid., p. 57.
22 L.-F. Céline, Letter to Joseph Garcin, September 1930. Reproduced in *Le Bulletin Célinien*, February 1984, no. 6.
23 R. Barthes, *Roland Barthes*, Paris, Seuil, 1975, p. 140.
24 "Interview avec Charles Chassé," *La Dépêche de Brest et de l'Ouest*, 11 October 1933. Reproduced in *Cahiers Céline 1*, J.-P. Dauphin and H. Godard (eds), Paris, Gallimard, 1976, p. 87.
25 Céline, "Hommage à Zola," op. cit., p. 23.
26 ibid., p. 24.
27 L.-F. Céline, *Voyage au bout de la nuit*, in Vol. II of *Romans*, Paris, Gallimard, coll. Pléiade, 1981. All further references to this work appear in the text. *Voyage* was first published in 1932.
28 P. Alméras, "Nature et évolution de l'argot célinien," *Le Français moderne*, October 1972, no. 40, pp. 325–34.
29 R. Barthes, *Writing Degree Zero*, trans. A. Lavers and C. Smith, New York, Hill and Wang, 1977, p. 30.
30 G. Holtus, "La Notion de code linguistique et son application au langage célinien," *Néophilologus*, 1977, no. 61, pp. 18–33.
31 M. Bakhtin, *The Dialogic Imagination*, M. Holquist (ed.), and trans. C. Emerson and M. Holquist, Austin, University of Texas Press, 1981, p. 304.
32 A. Guyaux, "La Poétique du glissement," in *Lectures de Rimbaud*, Editions de l'Université de Bruxelles, 1982, nos 1–2, pp. 185–213.
33 A. Rimbaud, *Poésies*, in *Oeuvres*, S. Bernard et A. Guyaux (eds), Paris, Garnier, 1983, p. 98.
34 J. Mukarovsky, *Aesthetic Function, Norm and Value as Social Facts*, trans. M. Suino, Ann Arbor, University of Michigan Press, 1970, p. 3.
35 ibid., p. 21.
36 Bakhtin, op. cit., p. 286.
37 ibid.
38 R. Terdiman, *Discourse/Counter-Discourse*, Ithaca, Cornell University Press, 1985, p. 337.
39 ibid., p. 283.
40 ibid., p. 286.
41 ibid., p. 309.
42 G. Altman, "Le Goût âcre de la vie," *Monde*, 29 October 1932.
43 P. Nizan, "Céline n'est pas parmi nous," *L'Humanité*, 9 December 1932. Reproduced in *Cahiers de L'Herne 3*, op. cit., p. 145 and *Cahiers de L'Herne 5*, D. de Roux (ed.), Paris, L'Herne, 1965, p. 143.
44 P. Scize, "La Vérité sur Léon Daudet," *Le Canard enchaîné*, 14 December 1932.
45 R. Fernandez, "Le Livre de la semaine," *Marianne*, 16 November 1932.
46 H. L., "Louis Ferdinand Céline: *Voyage au bout de la nuit*," *Le Libertaire*, 30 December 1932.
47 L. Trotsky, "Céline and Poincaré: novelist and politician," in *Leon Trotsky on Literature and Art*, P. Siegel (ed.), New York, Pathfinder Press, 1970,

pp. 191, 200. The essay was first published in *Atlantic Monthly*, October 1935.
48 ibid., p. 202.
49 L. Daudet, "L.-F. Céline: Voyage au bout de la nuit," *Candide*, 22 December 1932.
50 P. Loewel, "La Vie littéraire," *Ordre*, 2 November 1932; M. Bromberger, "Le Docteur X," *L'Intransigeant*, 8 December 1932; M. Augagneur, "Voyage au bout de la nuit," *Gringoire*, 2 December 1932.
51 A. Rousseaux, "L'Homme du jour: M. Louis-Ferdinand Céline," *Candide*, 8 December 1932.
52 A. Rousseaux, "Le Cas Céline," *Le Figaro*, 13 December 1932. Reproduced in *Les Critiques de notre temps et Céline*, J.-P. Dauphin (ed.), Paris, Garnier, 1976, pp. 13–19.
53 G. Bernanos, "Au bout de la nuit," *Le Figaro*, 13 December 1932.
54 P. Bourdieu, "Vous avez dit populaire?" *Actes de la recherche en sciences sociales*, March 1983, Vol. 46, p. 100.
55 J. Habermas, "Modernity–An Incomplete Project," in *The Anti-Aesthetic: Essays on Postmodern Culture*, H. Foster (ed.), Port Townsend, Bay Press, 1983, p. 5.
56 Interviewed by P.-J. Launay, "L.-F. Céline le révolté," *Paris Soir*, 10 November 1932.
57 R. de Saint-Jean, *Journal d'un journaliste*, Paris, Grasset, 1974, pp. 109–11.
58 A. Rousseaux, "Propos du Samedi," *Le Figaro*, 30 May 1936.
59 S. Jourat, "Interview avec L.-F. Céline," *La Meuse*, 5 July 1961. Reproduced in *Cahiers Céline 2*, J.-P. Dauphin and H. Godard (eds), Paris, Gallimard, 1976, p. 222.
60 M. Léger, "L.-F. Céline achève à Meudon son voyage au bout de la tristesse," *Semaine du Monde*, 23 July 1954. Reproduced in *Cahiers Céline 1*, op. cit., p. 157.
61 Interviewed by A. Brissaud, *Bulletin du Club du Meilleur Livre*, October 1954, no. 17. Reproduced in *Cahiers Céline 1*, op. cit., p. 164.
62 L.-F. Céline, *Exposé enregistré: Louis-Ferdinand Céline vous parle*, Disques Festival, 1958.
63 L. le Cunff, "Qui êtes-vous Monsieur Céline?" *Le Monde et la vie*, November 1960, Vol. 90, pp. 46–7. Reproduced in *Cahiers Céline 2*, op. cit., pp. 180–6.
64 Céline, *Exposé enregistré*, op. cit.
65 L.-F. Céline, Letter to Milton Hindus, 15 May 1947, in *Louis-Ferdinand Céline tel que je l'ai vu*, L. Deffoux and J. Royère (eds), Paris, L'Herne, 1969, p. 138.
66 L.-F. Céline, *Conversations with Professor Y*, trans. S. Luce, Hanover and London, University Press of New England, 1986, pp. 63, 65.
67 ibid., p. 73.
68 ibid., p. 104.
69 ibid., p. 110.
70 T. Adorno, "Commitment," in *The Essential Frankfurt School Reader*, A. Arato and E. Gebhardt (eds), New York, Urizen, 1978, pp. 300–19.
71 ibid., p. 305.
72 ibid., p. 314.

226 *Political Stylistics*

73 ibid., p. 302.
74 Céline, *Conversations with Professor Y*, op. cit., p. 16.
75 Adorno, "Commitment," op. cit., p. 314.
76 ibid., p. 315.
77 ibid., p. 303.
78 Trotsky, op. cit., p. 194.
79 ibid., p. 202.
80 Habermas, op. cit., p. 5; A. Breton, *Manifestes du Surréalisme*, Paris, Gallimard, 1973, p. 15.
81 Céline, Letter to Milton Hindus, op. cit.
82 J. Leenhardt, "Towards a Sociology of Reading," in *The Reader in the Text*, I. Crosman and S. Suleiman (eds), Princeton, Princeton University Press, 1980, p. 209.
83 Céline, *Conversations with Professor Y*, op. cit., p. 102.
84 J. Kristeva, *Pouvoirs de l'horreur: Essai sur l'abjection*, Paris, Seuil, 1977, pp. 206–7.
85 L.-F. Céline, *Les Beaux Draps*, Paris, Nouvelles Editions Françaises, 1941, p. 90. Cited in Kristeva, ibid., p. 206.
86 L.-F. Céline, *L'Ecole des cadavres*, Paris, Denoël, 1938, p. 140. Cited in Kristeva, op. cit., p. 206.

4 Queneau's *Zazie dans le métro*

1 F. Jameson, "Postmodernism and Consumer Society," in *The Anti-Aesthetic: Essays on Postmodern Culture*, H. Foster (ed.), Port Townsend, Bay Press, 1983, p. 124.
2 A. Touraine, *The Post-Industrial Society*, trans. L. Mayhew, New York, Random House, 1971, p. 51.
3 R. Hamilton, *Affluence and the French Worker in the Fourth Republic*, Princeton, Princeton University Press, 1967, table 4.7, p. 82 and table 4.9, p. 83.
4 ibid., table 4.22, p. 101; table 8.1, p. 161.
5 Touraine, op. cit., p. 265.
6 P. Guiraud, *Le Français populaire*, Paris, Presses Universitaires de France, 1965, p. 10.
7 *Grand Dictionnaire universel du XIXeme siècle*, Paris, Larousse, 1865, in the "Préface," n. pag.
8 *Larousse du XXeme siècle*, Paris, Larousse, 1928, in the "Préface," n. pag.
9 *Grand Larousse encyclopédique*, Paris, Larousse, 1960, in the "Avant-propos," n. pag.
10 C. Désirat and T. Hordé, *La Langue française au 20eme siècle*, Paris, Bordas, 1976, p. 43.
11 ibid., pp. 44–5.
12 Guiraud, op. cit., p. 9.
13 J.-P. Sartre, *What Is Literature?*, trans. B. Frechtman, Gloucester, Mass., Peter Smith, 1978, p. 209.
14 ibid., p. 230.
15 ibid.
16 ibid., p. 17.
17 ibid., p. 41.

Notes 227

18 A. Robbe-Grillet, *For a New Novel*, trans. R. Howard, New York, Grove Press, 1965, p. 32.
19 S. Heath, *The Nouveau Roman: A Study in the Practice of Writing*, London, Elek, 1972.
20 Robbe-Grillet, op. cit., p. 41.
21 Cited in J. Bens, *R. Queneau*, Paris, Gallimard, 1962, p. 12.
22 ibid., p. 13.
23 R. Queneau, *Exercises de style*, Paris, Gallimard, 1947, pp. 151, 75.
24 R. Queneau, *Exercises in Style*, trans. B. Wright, London, Gaberbocchus Press, 1958, pp. 192, 100.
25 R. Queneau, *Bâtons, chiffres et lettres*, Paris, Gallimard, 1965. *Bâtons, chiffres et lettres* was first published in 1950. All further references to this work appear in the text.
26 Désirat and Hordé, op. cit., p. 212.
27 ibid., p. 213.
28 ibid., p. 219.
29 ibid., p. 221.
30 ibid., p. 219.
31 J. Vendryes, *Le Langage: Introduction linguistique à l'histoire*, Paris, Albin-Michel, 1968, p. 303. *Le Langage* was first published in 1923.
32 R. Queneau, *Zazie dans le métro*, Paris, Gallimard, 1959, p. 9. All further references to this work appear in the text.
33 R. Queneau, *Zazie in the Métro*, trans. B. Wright, London, Calder, 1982, p. 11. All further translations of Queneau's text are taken from this work.
34 Jameson, op. cit., p. 120.
35 This quotation can be traced back not to Aristotle himself, but to Strabo's *Geography*, trans. H. L. Jones, Cambridge, Mass., Harvard University Press, 1950, Book XIII, p. 71. Queneau fragments the original passage, which reads: "For Homer said that the wall had only recently been built (or else not built at all, but fabricated and then abolished by the poet, as Aristotle said.)"
36 R. Barthes, "Zazie et la littérature," in *Essais Critiques*, Paris, Seuil, 1964, p. 125.
37 P. Robert, *Dictionnaire alphabétique et analogique de la langue française*, Paris, Presses Universitaires de France, 1952.
38 Barthes, op. cit., p. 125.
39 J.-P. Bordufour, "La Révolution langagière erratée," in *Cahier de L'Herne: Queneau*, A. Bergens (ed.), Paris, L'Herne, 1979, p. 183.
40 Barthes, op. cit., p. 127.
41 ibid.
42 Jameson, op. cit., p. 114.
43 Barthes, op. cit., p. 128.
44 A. Billy, "Raymond Queneau s'amuse," *Le Figaro*, 11 February 1959.
45 C. Roy, "Zazie dans le métro," *Libération*, 28 January 1959.
46 A. Berry, "De M. Queneau à Msieukeno," *Combat*, 12 March 1959.
47 R. Queneau, *Entretiens avec Georges Charbonnier*, Paris, Gallimard, 1962, p. 9.
48 ibid.
49 ibid., p. 69.
50 ibid., p. 70.

51 ibid., p. 89.
52 ibid., p. 36.
53 R. Queneau, "Errata," *La Nouvelle Revue française*, April 1969, no. 196, pp. 627–9.
54 F. Jameson, "Postmodernism and the Cultural Logic of Late Capitalism," *New Left Review*, July–August 1984, Vol. 146, pp. 53–94.
55 ibid., p. 88.
56 F. Jameson, "Reification and Utopia in Mass Culture," *Social Text*, Winter 1979, Vol. 1, p. 149.
57 Jameson, "Postmodernism, and the Cultural Logic of Late Capitalism," op. cit., p. 55.
58 ibid., p. 125.

5 Popular language as literary artifact

1 S. Fish, "What Is Stylistics and Why Are They Saying Such Terrible Things About It," in his *Is There a Text In This Class?*, Cambridge, Harvard University Press, 1980, pp. 68–96.
2 J. Searle, *Speech Acts: An Essay in the Philosophy of Language*, Cambridge, Cambridge University Press, 1969, p. 52.
3 Fish, op. cit., p. 85.
4 ibid., p. 91.
5 ibid., p. 69.
6 A. Rey, "Préface de la deuxième édition," in P. Robert, *Dictionnaire alphabétique et analogique de la langue française*, Paris, Les Dictionnaires Robert, 1985, p. xxii.
7 L.-F. Céline, "Hommage à Zola," in Vol. II of *Oeuvres de Céline*, F. Vitoux (ed.), Paris, Club de l'Honnête Homme, 1981, p. 23. Also in *Cahiers de L'Herne 3*, D. de Roux (ed.), Paris, L'Herne, 1963, p. 169.
8 A. Billy, "Raymond Queneau s'amuse," *Le Figaro*, 11 February 1959.
9 F. Jameson, "Postmodernism and the Cultural Logic of Late Capitalism," *New Left Review*, July–August 1986, Vol. 146, p. 65.
10 H. Etiemble, *Parlez-vous franglais?*, Paris, Gallimard, 1973, p. 227.
11 R. Barthes, *Writing Degree Zero*, trans. A. Lavers and C. Smith, New York, Hill and Wang, 1977, p. 79.
12 L.-F. Céline, Letter to Joseph Garcin, September 1930, reproduced in *Le Bulletin Célinien*, February 1984, No. 6.
13 G. Bernanos, *Ecrits de combat*, Paris, Gallimard, coll. Pléiade, I, 1971, p. 1040.
14 Barthes, op. cit., p. 1.
15 M. Bakhtin, *The Dialogic Imagination*, M. Holquist (ed.), and trans. C. Emerson and M. Holquist, Austin, University of Texas Press, 1981, p. 316.
16 E. Zola, *L'Assommoir*, in Vol. III of *Oeuvres Complètes*, H. Mitterand (ed.), Paris, Cercle du Livre Précieux, 1967, p. 915.
17 H. Godard, *Poétique de Céline*, Paris, Gallimard, 1985, p. 194.
18 J.-P. Richard, *Nausée de Céline*, Montpellier, Fata Morgana, 1973, p. 41.
19 M. Augagneur, "Voyage au bout de la nuit," *Gringoire*, 2 December 1932.
20 M. Foucault, *L'Ordre du discours*, Paris, Gallimard, 1971.

21 A. Wolff, "Gazette de Paris," *Le Figaro*, 5 February 1877.
22 A. Rousseaux, "L'Homme du jour: M. Louis-Ferdinand Céline," *Le Figaro*, 8 December 1932.
23 Billy, "Raymond Queneau s'amuse," op. cit.
24 L. de Fourcaud, "L'Assommoir de M. Zola," *Le Gaulois*, 21 September 1876.
25 Zola, Preface to *L'Assommoir*, op. cit., p. 599.
26 P. Nizan, "Céline n'est pas parmi nous," *L'Humanité*, 9 December 1932.
27 E. Pound, "Si c'est cela la trahison," in *Cahiers de L'Herne 3*, D. de Roux (ed.), Paris, L'Herne, 1963, p. 198.
28 Barthes, op. cit., p. 4.
29 ibid., p. 67.
30 ibid., p. 5.
31 L.-F. Céline, "Letter to Milton Hindus," 15 May 1947, in *Louis-Ferdinand Céline tel que je l'ai vu*, L. Deffoux and J. Royère (eds), Paris, L'Herne, 1969, p. 138.
32 Barthes, op. cit., p. 9.
33 Jameson, op. cit., p. 70.
34 Barthes, op. cit., p. 87.

Index

Adorno, T. 30-1, 146-8
Alexis, P. 51
Altman, G. 134
Auerbach, E. 56-7

Bakhtin, M. 32-3, 38-40, 122-31, 207
Baldwin, J. 16
Balzac, H. de 4
Banfield, A. 64
Balibar, R. 9
Barbey d'Aurevilly, J. 94
Barthes, R. 18, 29, 31, 110, 184-7, 204, 206, 214, 216
Bauche, H. 106-7
Bellay, J. du 8
Bernanos, G. 139, 205
Bernstein, B. 12
Berry, A. 192
Billy, A. 189
Bordufour, J.-P. 185
Bourdieu, P. 7, 11-12, 14, 17-18, 28, 31, 38
Brasillach, R. 104
Brombert, V. 27
Brown, R. 218

Chevalier, L. 21

Dancourt 89
Daudet, L. 137
Delvau, A. 23-4
Désirat, C. 11, 155, 164

Eagleton, T. 30

Engels, F. 77
Etiemble, H. 201

Fernandez, R. 134
Fish, S. 198-9
Flaubert, G. 100
Foucault, M. 211
Fourcaud, L. de 93-4
France, A. 95
Francisque-Michel 23, 25

Gilman, A. 218
Godard, H. 208
Goncourt, E. and J. de 48
Goody, J. 36
Guiraud, P. 155-6
Guyaux, A. 126

Habermas, J. 141, 149
Hamilton, R. 153
Heath, S. 158
Hindus, M. 144
Holtus, G. 120
Hordé, T. 11, 155, 164
Houssaye, H. 95
Hugo, V. 1-4, 27, 28

Iser, W. 30, 41

Jameson, F. 104, 152, 169, 187, 195-7, 215
Jauss, H. 19

Knappert, J. 7

Labov, W. 14

Larchey, L. 23
Leenhardt, J. 41, 150, 219
Leibnitz, A. 218
Loewel, P. 137
Lukács, G. 29, 85–6

Mailer, N. 16
Mallarmé, S. 100
Marcuse, H. 30
Mendès, C. 88
Millaud, A. 92
Mitterand, H. 88
Mukarovsky, J. 97, 130

Niess, R. 222
Nisard, C. 219
Nizan, P. 134

Perruchot, C. 67
Petrey, S. 221
Place, D. 55
Pontmartin, A. de 95
Poulot, D. 25, 53, 54
Pound, E. 214
Pratt, M. L. 5, 16, 18–19

Riffaterre, M. 39
Richard, J.-P. 208

Robbe-Grillet, A. 158
Ross, K. 72
Rousseaux, A. 139, 142, 212

Sainéan, L. 219
Sartre, J.-P. 157–8
Schor, N. 83
Scize, P. 134
Searle, J. 198
Spitzer, L. 60
Sternhell, Z. 103–4
Sue, E. 26
Suleiman, E. 218

Terdiman, R. 17, 21, 132–3
Touraine, A. 153–4
Trotsky, L. 136
Turgenev, I. 100

Vaugelas, C. F. de 9, 17
Vendryes, J. 167
Vidocq, E. 21, 22
Vissière, J.-L. 71
Vitu, A. 219
Volosinov, V. 21, 32

Watt, I. 36
Wolff, A. 89, 211

For Product Safety Concerns and Information please contact our EU
representative GPSR@taylorandfrancis.com
Taylor & Francis Verlag GmbH, Kaufingerstraße 24, 80331 München, Germany

www.ingramcontent.com/pod-product-compliance
Lightning Source LLC
Chambersburg PA
CBHW061442300426
44114CB00014B/1792